before they
EXECUTED HIM

before they
EXECUTED HIM

a wife's story of
DEATH ROW

Shari Bower

4:13
PUBLISHING
ARLINGTON, TX

© 2020 Shari Bower
Before They Executed Him: A Wife's Story of Death Row
First edition, May 2020

4:13
PUBLISHING
ARLINGTON, TX

ShariBower.com

Editing: Shayla Raquel, shaylaraquel.com
Proofreading: Lisa Thompson, writebylisa.com
Publishing and Design Services: Melinda Martin, melindamartin.me

This is a work of creative nonfiction. The events are portrayed to the best of the author's memory. While all the stories in this book are true, some names and identifying details have been changed to protect the privacy of the people involved.

Conversations in this book all come from the author's recollections. Though some may not be written to represent word-for-word transcripts, the author has retold them in a way that evokes the feeling and meaning that was said, and in all instances, the essence of the dialogue is accurate.

All legal scenes and courtroom testimonies have been taken directly from court transcripts, notes, and call logs provided by the judicial offices and other law enforcement agencies to provide authenticity to the story.

Unless otherwise indicated, Scripture quotations are taken from the Holy Bible, New International Version®, NIV®. Copyright © 1973, 1978, 1984, 2011 by Biblica, Inc.™ Used by permission of Zondervan. All rights reserved worldwide. www.zondervan.com. The "NIV" and "New International Version" are trademarks registered in the United States Patent and Trademark Office by Biblica, Inc.™

Scripture quotations marked (HCSB) are taken from the Holman Christian Standard Bible®, Copyright © 1999, 2000, 2002, 2003, 2009 by Holman Bible Publishers. Used by permission. Holman Christian Standard Bible®, Holman CSB®, and HCSB® are federally registered trademarks of Holman Bible Publishers.

The quote from Supreme Court Justice William O. Davis was used by permission. "Brady v. Maryland, 373 U.S. 83 (1963)," Justicia U.S. Supreme Court, accessed April 4, 2020, https://supreme.justia.com/cases/federal/us/373/83/.

ISBN: 978-0-5786680-9-3 (paperback)

WHAT THE PRESS IS SAYING

"During the years I covered the remarkable and remarkably tragic case for the *Fort Worth Star-Telegram,* Shari Bower became a source profound curiosity. Her husband, Lester Bower, had sat on death row for decades for a crime that he almost certainly didn't commit. Yet each time I met her, whether for interviews in her home or in corridors outside Texas courtrooms, Shari was the epitome of kindness, good humor, strength, and faith. How could that be?

Then the state of Texas killed the man who I and so many others came to believe was innocent. If anyone would have been entitled to bitterness, it would have been his wife. Yet Lester Bower's funeral was a celebration of his life and the life of his family. It was orchestrated by Shari. In the face of it all, she was the same.

That's why this book is such a gift. It tells the Lester Bower story as no one else could, and it takes us all into the heart and mind of this extraordinary person, Shari Bower. She is living proof that no darkness can ever fully extinguish the light of love. What's more, it is written with an elegance, a novelist's eye for detail, and a poet's insight. Once again, I'm asking: How can this be?

I guess it's time to stop wondering. It's enough to know that in this book, Shari Bower has given voice to her remarkable heart and we would all do well to hear it."

—TIM MADIGAN, Author of
I'm Proud of You: My Friendship with Fred Rogers

"Whatever you think about the benefits of having capital punishment, no one could possibly argue that executing an innocent man is in the interests of the state or our society. Our interests as lawyers and as people should be that our government, when in doubt, should not go forward with an execution. There is ample evidence to give people reasonable doubt about whether Les committed these murders. In my view, the evidence is compelling that he didn't."

—**ANTHONY ROTH**, Bower Appellate Team

"Lester Bower, who had a strong case of innocence, was executed on June 3, 2015, after thirty-one years on Texas death row. He spent more time on death row than any other person executed in Texas. Bower maintained his innocence to the end."

—**JORDAN SMITH**, *The Intercept*

"He [Judge Fallon] points out in pretty clear terms that this guy [Lester Bower] probably would have been found not guilty had this evidence been available at trial . . . But now, all these years later, he can't meet the new standard, which is actual innocence. That was not the standard at trial. Then it was guilty beyond a reasonable doubt."

—**MAURICE POSSLEY**, *Chicago Tribune*, Senior Researcher for the National Register of Exonerations

Dedicated to:

Peter Buscemi, Grace Speights, and Anthony Roth, three attorneys with the Morgan Lewis law firm in Washington, DC, who decided to take on a pro bono death penalty case in 1989. They had no idea the sacrifices they would make or the personal time with their families they would postpone or miss in order to work tirelessly investigating and defending this case as no one else had before.

This book is dedicated to the Bower Team, the moniker they soon became known by. They gave generously of their time, resources, and wealth of knowledge to battle the injustices that had been dealt to Les Bower in 1984. No one foresaw they would be fighting Les's battle for twenty-six years. No one imagined that Les Bower and the extended Bower family would become the close-knit group they did with the Bower Team, and all would be forever changed by the experience.

Thank you is not enough. We will always be eternally grateful to you and the many others at Morgan Lewis who supported us through your efforts.

Anthony C. Roth

September 9, 1957 to September 7, 2014

Anthony Roth became the "visiting" team member, the one who would visit Les on death row when the attorneys needed to talk to him about upcoming hearings. But he was much more than that. Anthony was a brilliant attorney, a man of faith who loved his family, his friends, and my husband, Les Bower. He and Les became very close friends—like brothers. They not only talked about the case but shared stories about their outdoor experiences, their families, and their hopes and dreams. They laughed together and cried together. Anthony and Les understood one another, which drew them even closer. When Anthony became ill in 2000, he continued to visit Les several times, often making bucket list trips along the way, visiting as many baseball stadiums as he could and seeing parts of Texas he'd never seen. He almost always stopped in Dallas to visit Les's extended family. We saw how ill he was, but he was determined to work on this case as long as he could.

Anthony was instrumental in obtaining seven stays of execution. He worked tirelessly to reverse what he believed was a failure of the judicial system, which resulted in a gross travesty of justice. For his efforts in this case, Anthony received his firm's Julie Noel Gilbert Award for Pro Bono Excellence. Even though his illness forced him to stop actively practicing law in 2011, Anthony remained involved in the representation of his client and visited him at the prison for the last time in July 2014, just two months prior to his death and eleven months prior to Les's execution.

CONTENTS

Foreword 1

Chapter 1: The End 7

Chapter 2: Romantic Visitations 12

Chapter 3: The Beginning 18

Chapter 4: Stages of Life 28

Chapter 5: The Longest Day 42

Chapter 6: Three Days 56

Chapter 7: A Fox in the Henhouse 60

Chapter 8: That Day in October 66

Chapter 9: You Don't Know Shari 76

Chapter 10: Desperate for Answers 87

Chapter 11: Do Your Homework 94

Chapter 12: A Deal with the Devil 106

Chapter 13: Now Entering the Twilight Zone 115

Chapter 14: The Rare Ammunition 137

Chapter 15: Juggling the Truth 160

Chapter 16: It's Our Turn 167

Chapter 17: The Defense Rests 185

Chapter 18: One Last Goodbye 199

Chapter 19: The Woman with No Name 211

Chapter 20: Witness #1 219

Chapter 21: Appeals 234

Chapter 22: The Girl in the Pigtail Braids 247

Chapter 23: Encounters 262

Chapter 24: That's What Sisters Do.. 268

Chapter 25: Forgiveness 277

Chapter 26: All My Love Forever 294

Chapter 27: Don't Mess with Texas 303

Chapter 28: The Day After.. 314

Chapter 29: The Memorial 317

Chapter 30: The Many Sides to Grieving................................... 320

Chapter 31: A Final, Hilarious, Fun-Filled Farewell
           (Les, You Would've Been So Proud!) 324

Chapter 32: Just Breathe 329

Chapter 33: Do I Miss You? 333

Gallery 339

Acknowledgments 351

About the Author 355

Foreword

"They killed him, Mom."

My daughter whispered those words to me on June 3, 2015, as I lay across my bed sobbing, waiting for that day to be over. I knew they were going to put Les to death sometime that evening before midnight—that's why I was alone in the darkness. I had known for a month or so that his execution was likely near but to hear those words was absolutely devastating. The finality of it all. No more future tense. Only past: "They killed him, Mom."

And there was nothing we could do anymore.

We had failed.

It was 1989 when Les and Shari Bower came into my life. I had just finished my maternity leave with my youngest child, when Peter Buscemi, a partner in the litigation group of our law firm, was notified of the need for legal representation in a death penalty case via the NAACP Legal Defense Fund and the Texas Resource Center. I remember Anthony Roth—who, like me, was a senior associate in the litigation group at that time—and I telling Peter a couple years before, "We want to work with you on a death penalty case. If you ever get one, let us know." Peter had handled several death penalty cases during his career. He did precisely that when the Bower case, involving claims of ineffective assistance of counsel, came to our Morgan Lewis law office in Washington, DC.

The more we researched the case, the less it made sense. Les Bower was happily married with two kids, had gone to college and played football, and came from a good family with a solid upbringing. And he had no criminal history. How could a guy like that have been charged and convicted of four counts of capital murder, which were allegedly committed during the course of stealing an ultralight hang glider? He didn't fit the bill. So we dug deeper and found that the lawyer representing the Bower family had done hardly anything in terms of investigation or putting on a decent case during the trial and penalty phases back in 1984.

We added these two factors together and knew it was the right case to take on. We each wholeheartedly believed we could save Les Bower's life from lethal injection.

And then twenty-six years went by. Twenty-six years, more than 15,000 *pro bono* hours of work, and seven stays of execution. All this time, and we failed to save Les, an innocent man.

But Les would scold me for saying that.

He'd say the same thing he said moments before the state of Texas killed him. During his last words, he thanked us for keeping him alive for as long as we did. I've read the media reports of Les's last words over and over again and tried to convince myself we didn't let him down. How many times did we say, "This has to make the judge change his mind"? We so believed in Les's innocence and still do to this day.

And so did his family. Shari and her children fought for Les. Even though it's been a very emotional and painful story for Shari to tell, she remains strong—so strong. When we knew it was the end, I cried. I couldn't help it. And she, the soon-to-be widow, consoled me: "You did the best you could do."

She tried to keep *me* from crying. There is no better person to take you, the reader, on this journey than Shari Bower.

After you've turned the last page, after you've had time to register the story you've been told, I hope you feel compelled to get active in the criminal justice system and to fight hard for people who are innocent like Les was—and is.

If you see an injustice, then do something. Stand up. Fight. Don't give up. If it could happen to Les Bower, I assure you, it could happen to anyone.

I'm often asked, "Will you ever take on another death penalty case after

Les?" I always vehemently shake my head and tell them, "Never again. It hurt too much to lose him. I can't go through that again."

I'll never take on another death penalty case, but I'll never—not for a moment—regret representing Les Bower and standing by his innocence.

—**GRACE SPEIGHTS**, Partner and Global Leader of the
Labor Employment Practice at the law firm of Morgan Lewis;
American Lawyer Magazine 2018 Lawyer of the Year

What Passionate Pleas

What passionate pleas, my heart doth cry,
When to the Lord, my soul asks, "Why?"
This pain no longer can I bear,
And silent cries I feel my prayer.
They're lifted up, but are they heard?
I long await, but ne'er a word.
I pray in heaven I might dwell,
But at this moment, I fear 'tis hell.

March 25, 1989

CHAPTER 1

The End

June 3, 2015

I stared at the white sheet covering my husband as he lay on the gurney less than eight feet from me in the Texas death chamber. The sheet, folded carefully beneath his neck as if he had just been tucked into bed, was a stark contrast to the seafoam green of the brick walls interrupted only by turquoise trim.

Nothing could have prepared me for the sight before me as I looked through the Plexiglas window. The sheet moved up and down ever so slightly with each breath he took. Tubes, which would soon deliver the lethal cocktail of drugs, dangled from his arms. They were strapped to extensions of the table, making it look as if he were on a cross.

Les had not always wanted me, or anyone else for that matter, to be there, but I could tell by the faint smile he gave us as my sister Kelli, Les's two sisters, Cheryl and Denise, and I entered the room that he was glad he wasn't alone. I knew I had made the right decision to be here, witnessing the killing of my husband of forty-seven years.

Eight times we'd faced execution dates. Eight times we'd prepared for the worst. And each time Les was emphatic. "I can't allow you to see me like that," he'd say. "That's not how I want to be remembered."

He wanted to spare me this pain, and that made me love him all the more. Each moment over the past thirty-one years had been unscripted. We held on to our faith, to our little family of four, to our hopes and dreams, to the future we were creating together. I knew not being with him in this moment would be far worse.

"I don't want you to be alone," I told him many times, holding back tears, trying to show how brave I was.

"I've been alone for thirty-one years," he responded.

"Don't say that." I held back a choked cry. "You haven't been."

But was it true? Was that what he felt?

The brick-walled viewing room would have been claustrophobic even if I'd been alone. We stood at the front closest to the window. There was just enough room on the front row for the four of us. Reverend Gayle Baucum—my mother's youngest brother and only six years older than me—had been Les's best friend and spiritual advisor. He stood behind Denise in the tiny room, watching the scene unfold.

Two prison chaplains and three reporters also joined us in the room. One of the reporters I recognized from the Associated Press. The other two were very young women, probably from *The Herald Democrat*, the Sherman/Denison newspaper. I had never seen them before, and we were not introduced. The chaplains' jobs were to make sure the family was okay and that the reporters did not ask us any questions. I wondered if this was their first time to witness an execution. In the next room, separated only by a brick wall, friends and family members of the murder victims stood in a viewing area identical to the one we were in.

Our two daughters had chosen not to be witnesses. I was glad they hadn't come, and so was Les. It was difficult enough for my husband to agree to have his wife and sisters there. It would have been unbearable to have his children witness his death as well.

A microphone hung from the ceiling just over Les's face, waiting for him to make his last statement. He spoke.

Much has been written about this case—not all of it has been the truth.

But the time is over, and now it is time to move on. I want to thank my attorneys for all that they have done. They have afforded me the last quarter of a century.

I would like to thank my wife, my daughters, family, and friends for their unwavering support, and all the letters and well wishes over the years. Now it is time to pass on.

I have fought the good fight. I held the faith. I am not going to say goodbye.

I will simply say until we meet again.

I love you very, very much.

I thought it was perfect. His scripture from 2 Timothy 4:7 was one he had quoted often in reference to what seemed like his endless battle to stay alive and finally be exonerated.

I continued looking at his face and back again at the crisp, white shroud. I found myself holding my own breath as I searched for signs of his breathing. I was not sure when the drugs had started to enter his body. Only one person knows that: the executioner. The state of Texas makes sure the executioner is never seen. That person is behind a wall, just behind the gurney where the inmate lies. A three-part "cocktail," as it's called, is used. The first drug is an anesthetic that causes the prisoner to lose consciousness. The second is a paralyzing agent to render him immobile. And the third is potassium chloride to stop the heart. At one point, my husband closed his eyes, his jaw going a bit slack, and he looked as if he were sleeping. Did it stop? No, there—it moved again. I couldn't be sure.

I could see the warden out of the corner of my left eye, his head never moving as he glanced up now and then, looking at something on the wall at the other end of the room, something I couldn't see. He stood motionless behind Les's head with his hands folded in front of him, staring straight ahead. He was immaculately dressed in a deep-blue suit. His tie and a handkerchief tucked in his pocket were a lighter blue, coordinating perfectly with his shirt. His shoes were polished. He looked as if he were going to a movie premiere rather than overseeing the death of an innocent man.

The chaplain of the Walls Unit stood at Les's feet, a small New Testament in his hand. I glanced over to see that it was open to Philippians. His other hand rested lightly on Les's right ankle. A door opened, and a man with a stethoscope around his neck entered the room and walked directly toward my husband. He lightly touched Les's neck, looking for a pulse. Still, the warden did not move. The man turned to look at whatever the warden had been glancing at and declared it was 6:36 P.M. It was Wednesday, June 3, 2015.

I had become a widow.

There were no wails from those of us who loved him most. There were eyes moist with tears of love, of loss, and of regret that he could not be saved. The room was silent except for the sound of someone quietly weeping in the back. One of the reporters had been brought to tears.

Silent tears rolled down my cheeks, and I wiped them away. The curtains on the Plexiglas window closed, separating me from the man I had loved since I was sixteen. The hot summer heat poured into the small, quiet room as the door behind us opened and we were ushered outside. It had only been thirty-six minutes since we entered.

For thirty-one years, Les and I had not been in the same room, breathed the same air, or touched or embraced. We had been told that he could not actually see us through the window. But as we entered the room shortly after 6:00 P.M., he turned his head toward us and smiled, knowing we were there at the end of this endless nightmare. It was over. The state killed an innocent man, just as they'd planned to do for thirty-one years.

It was the end.

Union

I came to you; you came to me.
God saw our love and let it be.
He joined us together as husband and wife
And blessed the union that began our life.
We shared our days, both good and bad.
We shared the hopes, the dreams we had.
We joined our love, and now we share
The love of children God placed in our care.
Now as we come to our middle years,
We share the grief, the hurt, the tears.
And as our lives are ripped and torn apart,
We face each day with a heavy heart.
But God has blessed this union so,
By placing us together so long ago.
So I trust in God and believe when I say,
He's in control and will lead the way.
Oh, thank you, God, for caring for me,
Even though most times I cannot see
The result of your gracious love,
Your constant guidance from above.

April 18, 1984

CHAPTER 2

Romantic Visitations

"Don't act like this is the first time you've seen me pee," he said, his eyes twinkling with mischief, revealing his characteristic sense of humor. "We've been together for thirty-seven years. Surely you've seen me pee during that time."

"Let me remind you," I replied, trying not to laugh, "that only fifteen of those years were actually spent together. The other twenty-two, we weren't exactly spending intimate time together—if you know what I mean."

"Oh, I know what you mean," he said, looking up slowly from the task at hand, still grinning at me. He seemed to be enjoying this way too much.

"But when you have a kidney stone and you're locked in a small room, you have to be prepared for emergencies such as this. I'm sorry if it bothers you."

"It doesn't bother me. If you want to know the truth, I find it rather humorous."

Again, he lifted his eyes to mine, letting them linger as he looked at me through the glass. I reached through his eyes and felt the wrenching pain I always did when we stopped, taking time to gaze, even for a second. He looked different. He wasn't the man in the photographs on my mantle at home. His youth had slipped away. Our youth had.

He returned his attention to what he was doing and lifted the once-empty Diet Dr Pepper bottle from beneath the desk shelf, screwed the lid back on, and placed it in the sack that had once held his vending machine lunch. He reached back under the shelf, buttoned a couple of buttons, and smoothed his pants legs, then folded his hands on top of the desk, leaned forward, his face as close to the glass as possible, and smiled at me with so much love and affection, sprinkled with his impish grin.

"Now when your friends ask you what you did on this fine, sunny Friday, you can tell them, in all honesty, you watched your husband piss in a bottle," he said, amusement crinkling the corners of his eyes, igniting a sparkle across his face as it so often did when he was teasing me. There he was! The boy I fell in love with. He was still there.

"Well, I didn't actually see you pee," I replied. "You've always been adept at making the best of a bad situation. And quite creative as well."

Neither of us in all the years of his incarceration had been overly emotional. Les had never been a big fan of public displays of affection even when we were physically together. Others in the visitation area would put their hands on the glass as if they were touching one another, the visitor on one side and the inmate on the other. The window, which had chicken wire between its panes, was old and dingy anyway, but oftentimes I had to clean it with paper towels from the bathroom just to get the handprints or lipstick off so we could see each other.

The two-hour visitation time we did spend together was short and precious. How much time had we wasted before he had been imprisoned? Did we take the time to look into one another's eyes during the past fifteen years and tell each other how much we loved one another with just a look?

I immediately knew something was wrong when he walked in the room that day. I could tell by the look on his face, the color of his skin, and the way he walked. He was in pain. It was obvious he hadn't slept well and was tired. Normally, he gave me a big smile before the guards even opened the door to the cubicle where he would sit to visit. On this day, however, it was forced.

His cubicle was about three feet wide by three feet deep. The door behind him was metal—solid at the bottom—and a basket weave pattern at the top allowed air flow. Below the woven and mesh metal was a slot that could be opened and shut from the outside. It was about two feet wide and six to eight inches high. The guards would unlock it, and the slot would drop down. Les would turn his back to the closed door and squat down so his hands could reach through the slot, and the guards would unlock the handcuffs so he could visit unshackled. The handcuffs left deep, red welts on his wrists. I tried not to look at them, as it was too painful for me to see.

The slot was also used to deliver vending machine items that I would purchase for him. Visitors were allowed to bring in only twenty dollars for the visit, which wasn't a lot of money, given the vending machine prices. Paper money wasn't allowed, so I usually stopped at a bank in town to get silver dollars. Visitors were not allowed to wear hats, shorts, or tank tops, which were considered too revealing, into the visitation area. I was once turned away and had to go into town to buy a pair of pants when I wore culottes that went to my knees, as they were considered shorts. Visitors couldn't carry in cell phones, purses, or food. I would put my car key, a folded tissue, and my silver dollars in a Ziploc bag when I went to visit. Anything else stayed in the car.

I would wait for Les to come in so I could ask what he wanted to eat before getting his food. I was allowed a one-time visit to the vending machines. There were different machines that offered sodas, sandwiches, fruit, yogurt, and, if you were lucky, fresh salad. The usual cookie, candy, nuts, and chips machines were available as well. Once I purchased his food, I couldn't change it or get him anything else. Some days, it would take an hour or more for them to bring him to the visitation area from his cell. I would spend my time waiting by checking out the selections of the day so I could rattle off a list of what was available—if I could remember. That became one of our running jokes as we grew older: whether or not I could remember what was available, as well as what he requested.

Once he told me what he wanted, I would tell the guard, and she would get a couple brown paper bags, marking them with his seat number. She and I would go to the machines, and I'd choose the items, insert the money, and press the button for each choice. The guard then removed it from the machine and placed it in the bag. I could not touch the food. All sorts of contraband flowed in and out of prisons—drugs, cigarettes, cell phones, and who knew what else—but the visitors had better not touch the vending items! Contraband didn't come in by way of the visitors. It was a marketable commodity between guards and inmates.

When our Washington, DC, appellate team came on board, Anthony Roth, one of the attorneys, would often visit Les when they needed to discuss an upcoming hearing. Anthony would purchase several candy bars and other items while he was waiting for Les to arrive. Les really wasn't fond of candy bars. Grateful for whatever he might get, he would never tell Anthony his likes and dislikes.

Usually, Les wanted a bottle of Diet Dr Pepper, a sandwich, chips, salad, fresh fruit (if available), and some kind of pie or dessert. On this day, he wanted two bottles of Diet Dr Pepper and a sandwich. Two bottles was an unusual request for him. He said his kidney stone was acting up, and he wasn't sure he could keep anything else down. I knew the soda wouldn't be helpful to the kidney stone; he needed lots of water to flush it out. But I also knew the plastic soda bottles were part of his grander plan for "just in case." He probably wouldn't be able to sit there for two hours, and once they told me that those two hours were up and I would have to leave, it could be *another* hour or two before they came to get him. So he prepared for whatever might happen. He could ask them to take him to the bathroom down the hall, but it usually took too long for them to get another escort, cuff him up again, and take him to the much-needed site of relief.

His kidneys lasted only an hour and a half that day, but his backup plan worked. And when they told me I had to go, his escort was at the door waiting to take him back to his cell. He wouldn't have to use the second bottle after all.

As we said our goodbyes and told each other "I love you," I choked back the tears, just as he was attempting to do. His eyes glistened with tears that he willed not to fall. Again, he was successful at keeping them at bay.

I felt older than my years as I always did on the long walk back to the front gate and my car. I reflected on how we came to be here. If I had known this would consume the majority of our life, had I known the pain and sadness we would experience, would I have chosen him anyway?

A Cold Winter's Night

Like a billowed cloud, the snowflakes lie
Among the forgotten past of springs gone by.
The magical, mystical wonders are seen as the sun shines down,
Causing a gleam of glorious colors, of sparling delight
That melts oh-too swiftly into the night.
Yet as darkness falls, the snow goes on gleaming,
For the moon up above through the night brightly beaming
Reveals to the world the beauty, glory, and delight that can
Be easily found on a cold winter's night.

November 1965

CHAPTER 3

The Beginning

October 23, 1965

When I was fifteen years old, my family moved to Tulsa, Oklahoma. I was starting high school in the fall and hoped we would stay put for a while. Our family moved a lot because of my father's work.

We joined Memorial Baptist Church. I began singing in the youth choir and went on group outings for pizza or to parties at other kids' houses after church. It was a beautiful summer, and I was making lots of new friends. The boys I knew were from church, and in September, I began to casually date Stan, who also went to the same school I attended.

Despite the fact that he was a senior and two years older than me, he was a bit immature. He had a car, which was cool, and ran on the varsity track team. He bragged a lot about being a great athlete. We had fun, but it wasn't serious.

By October, Stan had just about worn out his welcome at my house. He could be pretty obnoxious. He was always pulling pranks, making silly jokes, and just being childish. One night after church, we were at my house when he decided to see if he could put his head between the stair rails. He managed to put his head in, but then he couldn't get it out. He stood in the hallway, his hands gripping a rail on each side of his head as he twisted and turned. He tried to pull his head back out. Hearing the entire ruckus, Daddy appeared from the living room to see what was going on. Dad took one look at Stan, and his face became as red as Stan's. He looked like he was about to yank him out of there, no matter what.

He was furious. Stan was scared.

Mother ran to the kitchen, returning with a bottle of cooking oil. We began rubbing the oil on Stan's ears, head, and face as he continued to maneuver his way out of his self-imposed prison. He was finally able to release himself from the rails. Stan was told to go home.

As the door closed behind him, my father turned to me, still angry, and said I was grounded for two weeks. It was the first time in my life I had ever been grounded. I was the child who did everything by the book. I was confused. A part of me was glad that Stan had been sent home. I'd had enough of his childish ways myself. But it didn't seem fair that I was being punished for something *he'd* done.

Before the incident with Stan, I had noticed these two guys sitting in the back of the church every service. It was especially hard to miss them when I sang in the youth choir on Sunday nights. There they were—same back pew to the right. I never saw one without the other. The sound system for the church was located on the back wall, just behind where they sat, and I found out they were responsible for making sure it worked.

One Sunday evening, when I was hosting the teen social we usually had after Sunday night services, they showed up at my house. I learned their names were Les and Gary, but that was about it. I thought Les, the taller one, seemed older than the rest of the kids hanging out at the social. Obviously, he was too old for me. He was nice-looking, though, and athletic with short, almost-buzzed hair.

As Mother bustled around the kitchen, filling glasses and making sure there was plenty of ice, she leaned in toward me and asked, "Who is that good-looking guy over there leaning against the sink?"

"His name is Les," I told her. "I think he's older, maybe in college."

"He's cute," my mother responded as she walked over to fill a bowl with potato chips.

I turned to sneak a glance just as he looked up and caught my eye. We held each other's gaze for as long as we could. Realizing I was holding my breath, I tried to act normal as a rush of air from my lungs blew out and I started breathing again. His eyes were a perfect blue, and his smile lit up his entire face. I returned his smile.

He watched me as I walked across the room to where they were leaning against the kitchen sink.

"Can I get you something to eat or drink?" I asked them.

"We're fine," they both said in unison.

"So, what's your name and where do you go to school?" I inquired, even though I knew their names already.

"I'm Gary and I'm a senior at Nathan Hale," replied Les's friend.

"Oh, we go to the same school," I said, surprised.

"And what about you?" I asked, turning to Gary's friend with the blue eyes. "What's your name and where do you go to school?"

"I'm Les and I'm a senior at Will Rogers."

"I figured you were in college," I said to him.

"No, not yet."

"The football players at Rogers are just bigger than our football players," Gary chimed in, laughing. "They're state champions!"

After everyone left, Mother and I began cleaning up the kitchen. "He's a senior—not in college, but in high school," I said, bouncing around the kitchen. "I thought he was older."

"I think he's cute," Mother said. "You should go out with him."

"You don't just go out with someone," I answered incredulously, wondering why my mother didn't already know that. "The guys have to ask you first. As cute as he is, I can't believe he's not dating someone at his school. Maybe he is. I don't know. No one has ever mentioned it at church," I said rapidly as if I were trying to work out a puzzle. "And remember, everyone still thinks I'm dating Stan!" I said over my shoulder while tying up the trash.

"Don't remind me," she said, annoyed. "That can change."

Suddenly I sounded like a whiny teenager, which I wasn't, when I said in a voice almost in tears, "Don't forget. I'm grounded for two weeks. What if Les calls and asks me out?"

Three days later, Les did call. We chatted casually for a while about school and church activities, and then it was silent on the phone for a second. His voice lowered a bit before he spoke.

"I, uh, know you and Stan have been hanging out together the last few weeks," he said hesitantly, then a little quieter, "I wasn't sure if it was serious or not."

"No," I said. "It's not serious between us. We're pretty much done. He's not coming over anymore."

"I'm glad to hear that," he said, and I could hear the smile in his words. "I wondered if you would like to go out with me. The senior class play is Saturday, and I thought maybe you might like to go." He said "go" as if it had a huge question mark on the end.

My heart began to race at the prospect of the tall, cute guy with the blue eyes and the warm smile wanting to take me out. But I was grounded, and my dad was away for the week on business. My heart sank like a rock.

After a short pause, I said, "I'm not sure why, but I'm grounded. Stan did something really dumb, and my dad got so mad at *him* that he grounded *me* to get a break from him."

Les tried to hide the faint chuckle in his voice as he replied, "Oh, that's too bad." His tone was not very convincing. I was pretty sure he was glad Stan was out of the picture.

"It's over with me and Stan, but my dad is out of town. If you could call back tomorrow night, I might be able to get him to change his mind."

"Okay, I'll do that. I hope it works out."

"Me too," I said, meaning it a whole lot more than I let on.

I raced out of my parents' bedroom, where the phone was located, and ran downstairs, almost in tears, to find Mother. Frantic words poured out of my mouth when I saw her.

"That cute guy who was here Sunday night just asked me to go to his school play this Saturday. I really, really want to go, but Daddy grounded me, and I told Les I couldn't go. It's not fair that I'm grounded when I didn't do anything," I said a little too loudly and, again, too whiny. "I really want to go out with him. What am I going to do?"

"Don't worry," Mother said. "I'll talk to him and see what I can do."

She picked up the phone and called Daddy at the motel where he was staying. Before I knew it, he agreed to "unground" me and let me go out Saturday night with the good-looking football player from Rogers.

I was on pins and needles the next night, waiting to see if Les would call back. Sure enough, he did, and I told him I could go. We talked for a while, getting to know one another a little more. He told me about his football game the next night with Booker T. Washington, one of the other schools in town. Tulsa had seven high schools, and I was still learning all their names and where they were located. I told him I played in a bowling league that met every Saturday morning, confiding that I wasn't very good at bowling but that I enjoyed it.

I went to the bowling alley Saturday morning, and we were almost finished with our session when I looked up to see a tall guy with a Rogers High School letterman jacket coming through the door. A large bandage was wrapped across the right side of his face. I wasn't sure, but it looked like Les. He walked tentatively over to the lane where I was bowling and waited for me to finish.

"I thought I'd better let you take a look at me this morning," he said as I stared at his injured face. "I didn't want to scare you tonight by coming to pick you up looking like this."

"What happened?" I asked as I moved in closer to get a better look. He reached up and gently touched the bandage and winced a bit as he touched it. "I only had to get a few stitches, but I'm afraid I don't look like much."

I looked closely over his eyebrow, trying to see how much damage had been done.

"That must really hurt," I said, willing myself not to gingerly touch his face. "But you don't look all that bad." I hoped he wasn't going to cancel our first date. "I don't mind being seen with you looking like that. You'll be a hero. You took one for the team, right?" I asked, laughing. "I'm sure we'll be attracting some attention, though, so you might want to be prepared for that."

He looked down at me. We stood so close that we were almost touching. A sense of relief seemed to come over him as if he expected me to turn him away, not go out with him because of this. He paused for a moment, still looking at me, and softly replied, "You're probably right, but I think they'll be looking at you, not me." A tingle went up my spine as we stood looking at each other, and I saw no bandage, no stitches—just a very kind, thoughtful guy I could fall in love with.

We walked out of the bowling alley to where Mother was waiting to pick me up.

"See you tonight," he said.

"See you tonight," I responded. He opened the passenger door and said hello to my mother, and I got in the car, never taking my eyes off him, even as we drove away.

I was so excited for my first date with Les that I couldn't eat anything for dinner. Johnny Mathis was singing "Chances Are" in my bedroom, and I sang along with him as I slid into a bath filled with the fragrance of Estée Lauder's Youth Dew, my favorite scent.

I carefully applied my makeup and did my hair. Going to my closet, I took out the new dress that Mother had made me just the day before and just for this occasion. And then the doorbell rang.

Les had arrived right on time to pick me up. Bandage or no bandage, he was still handsome and polite. He walked me to his car and opened the door. I slid onto the passenger seat of his parents' 1958 Oldsmobile. We were alone for the first time since I met him.

Will Rogers High School was an older school than Hale. It looked like one of those classic, old museums or Ivy League colleges. We walked up the steps and through the doors, where I found myself surrounded by Les's football buddies and their dates. Gary was right. They were so big and tall.

Maybe I'd been hanging out with the sophomores too long at my school and hadn't really paid that much attention to the seniors at Nathan Hale High School. I felt as if I were in a different world. This was what state champions looked like.

We mingled in the foyer with the other students and their dates. The room was filled with trophy cases brimming with plaques, cups, ribbons, and lots of shiny trophies for every sport you could imagine. I felt comfortable on Les's arm and liked being with him. He seemed at ease, introducing me to his friends, looking out for me, making sure I was enjoying myself. I was so nervous; I hoped I didn't have to remember their names. He was a perfect gentleman and was funny in his own way. He had large hands with square fingers, and mine seemed to fit perfectly in his when he took it to lead me inside.

The play was enjoyable, and Les got me home that night just before my curfew. We talked for several minutes as we sat in his car outside my house. He gave me a smile, and his eyes twinkled from beneath the bandage across his right eyebrow, catching the glow of the streetlight.

"I bet that's going to hurt coming off," I said, pointing to the bandage.

"Yeah, I bet it is too," he answered as he turned to look at me. "I had fun tonight."

"So did I," I managed to say, despite the butterflies filling my stomach, making it hard to breathe.

"I'd like to see you again sometime." He looked down at me as I sat next to him in the middle of the front seat.

"I'd like that too," I replied, waiting expectantly.

He reached for the handle of his door, opened it, and got out. Walking around to the other side of the car, he opened the door for me and took my hand in his as I stepped out. He walked me to the door, then stopped and turned to look at me. I had to look up at him. Our eyes met for an awkward moment, and it seemed as if we were the only two people in the world.

"Maybe I'll see you tomorrow at church," he said, breaking the silence.

"Yes, I'll be there."

"Thanks again for going to the play."

"Thanks for asking me," I said softly, wondering if he would kiss me good night.

"Next time, maybe we can see a movie."

"I'd like that," I responded breathlessly.

Squeezing my hand, he turned and walked back to his car, pausing to give me a wave before he got in. He hadn't kissed me! Why hadn't he kissed me?

We would have three more dates before he kissed me good night. He didn't believe in first-date kisses. Some things, he said, are worth waiting for.

That was the beginning: October 23, 1965. The senior class play at Will Rogers High School in Tulsa, Oklahoma. Life would never be the same for either one of us again.

Almost fifty years later, I sat in the visitation room on death row, watching my husband of forty-seven years trying to spread mayonnaise on the sandwich I had just purchased out of the vending machine while also holding the visitation phone up to his ear. I finally asked him a question I had been curious about.

"Why would you ask someone out on a date who you knew was dating someone else?"

He stopped what he was doing and looked up through the glass. "You know I can't hear you if I'm not looking at you. What did you just ask me?"

"I asked, why would you ask me out on a date when you knew I was dating Stan?"

He furrowed his eyebrows as if it were the most ridiculous thing he'd ever heard. "What are you talking about?"

"You asked me out, knowing I was seeing someone else. Isn't that sort of against the rules?"

"You're asking me that now, after all this time?" he inquired.

"Yes."

He rolled his eyes as he oftentimes did with me. It was his way of teasing me, as if it were such a ridiculous question. I was never offended by it. It was part of our repertoire.

He looked back down at the $3.50 prepackaged sandwich, finished applying the mayonnaise, put the bread back on top, set it down on the plastic wrapper, and looked back up, wiping his hands on his pant legs.

"Was it some kind of dare?" I asked. "I know neither you nor Gary liked Stan very much, and I heard you were trying to break us up because you thought he was an arrogant show-off. Is that true?"

He shook his head, laughing to himself. He leaned in and looked me straight in the eye.

"You're right. We didn't like him very much," he said. "He was a show-off, and he brought his track medals to church. He was arrogant and immature."

There was a quiet pause as his face softened and his smile turned serious. My eyes began to burn as tears threatened.

"I asked you out because I liked you, I thought you were pretty, and I didn't think he was good enough for you. It wasn't a dare or a bet. I wanted you. And if I recall, you didn't have a problem saying yes to going out with me."

"No, I didn't," I said, still blushing a little just remembering how excited I was that he had asked me out. "I just thought if it was a dare, maybe you didn't know what you were getting yourself into," I said, teasing him a bit with a smile. If ever I wanted to go back in time, it was now. To do it all over again but with the knowledge of all the pitfalls.

"Oh, I knew what I was doing," he said quietly, as his laughing eyes became softer, somehow sadder, tears threatening to spill as well. "And let's not even talk about who got stuck with whom."

If You Love Me

If you need me, I'll be here.
If you want me, I'll be near.
If you love me, I won't go.
If you love me, please tell me so.
For love is patient, love is kind.
Love is in the heart, not of the mind.
So speak your heart and let me know,
Just as I speak mine, I love you so.

April 22, 1984

CHAPTER 4

Stages of Life

Life seems to present itself in stages. The first part of my life took place from the time I was born until I was eighteen. I was born, grew as a child, and became an adolescent and teen, learning more and more as each stage unfolded itself.

There was drama in my life, but the drama was through the eyes of a child, then a young person, who, although not rich or worldly, had been brought up with virtue, love, and a life without much want.

My second stage of life began when I married on August 24, 1968, a few months before my nineteenth birthday. I had been in love for almost three years and chose marriage instead of school. I think back to that time and remember how very mature I thought I was. I knew everything there was to know, or so I thought.

Two weeks later, we headed off from Tulsa to Texas A&M in what was now Les's 1958 Oldsmobile pulling the smallest trailer U-Haul had, loaded with all our wedding gifts. Les's dad had given him his car when Les Sr. bought a new Oldsmobile. We had no place to live, and neither of us had a job. We were two very grown-up people heading off to live our dreams, begin a new life, and find our future.

The only thing un-grown-up about this momentous departure was having my mother and my four-year-old sister with us. Our first stop would be in Abilene for my cousin's wedding. All four of my cousins closest to my age were getting married within forty-five days of each other, and we were all in each other's weddings. The Olds broke down halfway there, giving up its last breath, refusing all efforts to be brought back to life. My dad came to pick us up, and we continued on to the wedding, turning for a last look at the car we loved so much.

When people ask me where I grew up or where I am from, I tell them Anson, Texas, eighteen miles north of Abilene. I never lived there. I lived all over the country. But Anson, that's where I am *from*. That is where my roots are. I had spent a lot of time with my Anson grandparents, Joe and O'Fallon Baucum, both at the family farm and at the house Grandmother moved to in town after my grandfather, Daddy Joe, died.

Les and I were married just two weeks before and on our way to our first home. While we were there for the wedding, Grandmother took me grocery shopping with her at Wyatt's grocery, the place she had shopped for years. Wyatt's was about the same size as one of our smaller Dollar General stores. They still sold groceries on credit; if needed, customers could pay their bills at the end of the month, and their groceries were boxed, not bagged. There were times when Grandmother would call and tell Mr. Wyatt what she needed, and he would have it boxed for her when she came into town, or someone else would drop it off at her house for her.

She said her wedding gift to me was to send me off to my first home with everything I needed to "keep house," as she called it. By the time we had gone through the small store, I had a couple of boxes filled with flour and sugar, salt and pepper, Crisco, soda and baking powder, and any other staple items she thought necessary for a new bride's kitchen. When we loaded the boxes in our car, she placed seven handmade tea towels she had embroidered on top of the groceries, one for each day of the week.

A couple of days later, Les and I continued on our journey to College Station with a used Buick my dad had bought for us, towing the small

U-Haul trailer behind. We stayed a few days in the apartment of a cousin, Johnece Marchbanks, and her husband, Pete, while we looked for a place of our own.

We were on the waiting list for married-student housing, and our name finally came up. The houses were white, clapboard, two-story buildings with two apartments downstairs and two upstairs. We moved to an upstairs apartment of one of the many quadruplex buildings that faced Kyle Field. We were so close to the stadium that we could hear the football games from our living room.

The corps cadets marched down the street in front of our house during their training drills on Saturday mornings; the sound of boots hitting the ground and the chanting of their cadence as they passed by often awakened us.

The one-bedroom apartments, about eight hundred square feet, were quite roomy, and the rent was very reasonable at $62.50 a month, including utilities. The buildings had been built during the late 1930s and early '40s under President Franklin D. Roosevelt's Works Progress Administration project.

Women didn't go to A&M at that time, unless they were the wife of a student, a professor, or a daughter of a professor. I took a few classes while there but usually was the only girl in class. Every cadet in my class ran to open the door for me.

Les started classes, and I found a job on campus in the Department of Biochemistry, thrilled that I would be making $250 a month. Our plan was that I would work full time during the year and Les would work during the summer, making enough money for tuition, books, and anything extra we might want or need. I would later tell my friends I got my PhT, or Putting Hubby Through, at Texas A&M.

And so, Les and I began our life as newlyweds in College Station, Texas. From that time on, we struggled and succeeded, argued and made up, and our U-Hauls got bigger each time we moved to a new destination.

A lot of our friends there were hunters, so Les learned to reload, melting lead in a saucepan on our apartment stove and setting up his press on the kitchen table. Les would teach me how to shoot his .45 pistol at the Brazos River. Our targets were usually cans floating down the river, which made it more challenging.

We left A&M in 1971 and moved to Denver where our first daughter was born in February 1972. My middle name is Lea (pronounced Lee), so we named her Leslea by combining Les Jr. and Les Sr. and my middle name and my dad's name, Lee.

My parents and siblings were living there as well. After a couple of years in Denver, my dad was made an offer to run an insulation company in Alexandria, Indiana. He took the offer and hired Les to manage the warehouse and shipping and eventually sales. Once again, we found ourselves at the U-Haul store. This time, we had to rent a truck, as we had outgrown the small trailer we started out with on this adventure we called life.

Indiana was lovely, but it was strange to be in a state that was so small. We could drive an hour or two and be in another state in any direction we went. The winters were terribly cold and wet, which could chill you to the bone, unlike the dry cold in Colorado.

We lived in Daleville, Indiana, not far from Alexandria where Les worked. We had been there a couple of years when Hollie, our second daughter, was born in Muncie, Indiana, in late August 1975. An opportunity arose for my dad to purchase an insulation company in Fort Collins, Colorado, and he asked Alan and Steve (my two brothers) and Les if they would come help him run the business in Colorado and parts of Wyoming. We were all thrilled to go back to Colorado.

Hollie was four weeks old when we left Indiana and headed back to Colorado. Les drove the moving truck, and I followed along in our car with the girls in the back seat. Moving with a four-week-old baby wasn't all that bad, as she slept most of the time, waking up every few hours to eat and get a fresh diaper.

Living once again in Colorado, Les was able to take advantage of all kinds of sports activities. He had hunted some when we lived in Denver and had also taken up photography over the years.

In Fort Collins, he made close friends with a group of like-minded out-doorsmen at Arrow Dynamics, a local business that catered to bowhunters. He transitioned from hunting with a gun to a bow and enjoyed competitive black-powder shooting. He started teaching Leslea how to shoot a bow and arrow after he had a bow made to fit her small hands.

Jim Widmier, the owner of Arrow Dynamics, became one of Les's closest friends. Leslea sometimes hung out at the range with her dad and the other guys he bonded with over the years. Many of them are still friends of ours, and we are able to keep in touch through social media.

Les expanded his outdoor experiences by camping on weekends in rugged areas and hiking through the Rockies. He and his friends traveled up into the mountains, sometimes pulling horse trailers as far as the roads would go and then continuing up the mountains on horseback.

He always took his camera and would return with breathtaking pictures. Wanting to develop his own pictures, he built a makeshift darkroom in our hall bathroom where he could experiment with different mediums. His vivid color pictures were amazing, but his black-and-white stage, channeling his Ansel Adams within, produced some wonderful shots as well.

We wanted to live in the country, and in 1977, we found a log house on thirty acres northeast of Fort Collins. It was finished inside with drywall, indoor plumbing, and all the modern amenities. It just looked rustic from the outside.

A small creek ran through the property dividing the backyard from the acreage behind the house. Our driveway from the county road leading up to the house was just long enough to ensure our little corner of the world was quiet. It was just what we wanted.

The first night we spent in our log house, the girls were sleeping soundly in their beds as we turned out the light on the bedside table. It was so differ-ent from living in town, as there was not a sound to be heard. We lay quietly in bed and turned to look at each other. The room was pitch-black. I held my hand up in the air and couldn't see it in the darkness. I reached over, touching Les's face to make sure he was there, even though I could feel him next to me and hear him breathing. We laughed at the same time, making a mental note to get nightlights for the girls' rooms and hallway.

There were two concrete goose blinds in our alfalfa fields where Canadian geese often flew over. A small corral and barn sat at the far north end of the property, and another larger barn was about fifty yards behind the house.

The view from the picture window in our living room was Rocky Mountain National Park to the west. Sitting at our dinner table at the back of the house, we could see the fields where the geese flew over or an occasional pheasant strutting across the backyard.

Goats and horses grazed in our fields, and barn cats gave birth to kittens, much to the delight of our girls. One day, Les found two-year-old Hollie lying facedown in the dirt inside the barn, peering under a cast iron stove. She was trying to coax the new kitties to come out to play.

We loved living out there and so did the girls. Soon after we bought that house, Leslea started kindergarten at Timnath Elementary School, and I sent her off to school from the end of that road for several years. If the weather was nice, she, Hollie, and I would walk together to the end of the road to meet the bus. Hollie couldn't wait until she could go too. I remember the first day Leslea got on that bus. I cried and Hollie cried because Mommy was crying. Leslea looked out the window of the bus, waving excitedly, as she was ready to be a big girl. When it was rainy or snowing, I would drive her to meet the bus or sometimes drive her straight to school.

In 1980, after five wonderful years in Fort Collins, it was decided to sell the business. My parents and sister were moving back to Texas.

Les found a job with Thompson-Hayward Chemical Company in Grand Junction, Colorado, on the eastern side of the Rockies, or the eastern slope, as they call it. He would be working in the oilfields selling drilling mud. We both loved living in Fort Collins and thought this was the best place to live. But we had not been to Grand Junction yet and would soon find it was pretty great too.

We found a nice house on a cul-de-sac in the Redlands at the foot of the Colorado National Monument. Grand Junction was a different part of

Colorado than what we had experienced before. We had the mountains and Powderhorn Ski Resort to the east less than an hour away, and the desert and the Colorado River just twenty-two miles to the west. It was like the best of both worlds.

Les began his job with Thompson-Hayward, covering the territory in and around Grand Junction, up into northern Colorado and southwestern Utah. He drove a Bronco before anyone had ever heard of an SUV. He was in sales but wore blue jeans and boots to work, which suited him just fine. He had one of the first mobile telephones, a huge receiver that sat on a console bolted to the floorboard of the Bronco.

I went to work for Mesa College in the housing and counseling office. It was totally different than my other positions in the Department of Biochemistry at both Texas A&M and Colorado State University. I was more involved with the students and got to know so many more people. It was also a much smaller school than the other two had been.

Many of our friends were professors and students at the college, and we did a lot of things socially with them. At holidays, we would host dinners at our house, inviting students who couldn't make it home. Many a Thanksgiving we served a Canadian goose instead of a turkey. The meat was all dark and very tasty. One year we had venison; another year, elk and even bear that Les had shot with a bow and arrow that season. He named her Modine, and she hung on our wall for many years. The students always loved to come to the Bowers' for the holidays.

Christmas parties were a big deal at our house. We would have them early in December before the students left for Christmas break and before we packed up and traveled back to Texas and Oklahoma for our Christmas visits.

We soon got involved with the outdoor program at the college. Or I should say, Les did and I often tagged along. The outdoor program did all the adventurous things Les liked to do or wanted to learn. They rafted down the Colorado River, braving the roaring rapids between high canyon walls. They cross-country skied—some treks during the day and other breathtaking ones up on the ridge of the Colorado National Monument during a night with a full moon. Les preferred snowshoeing on those ventures and took Leslea along on a couple of those trips.

Outdoor survival classes were taught by Dr. Bruce Bauerle, a biology professor at Mesa, and Les took advantage of many of those. Bruce was almost the same age as some of the students and a really fun guy to go into the mountains or on the rivers with. They spent several frigid nights in "snow caves" that Bruce taught them to make after snowshoeing into the deepest parts of the mountains. I would see pictures of crossed snowshoes in front of what appeared to be a mound of snow and ice. That was an indication that someone had made his or her cave there. Les said once you were in your cave with your lantern, you had to take off your coat and thermals, as the glow of the lantern warmed the cave as if it were a crackling fire. I thought the one-man cave looked a bit too claustrophobic for my taste. I preferred a real crackling fire in the house.

They would find their food in the woods and cook whatever they shot or trapped in order to survive in a crisis. Les would perfect recipes for the group that he cooked over open fires or buried in the ground in cast iron pots.

He became a licensed gun dealer, allowing him to buy and sell guns for himself and his friends. And he continued to reload his shells as he did when we were at A&M. He also bought and sold cameras and other outdoor equipment, experimenting with new and different types of lenses and brands.

We camped, rafted, hiked, and fished, always on the go whenever we could, exploring new areas of the West. We started out with tents, and as our family grew, we graduated to a camper with real beds and a real potty. Something I much preferred, especially with small children in tow.

We took the girls camping to Four Corners, where we explored the ruins of the ancestral Pueblo cultures that lived on the side of the mountains for protection and farmed on the mesa during the day. While we were at Four Corners, several Indian tribes were having a powwow, and we were able to see them dance and perform in their native costumes.

Many Fridays, I would come home from work, and the camper would be packed, ready to go to Durango, Silverton, or Ouray, just a couple of hours away, where we would spend our weekends. Oftentimes, Les would hike by himself up into the higher elevations, scouting out his next hunting trip. There were a couple of times I got a bit concerned, as he would be gone for several hours. I never realized just exactly how far he would go until many years later. One particular year, 1981, he was scouting out what he hoped would be his big mountain goat hunt if he were lucky enough to draw a permit the next year.

Les whitewater rafted on the Colorado River as often as he could while we lived in Grand Junction. I went with him several times. My last trip down the river was in 1982. My brother Steve and his wife, Cathy, were with us on that trip, and we all experienced a lot more adventure than we had planned! We flipped the raft that day when a pretty big rapid got under the fourteen-foot raft and literally turned it upside down.

Ours was one of the larger fourteen-man rafts. This type was steered by one oarsman, unlike the smaller rafts where there are five or six rafters along with a guide crammed in as everyone paddles. Les had built his own frame and was the oarsman on our raft. We carried military ammo boxes that were waterproof and strapped down to the frame so that if the raft flipped, we wouldn't lose our cameras or gear that had been stowed in them. The ice chests were strapped down too—the passengers, not so much. We wore vests and tennis shoes and usually straddled the sides of the giant tubes, holding onto the rope around the buoyant sides of the raft as we tore through the rapids.

Floating the Colorado River could be peaceful and smooth in some areas, and then suddenly the roar of the river breaking over huge rocks could be heard just around the bend, the water no longer calm but rough and dangerous. Riding that raft was like riding a bull, or at least what I think riding a bull would be like. And sometimes I can't believe I did it—and on more than one occasion.

When she flipped that day, the raft went completely upside down. I remember the water surrounding me as if I were in slow motion. I thought, *This is what it feels like to drown.* I looked up through the swirling water and saw the raft above me and began to swim toward the surface. I came up under the raft, finding just enough space for me to get my head out of the water to breathe. The inflated sides of the raft kept the upside-down bottom just high enough above the water to make an air pocket. I swam over to one of the sides, grabbed the rope, and went back under so I could come up on the outside of the tube.

I found Cathy, and she looked as stunned as I felt. I told her to hold onto the rope and stick her feet out in front of her. The sound of crashing water around the bend ahead told me we were about to go through another rapid. Since we were on the outside of the raft, we needed to be able to kick off the rocks if necessary with our tennis shoes, as we could be easily crushed.

We bounced around in the water, this time on the outside of the raft, pushing ourselves off rocks as the roiling water tossed us to and fro. I had no idea where Steve and Les were.

After maneuvering that last rapid, the raft still upside down, we found our husbands on the other side of the raft. As we came around a bend, another raft in our group had pulled over to the rocks on one side of the canyon to throw ropes to us and pull us in and turn our raft upright. We finally got it flipped over, bailed out the water, and took inventory of what might have been lost or damaged. The biggest loss was Les's sunglasses and his noteworthy river hat.

I spent the rest of the trip through the canyon lying in the bottom of the raft with a pretty big knot on my head and probably a mild concussion. It was the end of the season. This would be my last trip; we didn't know then, but we would be leaving Grand Junction before the next rafting season. I never had the opportunity to get back on the horse, as they say. Frankly, I'm not sure I would have. We had small children. What was I thinking?

Not only had Les built his own raft frame, but he had also recovered two of our sofas and made his own backpack, tent, down jackets, and outerwear. My Singer sewing machine was practically worn out from him using it to make all these things. And we were constantly picking up goose down off the living room floor where he had packed his jackets before closing up the stitches. He loved every minute of being outdoors and in nature, especially with his friends and family.

Our life was idyllic in a lot of ways but certainly not without problems. We had been living in Grand Junction for a couple of years and were on one of our many camping trips. It was the summer of 1982, and Les and I were sitting in the Bronco parked beside a beautiful river high up in the mountains between Silverton and Durango. The girls were napping inside the trailer as we sat in the car discussing whether to stay married or not.

I can't remember why. Our biggest issues were communication, unmet expectations on one another's part, and occasional financial struggles. Our faith, love, and commitment to one another and to God seemed to always overcome whatever life threw at us.

We both loved each other, and we had too much to lose not to work on resolving our differences. We decided that day that neither one of us could imagine our life without the other, despite whatever problems we faced.

It was a conversation that neither of us thought we would ever have, but one probably every couple has at one time or another. We decided to stay together and work on those differences because the love we had grown into at that point was greater than the conflict we were experiencing.

Less than a year later, we found ourselves in the middle of the 1983 oil crisis. There was a surplus of crude oil that caused an economic downturn in the industry. The Grand Junction office of Thompson-Hayward was shutting its doors.

Les did some contracting work for a while, and I continued my job at Mesa College. He became Mr. Mom, and it was nice to come home from work and find dinner and homemade bread on the table. (He made an amazing beer bread that I've never quite been able to duplicate.) But it wasn't enough. He needed a more stable position. Businesses on the eastern slope were closing. The economy was bleak.

Thompson-Hayward had an opening for a salesman in Dallas, and Les was offered the job. It would be a transfer, but in a different division, not the oil industry. He would have to say goodbye not only to the Rockies, but also to his boots and blue jeans on business calls. He would be in corporate America now.

Moving back to Texas was not what we really wanted to do, but at the moment, it seemed like the best alternative. The girls were getting older, my parents lived in Weatherford, and his parents were in Tulsa. Maybe it would be good to be closer to family.

If leaving Colorado wasn't bad enough, we moved back to Texas in July, pulling our camper behind us. I had forgotten how hot Texas was in July. Grand Junction temperatures sometimes got into the triple digits, but the air was dry and we had large swamp coolers on our roof and slept with the windows cracked in the summer, the cooler pulling fresh breezes in through the windows.

Les's sales territory was Garland and Mesquite, on the east side of Dallas. I had lived in Arlington when I was in elementary school and still had friends I knew from those days. Arlington was closer to Weatherford than Dallas, so we decided to settle there.

One of his dreams had been to learn to fly. He went up in a glider in Colorado once and found it so exhilarating. If he could have afforded it, he probably would have taken up that sport. But the lessons and flying time didn't fit into our budget.

He began to read about ultralight aircraft and talked about maybe one day owning one. I knew how much he had enjoyed his outing in the glider but was not aware he was seriously interested in ultralights. I had never even heard of them before he started subscribing to magazines about them.

One night in the late summer or early fall of 1983, we were watching a *60 Minutes* segment on ultralights. Les turned to me and said he thought he would like to make this his next sport. I believe my exact words were, "Over my dead body." Probably not one of my finer moments.

The report had focused on accidents and deaths attributed to the small aircraft; I didn't think they were safe. I reminded him that he was a 240-pound, one-time offensive guard who used to play football with Joe Greene at North Texas State University. A small airplane, with what I believed was the equivalent of a lawn mower engine, was not sufficient to carry him safely up in the air.

He didn't bring up the subject of ultralight airplanes again after that, as he realized how serious I was about him not having one. Now his biggest problem was how he was going to break it to me that he had already bought one. Something I was not aware of.

We had my family over to our house on Thanksgiving Day, 1983. The kids and Les, along with my brother-in-law, Tracy, spent a lot of time out in the backyard. Les had told me he was going to build an ultralight that would be modified to his height and weight. That afternoon, he was showing Tracy some of the parts he had purchased and setting it up in the backyard. I poked my head outside to see what was going on. When I saw the half-assembled ultralight in the backyard, I just turned and went back inside. He knew I was still not keen on the idea, but he was working on changing my mind about its safety.

Despite my rather blunt opinion of his new interest, Les continued to read magazines and learn more about the sport. I did not know he had bought a fully assembled plane at this time, so I'm just speculating when I say that. I think after he did more research, he realized his rush to purchase this particular plane was a mistake; the engine was not going to work for him. He would have to either get another one or modify the one he had. But first, he had to get me on board with the idea.

I woke up Friday morning, January 20, 1984, to Les's arms wrapped around me as we lay there like two perfectly formed spoons joined comfortably together in a kitchen drawer. I felt the warmth of his body mingling with mine, thinking I couldn't remember being happier than I was at that very moment. Our conversation eighteen months earlier while camping in the mountains about whether we would stay married or get a divorce was merely a far-off memory of a small bump in our otherwise peaceful life. I had no idea the happiness I felt would crumble before the strike of midnight.

Serenity

When the world around us seems more than we can bear,
There's someone who can help, our troubles He will share.
He's there when things go easy, and He's there whenever we fall.
He's there to carry the burden; all we have to do is call.
When all is dark around me, and even darker inside,
It's then I need Him most; it's to Him I run and hide.
He lifts me in His arms and holds me close to Him.
He carries me through the dark and gives me peace within.
Thank you, Lord, for being there. With you, I'm never alone.
Thank you, Lord, for loving me and making me your own.

April 24, 1984

CHAPTER 5

The Longest Day

January 20, 1984

On Thursday, January 5, Les and I were driving from Arlington to Dallas to meet Jim and Pat Widmier from Fort Collins. They were in town for the gun and bowhunters convention, and we were meeting them for dinner. On the drive over, Les told me the FBI contacted him twice at his office regarding four men who had been murdered in a small town north of Dallas. Les said he told them he talked to one of the men on the phone the week of the murders, inquiring about an ultralight the man had advertised to sell. The FBI contacted him through phone calls he had made to one of the victims and hoped he might have some information about the murders. I wasn't happy that he hadn't told me when they first contacted him, but I wasn't too concerned about it either.

Les told me he didn't want to worry me about it, so he hadn't mentioned it. Now he had received a phone message from the FBI requesting that he come to their office for a polygraph test. They told him he was not a person of interest but hoped he could offer some information that might be helpful to their investigation. He wanted my opinion on what he should do.

I immediately told him I didn't think he should do it. The idea of their asking him to take a polygraph just because he had talked to some guy on the phone seemed ridiculous to me. We decided he needed to call his high school friend Gary, who was now a lawyer in Oklahoma City. We did after we got home, and Gary agreed with us that it wasn't a good idea to take the polygraph. However, he was not a criminal attorney and advised Les to talk to a lawyer for another opinion. Les made an appointment to talk to Richard Klein, a criminal attorney he was referred to.

Richard advised Les not to do it as well, citing some of the same reasons Gary had advised against. The courts did not consider the technology as evidence. Machines and operators were not reliable, and often mistakes were made in the testing. As far as I knew, that was the end of it.

Les had no appointments for Friday, January 20, so we planned to spend the day together. After getting the girls ready and off to school, Les and I went to Stitch Niche to get material, patterns, and thread for him to begin his new craft project: counted cross-stitch. From the outdoors to sports, from recovering furniture to cooking, Les always had a project going on. He never wanted to be idle. Now he was going to try his hand at something entirely new.

After picking out a wildlife pattern and the supplies for him to begin, we shared a leisurely lunch together at Schlotzsky's next door to the craft store. Once we got home, he went to run some errands, and I picked up the girls from school, dropped our soon-to-be twelve-year-old daughter Leslea at a friend's house to spend the night, and Hollie, our eight-year-old daughter, and I went to the grocery store to pick up something for dinner. I also went to the rental store, as they were now renting movies in a box that had the tape inside, as well as the machines you could play them on. I picked out a mystery movie about the FBI.

The three of us ate fried shrimp, potatoes, and salad, cleaned up the kitchen, and settled in to watch a movie in our pajamas and bathrobes. Just a typical Friday night at home.

About 7:30, the doorbell rang. I opened it to find two Texas rangers standing on our front porch. They informed me that they had warrants to search our house, our car, and my husband's person.

One of them handed me the warrants just as Les walked up beside me to see who was at the door. Immediately, twenty-three officers descended upon our house—Texas rangers, the Grayson County Sheriff's office, the FBI, and even two Arlington police officers stormed our living room.

Les went to the phone to call Richard Klein, the attorney he had conferred with earlier that week regarding the visit from the FBI at his office and their request for a polygraph. Richard told Les we would need to comply with the search warrants but not to answer any questions they might ask him. While he was on the phone with Richard, I gathered Hollie and went to her room to find something to distract her. There was an agent with each of us wherever we went.

I walked back in where Les was. His face was contorted, now deep in thought, clearly concerned. I started toward him when FBI Agent Jim Blanton asked if there was someplace I could go, somewhere I could take Hollie and stay for a while. I couldn't take my car, he said, as it was part of the search warrant. It was obvious the agents were trying to separate Les and me, but I continued to try to catch his attention. I finally walked *around* the agent blocking me and asked him what Richard had said and then told him I was going to take Hollie to Sharon and Fred's house. He agreed that was a good idea and told me to call my parents to come get her and Leslea. I left Hollie with him and saw him trying to assure her everything was okay. She clung to him, crying as I went to the phone. I called Sharon and asked her to come pick us up. Then I went to our bedroom to change into my clothes and found the room filled with officers already searching everything. There were at least five of them, some in the bathroom, others opening drawers and closets.

Blanton stood over six feet, three inches and was lean with close-cut hair. He was probably in his fifties or so. He stayed near me the whole time, following me wherever I went. I could see that I had no privacy and he was not going to leave me alone, even to change clothes. I picked up my clothes from the end of our bed where I had laid them when I changed into my nightgown and robe. I went into my walk-in closet, shutting the door with him standing outside.

He was still standing there waiting for me when I emerged. I held my purse in my hand as I stepped into the bedroom and headed toward the door. He stopped me before I got there, took my purse from me, and riffled through it, making sure I didn't carry anything out they might be looking for. Les was surrounded by other agents and officers and looked up as he saw me emerging from our bedroom. He was still in his jeans, T-shirt, and robe. His face was grim. I walked toward him, and it was as if they all circled up and were making a concentrated effort to keep us apart. I reached into the circle and picked up Hollie and looked straight at Les to say something to him just as the agents turned him around and walked him into another room.

He was gone before we could speak.

I took our daughter, walked outside, and piled into my friend's car. We drove off to Sharon's house, a couple of miles away.

The two hours I stayed away from my house and my husband were excruciating. I paced the floor, trying to remain calm for Hollie. I couldn't believe I had gone off and left Les there alone. I needed to know what was going on. I needed to be there with him. After much debating with Sharon and her husband, Fred, regarding whether to stay or go back, I convinced her to drive me back home. I left our daughter, sleeping with one of Sharon's kids, and she promised to look after her for as long as I needed. I had no idea how long that might be.

I could feel the eyes of all the men—who had only hours before invaded my home—watching me as I returned to the place that should have been our sanctuary. I found my husband had switched his bathrobe for a flannel shirt and was sitting on our couch in the front living room. He looked up at me as I walked through the front door, our eyes met, and I wondered if he saw in my eyes the shock, confusion, and fear that I saw in his. Easing myself down beside him, we sat silently, holding hands for a few minutes. A Grayson County sheriff's deputy sat less than two feet away from us on the piano bench.

Throughout the house, officers were searching every drawer, every closet, and every corner. They were in the garage, in the backyard. I had no idea what they were looking for. Some peered around corners from other rooms, trying to see where we were and what we were doing. Others would casually walk by now and then. We sat there for what seemed like hours. From around the corner, I stole a glance into our bedroom and saw a couple of men lying on our bed, taking a break it seemed, from their search. Laughing and talking to one another, they lit up a couple of cigarettes.

Under the living room's window seat, plastic bags with labels marked EVIDENCE sat on the floor. I had no idea what that meant. I should have, I suppose, but I didn't. The few items I could see inside the bags seemed like benign, everyday objects, nothing of importance. *Evidence of what?* I still had no idea what was going on, what brought this on, why they were here. Les and I just sat there and stared at the bags.

He turned to me and quietly told me while I was at Sharon's house that they had taken him to Arlington Memorial Hospital. I was shocked. A doctor had removed hairs from his head, his beard, his arm, and his leg. Evidently, that was what the search warrant "for his person" meant.

I stared at him, unable to respond. The thought of him going through all of that alone, even though I knew they would never have allowed me to go with him, broke my heart. We continued sitting silently, holding hands, speaking only in low tones now and then.

The deputy on the piano bench never left. I wondered if he didn't have something better to do. He tried to engage us in conversation, but we were too shocked and deep in our own thoughts to give him any mind. I know now that he didn't just happen to be there but had been strategically placed in order to keep an eye on us, in hopes that we would say something incriminating.

The thought of Les being arrested never crossed my mind. Even as I write this, I see how incredulous it sounds. I saw the bags of evidence lying on the living room floor. That should have alarmed me, but I wasn't putting the meaning of everything together. My brain did not comprehend what was going on. I thought they were going to finish what they were doing and leave.

Weldon Lucas, one of the Texas rangers, asked Les to step into one of the girls' bedrooms with him. It was then that reality hit me. They were not leaving there without my husband. It was a little after 11:00 P.M., and they were about to take Les out that door.

Within a few minutes, Lucas came back into the living room where I stood planted firmly in the middle of the room, my coat draped over my shoulders. It was freezing cold in the house, but the look in Lucas's eyes, and my sudden realization of what was about to happen, chilled me to the bone.

The front door had been standing wide open for some time, people coming and going, the heater frantically working, trying to keep the house warm in the middle of that cold January night. But the ice I felt emitting from the man standing in front of me was more than any cold I had ever felt before.

Silence overwhelmed the room. Twenty-three pairs of eyes focused on me, watching, waiting for my every move, my reactions. I held my breath, waiting to see what would happen next. They did the same. Lucas, a cocky and arrogant man in his late forties, was slightly taller than I was. He walked right up to me, standing only inches away, a smirk on his face.

"Mrs. Bower, we have just arrested your husband on four counts of capital murder. He will be taken before a Tarrant County judge and then transported to Sherman in Grayson County, where he will be arraigned and held at the Grayson County Jail."

He paused for a minute, letting his words register. I watched the twitch of his mouth, the lines on his forehead, and observed the coldness of his eyes.

He cocked his head slightly, frowned a bit, and moved his face closer to mine. "Mrs. Bower, do you understand what I just said?"

I stared back at him without blinking an eye. "Yes. I understand. May I see my husband?"

His face darkened and the furrow in his brow deepened as he continued to look at me a few seconds more, our eyes not leaving each other. His composure seemed to change from one of arrogance and all business to one of annoyance. He appeared genuinely surprised by my question as a look of disbelief came over his face. He then gathered himself, the smirk returning slowly to his face, looked at me, and said, "No, you may not! He's been read his rights, and you may not see him."

His face was still only inches from mine. I could smell the fading of that morning's cologne that his sweat had overtaken, leaving a musty scent instead. He frowned, and his eyes moved closer together as he studied my face. Several seconds ticked by.

"Mrs. Bower, do you understand what I just told you?"

"Mr. Lucas, may I talk to my husband, please?"

"Mrs. Bower, I don't think you understand the severity of what I have just told you." His voice now louder. I was not making him look good in front of his audience, and he did not like that.

"Do you understand what I said?"

"Yes, I understand what you said. But I still want to see my husband before you take him away."

And with that, he marched off, leaving me standing in the middle of the freezing room, all eyes staring at me, waiting, watching to see what would happen next.

I sized up the situation, concluding there was only one way they could take him out of our house. I made a quick, calculated decision and placed myself by the front door so that Les would have to pass right by me on his way out.

Within a few minutes, Les appeared at the end of the hall toward the bedrooms, flanked by two other Texas rangers. He had added a jacket on top of his flannel shirt, and he looked weary and tired. More so than I had ever seen him. They stood there for just a minute, talking to each other and to Les. Les was standing in the corner of the hall, the rangers in front of him, their backs to me, as they talked to each other. Les was looking down. He was about fifteen feet away from me, and I stared at him in an attempt to catch his eye.

Les looked up, our eyes met for a second, and we just stared at each other. It was only for a split second, as one of the rangers saw this and moved to stand in front of him, blocking his view of me. He began talking to Les again, distracting him from me.

Suddenly they began walking briskly toward the end of the hallway, his hands cuffed in front of him and a ranger at each elbow. Les kept his eyes on me as he walked down our hallway. They turned right to the entry hall, where I stood on the edge of the carpeted living room, just inches from where they were ushering him out the front door. Les looked directly at me while continuing to walk and asked, "Do you know where they are taking me?"

"Yes."

"Do you know what to do?"

"Yes."

"Listen to me! I did not—"

"I know."

"Do you understand? Listen to what I am saying. I did not."

"I know."

And then he was gone. The door stood open as the cold, biting air of January blew in and the heater churned away, trying to heat a house that was cold and empty yet full of people.

The minute Les stepped over our threshold, two FBI agents were by my side, asking me questions. I might've been new at this, but I had the good sense to tell them, "No, not till I've spoken to an attorney."

My hands trembled slightly as I called Richard Klein, the same attorney Les had called earlier in the evening. By now, it was almost midnight. After telling him what had happened, he said arresting a suspect was often done on a Friday night so they would have to stay in jail all weekend before appearing before a judge. We made arrangements to meet him in his office Monday morning. He advised me not to talk to anyone or interfere with the officers still there. I'm sure he went back to bed after we hung up. That wasn't going to happen for me and probably not for Les.

I placed the phone back in its cradle and thought to myself, *Monday is three days away. That's all we have to wait. Three days.* I felt panic rising within yet assured myself, *I can do this for three days. God, help us do this for three days! This? What is this? God, how do I do this? I don't know what* this *is.*

I was alone except for the fifteen or so officers still combing through our house. I had called my parents earlier in the evening, but two Texas rangers were at their house in Weatherford, forty-five minutes away. I would learn later that their visit to my parents' house was strategically planned to keep them from coming over immediately. And it gave the rangers the opportunity to question them as much as they could before arresting Les.

Around midnight, Mother and Daddy finally arrived. I had done what I always did in emergencies: I was a rock. Doing what needed to be done, the adrenaline carrying me through whatever I had to do in a crisis. Then, when someone else came onto the scene that I believed would relieve me of the responsibility, I would melt into a puddle of tears and pent-up anxiety, turning into grief.

There had never been an emergency like this. I had felt the presence of God the whole time, His arms wrapped tightly around me, giving me the strength to do what needed to be done. Les and I had held each other close, watching helplessly as if someone had taken our world and turned it upside down like a ragdoll, shaking and pulling it as hard as they could to see if it would fall apart. Despite the strength I had been given, I was still a vulnerable, scared young woman whose life had just been shattered.

I was standing in my kitchen when my parents walked through the door. I felt myself begin to crumble as if I were in slow motion. The agony and pain crawled from the pit of my stomach up through my throat and into my face. Tears came as I went to them, ready to fall into Daddy's arms. I felt the strength I had held on to for so long slowly ebb from my body. He walked quickly to me, took me by the shoulders, looked me in the eye, and said, "Don't you let them see you cry!" And so I didn't.

It was after 2:30 A.M. before all the officers finally left our house. Mother, Daddy, and I stumbled to bed in shock and disbelief. I wanted to crawl into the bed Les and I had shared for so long, the bed law enforcement officers had only hours earlier been crawling all over, lying on while the search was underway. I could still smell cigarette smoke in the room, unable to believe that they had defiled my home, smoking and lounging on our bed.

I wasn't sure I could bear to lie down where they had been. Stripping off the bedspread, I threw it to the farthest corner of the room, trying to erase any sign of their presence. Tears streamed down my face. There was no one there to see me crying now. I slid between the sheets, burying my head in Les's pillow where I could still smell the faint aroma of him: a light touch of Irish Spring soap and the scent of his body, *his* scent. I drew the pillow closer, clutching it in my arms. The bed was cold. It felt dirty. But it was the only place I wanted to be, to feel close to him, to feel he was still there.

Continuing to cry until my whole body ached with anguish, I wondered where he was at that moment. As if he were thinking the same thing, the phone rang. It was 3:30 A.M. I answered it on the first ring. It was a collect call from the Grayson County Jail, from Les, and I was so glad to hear his voice.

"Are you all right?" I asked, holding back the tears that threatened. There was a pause, as if to gain his composure.

"Yes, I'm okay, but I'm exhausted, and my eyes are bothering me." He had his contacts in all day and they were very dry. "Are you okay?" he asked softly, a crack in his voice.

"Yes. They are finally gone."

He suddenly seemed rushed, as if we didn't have much time, and began giving me details regarding visitation that would take place later that day, now Saturday. He told me what time visitation was and what I could bring and a list of things he needed.

"Have you called the lawyer?" he asked.

"Yes," I said, my voice just above a whisper. "I'm meeting him on Monday."

There was a brief silence, and I heard him quietly sniff before he continued. "Are you listening to me?"

"Yes."

"Are you listening to me?" he repeated, urgency in his voice.

"Yes," I answered, tears rolling down his pillow.

"I did not!" he said emphatically.

"I never thought you did."

Slowly, he released what seemed to be a sigh of relief. "I'll see you in a few hours," he said. "I love you so much."

And then he was gone again. The call had been disconnected. Our time was up.

I lay staring at the ceiling through the darkness of the cold, smoke-tainted bedroom that only the night before had been our sanctuary, our private place. But now it had been invaded, violated, never to be the same.

My mind was racing with thoughts and questions, but I had no answers. All I could think about, all I could do at that moment was to begin putting his things together. His glasses, his contacts case, some underwear and socks, the things he had asked for.

Sleep would not come. In just a few hours, I would get in my car and drive to Sherman, Texas, for the first of many more visits to come. I had no idea just how many more there would be. No one slept much that night at my house. Or probably in the Grayson County Jail.

I was thankful that Leslea was sleeping over at her friend's house and that Hollie was still at Sharon's. They had been spared the trauma of seeing their daddy handcuffed and escorted out of our family's home.

I worried about Hollie, our youngest daughter. I had only been with her a couple of hours, soothing her worries, distracting her with television and Sharon's children to play with. I wondered what must have been going on in her mind. I was an adult and I was afraid. I thanked God that Sharon had been there to take her and keep her from everything else that went on that night. What lasting effects would all this have on both our girls?

The next morning, my dad and I headed off early to Sherman to visit Les. Leslea and Hollie were not home yet, but they soon would be. So Mother stayed at my house to be there when they arrived. I'm not sure which one of us had the harder job, Mother or me. *What would she tell them?*

I don't remember much about the trip other than I thought we would never get there. The four-story courthouse stood in the middle of the town square like many Texas courthouses do in every county seat. There wasn't much activity going on at that hour on a Saturday morning. But for some reason, I felt my presence was known by the few who were there.

We met Les's parents in the lobby. They had driven from Tulsa that morning, obviously as shocked and confused as we were. The four of us entered the run-down elevator and stood in silence as the creaky antique crawled to the fourth floor, the highest floor in the courthouse, where the jail was housed. I stared at the crumpled and torn list of visitation rules taped to the wall in the elevator, committing them to memory. In the next few months, as Les wrote to me from jail, many of his return addresses on his letters would simply say PENTHOUSE, SHERMAN, TX. Somehow, he managed to keep his sense of humor alive.

As we exited the elevator and approached the visitor check-in, it seemed the guards stopped what they were doing and looked up, staring at us. Officers peered around corners to get a glimpse, and quiet whispers faintly echoed through the dirty hallways. The family of the Dallas man they had been looking for was here, and they wanted a good look. Plus, this was a capital case. This didn't happen often in their jailhouse.

This was my first experience inside a jail. We agreed I would see him first, alone. My dad and Les's parents would visit after. One of the deputies took the things I had brought for Les. Then a captain came to escort me down a narrow, winding, and very dimly lit corridor that reeked of body odor, urine, and old, musty wood and mattresses. Paint peeled from the walls, revealing the many layers that had been applied over the years, one color on top of another.

Finally, we reached the end of the corridor where a single cell was tucked away in the farthest recesses of the building. They were holding him in isolation for a few days, watching him around the clock. My stomach lurched when I saw Les on the other side of the bars, a sight I never dreamed I would see.

The captain stopped me as I stepped forward, instructing me to stand three feet from the door, not to go any closer. "You've got fifteen minutes," he grumbled to me. He moved toward the cell and unlocked a one-foot-by-one-foot window so Les could talk to me.

Les stood up and came toward the window. I could see he had been crying. When he saw me, he began to cry even harder. I wasn't sure I had ever seen Les cry before. Not like this. I had seen tears in his eyes, but he was crying as if the weight of the world were spilling out and he could hold it no more. All I wanted to do was put my arms around him and hold him. But I couldn't. I couldn't even touch him or hold his hand, the hand I had been holding only twelve hours earlier in our living room.

All I could do was cry with him. It must have been a pitiful sight. My big, burly mountain man holding tightly to the bars of his cell, crying as he never had before, while I stood fifteen feet away from him, my arms wrapped around myself, crying as hard as he was, totally helpless to comfort him. I had waited for this moment to see him again. Now it was here, and our time was much too short.

We talked quietly, and I told him about my conversation with Klein. We focused on making it until Monday, the day after tomorrow. We were helpless to do anything before then.

Things would get better, I told him, once we had some answers. I truly believed if we could only make it to Monday, this would all be over. We'd be okay.

He looked at me with red-rimmed eyes and asked how the girls were. "When I think about them," he said, "and what this must be doing to them . . ." He couldn't even finish his thought before the tears overtook him again.

My husband was a stoic man and kept his emotions to himself. But the tears I witnessed as we stood in that dingy jail were tears of grief, fear, and helplessness. There had never been a time in our nearly sixteen years of marriage that we had ever felt this much despair. We had only fifteen minutes, and then I would have to turn and leave him there all alone. I watched over my shoulder as the captain escorted me out. Les stood, his hands wrapped around the rusty bars, his eyes following me as I walked out. We turned the corner, and I could no longer see him. My heart broke just a little more as I cried all the way back to the waiting room.

Tears on My Pillow

I'm crying myself to sleep tonight because I feel so all alone.
The feelings that I feel right now are ones I've never known.
One day I seem so happy, and the next so sad and blue.
I'm so tired of feeling lonely, I'm so tired of missing you.
I need someone to put their arms around me and tell me it's all right to cry.
But all I hear is how strong I've been, and how well I'm getting by.
All I know is I want to scream. I want someone to make it right.
I'll be all right tomorrow, if I can just make it through tonight.

March 12, 1984

CHAPTER 6

Three Days

January 21, 1984

Not long after returning home from my visit with Les, I got a phone call from my uncle, Gayle Baucum. Gayle was able to visit him outside of the visitation hours because he was a minister. During the visit, Les told Gayle what happened on October 8, 1983. He hadn't told anyone what happened that day. Not even me.

Gayle asked Les if he could share with me what Les had told him. Les agreed, telling him I would need to tell Klein as well. Gayle proceeded to tell me what Les shared with him that afternoon.

It seemed minutes passed before I could speak. The phone line between us was silent as Gayle waited for me to respond to what he had just told me. The scenario, still reeling in my head, made no sense. I felt as if all the breath had been knocked out of me. My knees seemed ready to buckle from under me, but I willed them not to. My disbelief turned to shock and my shock to anger. How could Les not have told me this before?

Suddenly my survival mode snapped back into autopilot. I thanked Gayle for calling and telling me. I appreciated it very much. Gayle asked if I was all right. I assured him I would be. I just needed to process this new information.

As I ended the call, I thought about what Les was going through at this moment, knowing Gayle and I were having this conversation. But what about everything I was going through right now, trying to make sense of it all? No wonder Les was so distraught.

He'd had three months to tell me the whole story. *Would things be different right now had he told me earlier? Possibly. No, definitely! But we'll never know now.* I was caught between being mad as hell at him and worrying about him. But that would have to wait. I didn't have time to worry about him. I had to tell Klein. I had to tell our families.

This changed everything.

After telling the family members who were at my house at the time, I called Klein and told him the story. He seemed annoyed that Les had told Gayle. And annoyed that I had told our family at the house. I urged him to go as soon as possible to see Les and talk to him. Klein gave me specific instructions to tell our family not to speak of this to anyone.

I hung up the phone and quietly slipped out of the house into the cold night air to find someplace to be alone. I needed to think. The driveway and street in front of our house were full of cars. My parents, Les's parents, one of Mother's brothers, and his wife were there. I don't remember who else was there. I trudged through the maze of cars, stopping at Mother's car.

I'm not sure why I stopped there. Perhaps because it was parked off the street in the grass, a little farther away than the others. I needed to be alone. Somewhere no one would see me or interrupt me. Someplace I could think and process what I had just learned.

As I quietly opened the driver's door, slipping into Mother's tan Toyota Cressida, the overhead light came to life. Closing the door, I felt the butter-like leather seat against the chill of my arms. I let my head fall onto the headrest as the automatic seatbelt whirled from one side to the other, wrapping itself across my body, cocooning me, as if I were being held tightly within its arms, not just sitting alone in an empty car.

I began to cry. Hysterical sobs that I could not hold any longer. It was a gut-wrenching, ugly cry. I beat my fists against the steering wheel, yelling at my husband who was too far away to hear my wails.

I was furious with him. I screamed at him. I screamed at God. I asked them both *why*, knowing full well I would receive no answer. Not then, maybe not ever.

I needed to vent the anger, frustration, sorrow, hurt, and betrayal I was feeling at that moment. It seemed to go on forever. And then it was done. I was done.

As the echoes of my screams subsided around me, I fell into God's arms and begged Him to take this away and make it all right. I felt exhausted. I felt helpless. But I also felt protected in God's embrace, knowing He was big enough to take away my anger. He was greater than all my fears, and He was in control. I knew I certainly wasn't. And neither was Les.

Once the papers had Les's identity and the news hit the Associated Press wires, the phone began ringing. Friends all over the country could not believe the Lester Bower they knew could ever be considered a murderer. By the end of the day on Sunday, January 22, we had received over two hundred phone calls. Only one or two calls were from strangers who wanted to tell me how evil Les was and ask how I could support my husband and believe in his innocence after the horrible things he had done.

The Sunday papers were full of headlines, pictures, and speculations. The *Fort Worth Star-Telegram* read "Arrest Stuns Suspect's Neighbors." The *Sherman Democrat Headline* said "Suspect Arrested in Tate Ranch Murders, Arlington Salesman Charged on 4 Counts." I was shocked by the audacity of many reporters, both print and media. Pictures of our house were printed in papers and flashed on television. One paper had a map listed under a picture of our house with the address at the bottom. It was just the beginning of our relationship with the press.

Monday would come, I told myself, and I would be able to bring my husband home. We could hold each other and cry some more. This terrible mistake would be discovered. We'd get it all straightened out, or at least get him out on bail. I could not think about anything past Monday.

No More Tears

The tears are all gone, I've cried them all.
There's no more to cry, there's none left to fall.
But the pain is still there, and it hurts so inside.
The pain won't go away, and there's no place to hide.
Will the pain someday stop, or will it always be there?
Will it stop like the tears, or turn to despair?

March 23, 1984

CHAPTER 7

A Fox in the Henhouse

January 23, 1984

Richard Klein was a man of average stature, lean with black-and-gray-peppered hair. He was dressed in an immaculate suit, along with what appeared to be very expensive cowboy boots.

He began by giving us his verbal résumé. He had worked in the Dallas County prosecutor's office at one time and was quite proud that he was part of the prosecution team in a very well-known trial. He claimed it was one of the most infamous trials in Dallas County and he was the only attorney who had ever beaten the defense attorney he was up against.

I had no idea who or what he was talking about, so his bragging about it didn't impress me, especially since he was an assistant prosecutor at the time, not a defense attorney.

The word *famous* was tossed around quite a bit, and I wondered how he could be the *only* attorney who had beaten the opponent if he was part of a prosecutorial team and not the district attorney. My logic seemed somewhat intact, but I couldn't get the logical questions verbalized. The statement alone and the fact that I questioned it in my mind should have been a major red flag for me, but my red-flag radar was broken.

In hindsight, I should have stopped right there and called this other attorney to check him out. Or better yet, checked Klein out. Years later, I looked up the attorney he mentioned, and his credentials were as good as Klein had said, certainly better than his own.

Klein had a contract waiting for us. He wanted Dad and me to sign it with a one-hundred-thousand-dollar up-front retainer fee. He explained he would be contracting with us, not with Les, to conduct the defense. Why, oh why, wasn't my red-flag radar working?

Obviously, he wanted us to be liable for the cost, as Les was in jail, no longer employed, and facing a four-count capital murder trial. Les was basically indigent. I'm sure Klein had already figured my dad was good for the fee more than Les was.

None of us had discussed or checked around to see how much a defense attorney for a trial of this nature would cost, but what he was asking was more than we imagined. We knew our other option was to use a court-appointed attorney, maybe someone straight out of law school and most likely practicing in Grayson County, where the murders took place. We felt that might be too risky.

My dad had been a salesman all his life and began to negotiate with Klein. Dad mentioned property in west Texas he owned and some family oil rights. It wasn't long before Klein had agreed to take a partial payment up front and the rest in installments. He also agreed to waive the entire fee in advance, with the understanding that payments would be made along the way.

Klein said that, because this was a capital case, he would need to shut down his office, devoting all his time to Les's case. He had included that clause in the contract. He also promised to hire a private investigator, as well as a co-counsel in Grayson County to help him locally.

By that afternoon, he was giving interviews to the press, stating he would be closing his office in order to concentrate solely on Les's case. He made references to this same promise in several subsequent interviews as well.

Klein would also become one of our biggest adversaries, speaking to the press way too often, revealing things that were privileged, and saying things that created more problems than solved them. I began to believe that

Klein was one of the best tools the prosecution had in their arsenal. Before the trial was over, he seemed to be working for the prosecution rather than the defense.

Offers were made by at least two local Grayson County attorneys to assist with the case, but Klein never accepted their offers. One of them wrote to Klein, introducing himself and offering insight into a case he was involved with that might help shed some light on what Klein might expect from the prosecution and many of the past indiscretions, tactics, and tricks used by local law enforcement to get convictions—no matter what.

According to the local attorney, two men had been convicted of murder and "were totally and demonstrably innocent of murder."

He wrote to Klein that he had been appointed by the US Attorney's Office to conduct an investigation of local law enforcement on allegations of coercion, perjured testimony, and misrepresentations of the facts in order to obtain convictions.

The writer said he felt Klein should be acquainted with the Grayson County law enforcement officials' propensities in other cases. His investigation of these two cases had resulted in a new trial and the release of one of the defendants. He was working on getting the second innocent man released from prison. He said:

> It occurs to me that both the sheriff and county attorney are in a position to totally require a little "face-lifting" as the result of a rather pronounced "black eye" stemming from this investigation and the coverage by an investigative reporter from a Dallas news station about their wrongdoing. As a result of this, the county has appeased itself by suing myself and the reporter for the tidy sum of $12 million.

He went on to offer Klein office space where he might work while he was in town at no charge.

> I simply invite you to feel free to make such use of my facilities as you may see fit during your ongoing representation of your

client. In parting, let me again admonish you to "keep your head on a swivel."

P.S. One of the witnesses in the case I referred to committed "suicide" while in the Grayson County Jail.

Not long after Les's execution in 2015, I decided to see if I could find this attorney, as I had never spoken to him personally. It had been thirty-two years. He was easy to find, as he still had his office in the same building and was still practicing law. He was surprised to hear from me—as surprised as I was that he took my call.

I confirmed what I already suspected to be true: Klein did not have any further discussions via mail, phone, or in-person with this attorney. Nor did he take him up on his offer to use his office space or follow up on his request that he testify as to the reputation of the Grayson County attorney and sheriff's office.

Klein ignored the significance of the information provided to him about the misconduct of the Grayson County Sheriff's Department and the Grayson County prosecutor's office in connection with other cases.

A Grayson County deputy sheriff pressured a witness into giving a statement by threatening to put her in jail if she didn't. The resulting statement drafted by two deputies failed to accurately reflect the statement she had given.

A second witness was pressured not only by a Grayson County deputy sheriff with the same threat of imprisonment but was pressured by the Grayson County prosecutor. The witness argued that the statement they wanted him to sign was not what he had said. The deputy sheriff had written the statement to his liking rather than to the witness's accuracy. When the witness protested, the Grayson County prosecutor threatened the witness that if he did not cooperate and say what he was told to say, the county would "take the deal back and give him the death penalty."

Two other affiants were pressured into giving false statements, which the deputies from the Grayson County Sheriff's Department "suggested" to them.

In light of considerable evidence that, historically, investigative reports prepared by the Grayson County Sheriff's Department were not reliable and that witnesses' testimonies were shown to be altered or modified by the deputies, Klein merely accepted the statements provided to him by the Grayson County Sheriff's Department in reference to Les's case and never interviewed a witness. He would claim later he did interview them, but follow-up investigations during the appeal process showed he didn't.

Two days after Les's arrest, Klein, holding another press conference, stated adamantly that discovery of the state's investigative files was one of his top priorities. I knew Klein hadn't seen the evidence, yet he told the press he knew what evidence the county had against Les and didn't believe they had enough to convict him. I was floored when I heard him say that, as I knew it wasn't true.

After many pleas on my part, he finally filed a motion for discovery. Les and I both wanted to see what evidence they had. Our discovery motion was granted on March 19, 1984, two months after Les's arrest, and only three weeks before trial was scheduled to begin.

Klein didn't file for additional time to prepare for trial given that late date and continued to adhere to his schedule of trying the case within the ninety-day window he was shooting for, attempting to give Les his right to a speedy trial.

Life's Path

This life is not as I would have it to be.
But this is the life you've chosen for me.
If only the way of life's road I knew.
But that path is known only by you.
I ask only for wisdom to show me the way.
And to grant me your grace to get through each day.
I'll cling to your promise through my trouble and strife.
The promise you've given of a more abundant life.

March 17, 1984

CHAPTER 8

That Day in October

February 4, 1984

February 2, 1984

Dear Leslea:

I'm not one of the best letter writers in the world . . . well, let's be honest, I haven't written a personal letter in over 15 years, but it seems this will be the only way we can talk for a while. If you'll write me, I'll sure do my best to write back as often as I can.

Sometimes life deals out problems that seem to have no solutions. But you must remember that through faith, all problems will work out for the best. There is something I need you to do for me. In my absence, you and your sister must keep your things cleaned up, and fights between you and your sister must be kept to a minimum.

At night before you go to bed, I want you to say a prayer for our family in this time of trouble. In the Bible, it says if you have a problem, you need only ask the Lord to take care of it and He will.

Remember two things: I love you very much, and no matter what you hear or see, I am not involved in the crime I have been charged with.

Love and kisses,
Dad

At Klein's request, I asked my uncle, Gayle Baucum, to meet with Les on February 4 and to ask Les to write an account of what he had done on Saturday, October 8, 1983, the day the four men were murdered—the same story he had told Gayle at their meeting the day after his arrest. Gayle was to arrange a date to pick up the statement from Les and deliver it to me personally. We did not trust the jail to mail it out.

All inmate letters going out were unsealed, and the mailroom employees sealed them after inspection. Incoming mail was opened and subject to perusal or actual reading. Once Gayle gave me Les's handwritten story, I made a copy of it and turned over the original to Klein the day after I received it.

The following is Les's written account of his activity on October 8, 1983, the day of the murders, which was written from Grayson County Jail on February 4, 1984:

February 4, 1984

Saturday started out wet, and I went out to the shooting range in Mansfield to see if I could drive in or not. I had breakfast at the Hungry Farmer about 6:00 or 6:30, went out and hung out at the range till about 8:30 or 9:00, but I didn't see anyone at the range or going back out. I was down at the archery barn, and no one really goes down there anyway.

I drove from Mansfield back to I-20 East to Loop 12, then north to 635 and east to Highway 75, and north to Sherman. I got into town about 11:00 A.M. and sat in the parking lot of a mall just off the highway and listened to the baseball game till noon. I went down to a Burger King or McDonald's or some hamburger joint and got some lunch, took it back to the parking lot, and ate lunch and listened to the baseball game.

About 2:15, I left the parking lot and drove out to the hangar, which I had been told belonged to Bob Tate. I arrived about 2:30, and no one was there. The hangar is located about a quarter of a mile off the road out by a wooded area. A house was under construction out at the road, and there was a travel trailer on the east side of the driveway, and the house was on the west. The closest house to the entrance to the hangar was back west toward town about a quarter of a mile.

I walked around the hangar waiting for someone to arrive and looked over the landing strip. It is a good one with no power lines or large trees to give you trouble and, except for the hangar and the house under construction, the closest house looked to be over a quarter of a mile away. There was a tractor and a dry tank to the east of the hangar and light timber beyond that.

A Chevy Suburban drove up with Good and another gentleman in it; we were introduced, but you know me and names. He was 50'ish, 6' tall, thin, with a receding hairline. He and Good had been somewhere else putting wing finish on a Mitchell ultralight, and we walked around and talked flying till Tate arrived maybe 15 to 20 minutes later with the keys to the hangar. We went into the hangar through a regular metal door on the east side under an overhang. We walked around the plane I wanted to buy several times, chatting about several things, and then we went to an area on the west side of the hangar where there were some chairs and tables. There were flying magazines all over the table, and we just talked about the aircraft and flying for maybe 30 minutes. It seemed to me that Tate wanted to leave. He had to go get ready to go out to dinner, or he had to meet someone or something, so I went ahead and made my purchase pitch.

Tate wanted $4,500 for the plane, but I thought it was worth about $4,000 and I told him so. I had taken from a previous meeting with him that he really needed to sell the plane for some reason. I told him I would pay him $4,000 cash if I had it, but I didn't, so I made him this offer. I took a letter out of my back pocket, which had $3,000 in $100 bills, and took the money out and told him I would pay the asking price of $4,500 if he would take $3,000 down and allow me to pay the balance out at $150 per month for ten months or at a sooner time if I came into some unexpected wealth. Tate thought about it a minute and said if I would give him my address, business card, and phone number, he would take the offer. Good said he would teach me to fly the plane and give me ground school for $150, which was less than the $350 he normally charged. We discussed the problem of my weight at 260 pounds, and the opinion was expressed that it would be a lot easier if I would lose 20 pounds. I expressed one other problem I had, and that was how I was going to explain to you how I got this plane. Tate offered to let me keep the plane at the hangar at no charge for a while if that would help.

I had already thought about this problem and had come up with the idea of taking the plane back to Arlington and taking it apart piece by piece and reassembling it piece by piece over several months under the disguise of me designing it and building it piece by piece. The reason I wasn't worried about my design plans were because I was putting together a production plane. While I was putting the plane together, I could work on losing the 20 pounds. Tate agreed to this, and Good warned me not to put it together and go fly it without coming back to *him. He offered to train me for $150, which was cheaper than I could train myself, and he knew it.*

For having only met twice, there seemed to me to be a great deal of trust between the three of us. It may seem foolish for me not to have asked for a receipt on the $3,000, but then Tate didn't ask for a promissory note on the $1,500. I handed Tate the $3,000, which was in a legal white envelope with my name, address, and phone number on the front, and I put one of my business cards inside. All this conversation took maybe 20 to 30 minutes.

Tate indicated he needed to be on his way, so we started to tear down the plane. I say "we," but I just stood around and watched the three of them lift the wings off the landing gear, fold the front of the nose back, and the wings just laid back like they would on an insect. The wings, all the cables, and everything but the engine, prop, and landing gear fit into a long blue bag about 18' long and about 14" across. All this work was done in about 20 to 30 minutes, and we carried it out and roped the long bag down on top of the Scout and put the landing gear and engine in the back.

Everyone seemed to want to be on their way, so we said our goodbyes and I drove out of the property and headed home. I got on Highway 82 and went west to Gainesville and then south on I-35 all the way to I-20 and south on 287 to Mansfield. I left Sherman about 4:00 P.M. and drove nonstop to Mansfield, arriving about 5:30 P.M. I went out to the range and dropped off the plane behind the archery range barn and came home about 7:00 P.M. There was a large weeded area behind the barn, and I knew no one went down there because of the chiggers.

Over the next couple weeks, I went out to the range and took the plane apart piece by piece and transported it back to the house and put it in the attic until I needed each piece, and then I brought it down into the garage.

I don't remember any carpet in the hangar at Sherman. The only people I saw at the hangar were Good, Tate, and the man I described. I stopped for no gas. I ate breakfast in Mansfield and lunch at some fast-food joint in Sherman. The extra time I spent in Sherman waiting was spent in a parking lot behind a large shopping center just off the highway in Sherman. I didn't see anyone at the range.

To the best of my knowledge, this is all that happened and all I saw on that Saturday in question.

The day after the murders, as we got ready for church, one of us brought the Fort Worth Star-Telegram *inside. On the front page was a picture of an airplane hangar along with a story of how four men had been murdered in Grayson County the day before.*

—Les Bower

Les told Gayle he was terrified when he saw the front page of the *Fort Worth-Star Telegram* on Sunday, October 9, the day after the murders. We were getting ready for church when he saw the headlines about the murders at the ranch in Denison, where he had been the day before. The story said four men had been killed. He knew he hadn't killed them. And he also knew there were only three men at the ranch when he left, not four as it stated in the paper.

The story alluded to possible drug activity, which frightened him even more. His first thought was whoever killed them might come after him or his family if they knew he had been there and were concerned Les might have seen something or knew something. He felt confident that the authorities would find who murdered those men and he wouldn't have to get involved, possibly putting himself or us in harm's way.

I remembered that Sunday, October 9, 1983, as well. I had brought in the paper and glanced at the front page where I saw a picture of an airplane hangar, along with a story of how four men had been murdered in Denison, just outside of Sherman, the day before. Having recently seen ABC's *20/20* program on ultralights, and my negative reaction to Les buying one, I took the time to read the story. The article stated that the four men were killed when an unknown assailant, or assailants, had stolen an ultralight airplane from the hangar. It also alluded that a drug deal might possibly have been a motive.

Les walked into the room just as I was finishing the article. I handed the paper to him. "See, there's another reason not to take up that sport," I said over my shoulder, as I walked toward the door. "Evidently, those airplanes are used to transport drugs, and now these guys have been murdered."

Les stood there for a moment, staring at the paper as I gathered the girls and went outside to put them in the car. Within a few minutes, he followed us out, we got in the car, and we drove to church.

After meeting with Klein on Monday, January 23 to finalize the contract, I returned home to find that the calls were still coming in. I also found out that Les had been put on a leave of absence from Thompson-Hayward, the company he worked for. We could expect one more check, and our insurance would be gone. The leave of absence did not fall under disability, nor could he collect unemployment. Sharon and I had just started our business, and it was still struggling to get off the ground. There was potential, but I had just begun to venture out with new and innovative ideas. I knew I could make something of it, but I still needed time.

I could count on four hundred or five hundred dollars a month then. Our rent was six hundred dollars, and my car payment was three hundred dollars. We had no money in the bank, no savings, nothing to borrow against, no house to sell. I began selling everything I could. Furniture, wedding crystal, Les's car. Anything that we could do without.

Joe Halifax, our friend from when we were at A&M, came out from Odessa and helped me go through all of Les's hunting, camping, and photography equipment to sell, including the fourteen-man river raft we had moved from Colorado to Texas. There were no rivers we knew of here that would accommodate a raft that big, so there were probably no prospective buyers. I called our friends at the outdoor program at Mesa College in Grand Junction. They got busy and found a buyer pretty quickly, and I shipped it via a freight hauler.

Sometime in early February 1984, I received a letter stating we had to move out of our house. My first reaction was it being a result of Les's arrest. But after talking to the agent, I found the owners were selling and wanted it vacant. So on top of everything else, we were going to have to move in thirty days.

Les's cousin Paul and his wife Nancy lived in Arlington and had recently purchased a house for rental property. They offered to rent it to us until the trial was over at a very affordable rate. It was an answer to prayer.

Although we were moving outside the school area where the girls were currently enrolled, the school made arrangements so my daughters could remain in their classrooms for the rest of the year to avoid any further disruptions in their lives.

Arrangements were also made between Bob Windham, the principal of Ditto Elementary, and Billy Bob Burnett, the principal of Young Junior High, for Leslea to graduate and follow her sixth-grade friends and classmates to Young Junior High, rather than have to start the next school year across town with kids she didn't know. This was one of the greatest gifts we received to relieve some of the trauma that Leslea might experience.

The teachers, counselors, and principal at Ditto Elementary were amazing during all of this. On Monday, after Les's arrest, Bob Windham met with the sixth-grade classes. Leslea was not in class that day. He asked if they had ever been accused of something they didn't do. Many of the kids nodded—yes, they had. He went on to tell them that they were going to hear a lot of things in the news, from their parents, and from other kids about Leslea's dad. It was important, he said to those twelve-year-olds, to remember that we don't always know what's true and what isn't true, and that according to Leslea's family, her dad was accused of something he didn't do. He asked them to please remember that.

"If you are a friend of Leslea's, be her friend and be there for her if she needs you. If you aren't her friend, then don't ask her questions and make this any harder for her than it already is."

I had really liked him before. Now I loved him. It was the greatest gift he could have given our family.

Comments I heard made by some second-graders were another matter. Some of them were harsh and hurtful. I knew seven- and eight-year-old children didn't come up with those comments on their own. They were merely repeating things their parents had said after making judgments based solely on what they had read in the papers or seen on TV. Hollie was fortunate, though, as she had Sandy McNutt as her teacher. Sandy is legendary in Arlington. She was an amazing teacher, and it seems everyone in Arlington has kids who have benefitted from her in one way or another. She went on to become a principal and was eventually honored by the school district when they named one of Arlington's new elementary schools after her in 2017.

We had only been in Arlington for six months. I was glad that we immediately found a church home, and the pastors and members of our Sunday school class at Fielder Road Baptist Church stepped up as well to support and help us through this difficult time. The church set us up with a member, Patsy Harry, a private practice counselor in Arlington, who the girls and I were able to talk to. We had a long-term relationship with Pat over the years, and then a close friendship once I stopped seeing her professionally. Our Sunday school class was awesome. Our group, led by Don and Gena Rogers, made sure we had occasional gift cards to Kroger and that the girls had Christmas gifts that year.

Mirage

Darkness surrounds me as night closes in.
The lights are turned off, the day's at an end.
I lay in my bed, scared and alone.
I reach out to touch you, but you're not at home.
My mind races back to the times you were there.
The gentleness of your touch, the smell of your hair.
I close my eyes and feel your body next to mine.
I feel your kiss on my lips, and your caress so divine.
But it's all a mirage, my mind's playing tricks on me.
There are tears on my cheeks, where your kisses should be.
Oh, please hurry back; no longer can I fight.
The days I can handle, but God help me at night.

April 20, 1984

CHAPTER 9

You Don't Know Shari

January 24, 1984

We arrived at court early Tuesday morning for the bond reduction hearing we had requested. Bail had been set at four hundred thousand dollars. This would be our first time in the courtroom and the first time with reporters. Klein told us what to expect and what motions he intended to file. Yet he never provided us with copies of any of those motions. He said he didn't believe the state had the evidence necessary to convict Les, despite never seeing any evidence. I questioned him as to how he could make that conclusion without seeing what they had against him. He assured me he would know if they did. That didn't make me feel any better.

When we asked Klein if he would request a change of venue, he replied that we had nothing to hide and felt we should "try it in the den of the lion." Each day seemed to present itself with a nightmare of its own.

Les was brought in wearing the same jeans and flannel shirt he had left the house in four days before. I could see the tension in his face, and he looked as tired as I felt. Sheriff's deputies led him to the defense table, his hands cuffed in front of him. His eyes darted around the room as he tried to find me. He smiled slightly when he did.

I sat on the end of the third row, directly behind him. It was as close as

I was allowed to be. I couldn't tell you who else was with me, or how many people were in the room that morning. My eyes stayed fixed on my husband, and I wasn't aware of anything else going on around me.

The judge, Klein, and the county attorney spoke to one another at the bench, and then I heard a bailiff call my name. I rose slowly from my seat, walked past Les, and sat in the chair next to the judge. Then Klein addressed me.

Klein: Mrs. Shari Bower, can you tell the court where Mr. Bower was employed prior to his arrest?

Bower: He was employed by Thompson-Hayward Chemical Company, whose offices are in Dallas.

Klein: And what was his salary there?

Bower: His salary was approximately eighteen thousand dollars a year plus commission.

Klein: How many children do you have, Mrs. Bower, and what are their ages?

Bower: Leslea, our oldest daughter, is twelve, and Hollie, our youngest, is eight.

Klein: Tell us a little bit about your home life, if you will.

Bower: Les and I have been married for fifteen and a half years and dated for three years prior to that. We have what I consider a fairly normal home life. He works five days a week, the children have school right across the street from our house, and I have recently started a business with one of my childhood friends who lives in Arlington.

Klein: What kind of business?

Bower: Right now, we clean houses for people. We drop the kids off at school, and the two of us can do at least two houses a day by working together. I have plans to expand the business to other services for our clients, like picking up their dry cleaning for them, doing grocery shopping, catering parties, and any other things a family with two working adults might need help with.

Klein: Are you making good money doing that?

Bower: Not right now. Certainly not enough to maintain a household without my husband's income or help. And it's even more difficult now, as I have to come up with extra money for his defense.

Klein: Mrs. Bower, tell me something about your husband, Lester. What kind of man is he?

I looked over at my husband and kept my eyes focused on him while I told the court about Les—*my* Les. I watched as he tried to hold back the tears while still looking at me. He never ducked his head but stared straight at me, giving me the strength I needed to carry on.

Bower: Les is a loving, devoted husband, father, son, brother, and friend. We've known each other almost half of our lives; we met in high school. He is a kind, generous man; a man of his word, and not someone who would skip bail or abandon his family for any reason.

The prosecution presented testimony as to the severity of the crimes Les was accused of, and why they felt the bail was adequate. Despite the fact that he had no prior record and had an extended loving and caring family, law enforcement officials still considered him to be a flight risk.

Texas Ranger Weldon Lucas later that day told my uncle, Gayle Baucum, that in his opinion, Les was a flight risk because of his connections in Colorado, his hunting buddies, and the wilderness and survival training he had received while living there. He fully expected him to run off and hide someplace in the mountains, possibly even harming the children and me in order to save himself.

We were standing outside the entrance to the courthouse when Gayle told me this. I was so furious at what he had said that Gayle had to grab me by the arm and hold me back from going to find Lucas.

"How could he make such a statement like that? And how many other people has he shared his theory with?" I asked out loud to no one in particular. "Opinions like *that* . . !" I said, unable to even finish the thought. "And they are *only* his opinions, as he has no degree or knowledge to make such a statement. If he goes around saying things like that in the courthouse or sheriff's office, it could very well influence the judge's decision in any further matters. Or influence a jury later!"

Lucas also told Gayle he might want to have a psychiatrist look at me. Gayle laughed as he asked Lucas why he would say such a thing.

Apparently, Lucas had told him, "There is something wrong with her. She was way too calm the night we arrested Les. She didn't even cry. And she got up in my face. If it had been my wife," he said, "she'd been hollering and screaming."

Gayle just shook his head and said, "You don't know Shari! She's one of the strongest women I know. She would never give you the satisfaction of seeing her fall apart."

The judge did not even take a break to consider the issue but immediately ruled against us on the motion for reduction of bail. The deputies stood and prepared to take Les back to his cell. As they started walking toward the doors in the back, Les looked at me from only a few feet away and smiled ever so faintly. He looked so tired. As they neared where I was standing, I stepped into the aisle, surprising not only Les, but also his captors, as I threw my arms around his neck and held him for just a moment. He put his cheek up to mine, then pulled back, looking at me straight in my eyes as he told me, "I love you." We kissed each other as if it were our last. The officer pulled him away, and Les turned once more to look at me over his shoulder. I raised my hand to wave, telling him I loved him too. We had broken all the courtroom rules. Neither of us cared. Everyone was in shock. Except one cameraman who captured that moment for the next edition of the *Dallas Morning News*.

Any hope of bringing him back home while we prepared for trial had just vanished. Since Friday night, when he had stepped over our threshold, I had held on to the hope that he would be able to come home in just three days. Now that hope was gone.

My job, at least for the next few months, was to keep what family I had left together, pack to move, and make the 190-mile round trip to Sherman on Wednesday and Saturday to see Les for fifteen minutes.

I continued to clean houses for the few clients I had, ran errands, and catered parties. God provided in so many ways those first few months so I could be available, and then He provided with full-time employment thereafter.

Some days, I would go to the mailbox and find an encouraging card from a friend with a check or cash included. It would be just what I needed for that week. People at church would shake my hand, and I would pull it away, finding a twenty-dollar bill inside my palm. I was grateful for every kindness, no matter how big or small.

I was shopping for groceries one day, my twenty-dollar bill in one hand and a calculator in the other, making sure I didn't go over. I found myself standing in the freezer aisle of the store, staring at ice cream. *The girls would love to have some ice cream,* I thought, but it wasn't going to fit in the budget. Not this week. I needed hot dogs, fish sticks, and macaroni and cheese.

A woman stood near me with a coupon in her hand, looking in the same freezer. "Have you tried this ice cream?" she asked.

"Yes," I replied. "My kids love it."

She looked down at the coupon and back up to me.

"Here, I have a coupon for a free half gallon. I don't think my family will eat it. Why don't you use it?" She smiled as she handed me the coupon.

I stared at it and then turned to her as she walked away. "Thank you," I called to her, a knot forming in my throat. Tears welled up in my eyes, as I silently thanked God for reminding me He was still with us.

Les and I had agreed I would not bring the girls to visit him, as the Grayson County Jail was so awful. We felt it would be harder on them, and probably Les, to see him in that environment. They wrote letters to each other often. He was able to call on Wednesday nights, and sometimes I would give them the phone to talk to him, but that seemed upsetting to them as well, especially to Hollie.

We only had a short amount of time for the calls. In 1984, there was no call-waiting, no messages, no cell phones. So we sat by the harvest-gold phone on the kitchen wall, waiting for the collect call to come through. I told all my family and friends not to call me on Wednesday night. The girls did their homework on the kitchen table as I cooked dinner. We were all waiting for the phone to ring.

When it did, I practically jerked the phone off the wall to get to it. Les and I would talk for a few minutes, many times about legal issues, but sometimes about personal things. He was always concerned about our well-being and if we had enough money to live on, or if I'd found a job. Then I would hand over the phone to one of the girls, and she would take her turn to talk to Daddy. Hollie always asked him, "When are you going to come home, Daddy? I miss you." And then she would cry, and I was sure he was crying too, without letting her know.

Sometimes if they were done with dinner and homework, we would sit at the table and write letters to him. It seemed to help, just a little.

Law enforcement officers and prison guards are trained not to interact with visitors, to toe the line, keep the rules, and make sure visitation day ran like a finely oiled machine, churning away and spitting out each outsider as quickly as they could. I came to realize that I was one of the most frequent visitors they had at the jail, so naturally we eased into a kind of pattern, as I came about the same time of day, every visitation day, Wednesday and Saturday, for three months. Some of the deputies were friendly to me; some kept their distance.

I felt I was treated a little differently, not special, but more respectful. They had spent some time with Les and with me, getting to know what we were like. Some noticed, others didn't care, and then a few higher up in the ranks were silently hostile.

One guard privately told me he didn't think Les was guilty. He said we were different, but he didn't want anyone else to know he felt that way. It was as if it were a bad thing for him to feel that way or have an opinion about Les—at least a positive one.

"You just seem like good people," one of them said to me. "And him—he's not like the others we have up here. I don't believe he's guilty."

Six or seven inmates shared a pretty good-size cell that had a toilet and a shower in it. I only know this because of Les's descriptions to me. Les got to know some of the men who were in his cell pretty well. Some would come and go, and others stayed a few days or even weeks. A few times, he became a spiritual mentor to some of them. He had an in-house church meeting on Sundays, leading one young man to Christ just before the guy was released. A few weeks later, he received a note from the young man's wife, thanking Les for taking care of him while he was in jail and for helping him as he had. She said Les had helped Kenny turn his life around.

Les had a very good sense of humor and, without pushing the boundaries too far, would every now and then pull pranks. One Friday night, he and his cellmates all crowded into the shower area so they couldn't be seen when the guard went by to check the cells. Before they huddled behind the shower wall, they hung a sign on the bars that read GONE FOR PIZZA. BE RIGHT BACK. Les told me they were about to suffocate, as they were packed like sardines in those small quarters before the guard finally came by for roll call. The guard almost panicked before hearing snickering coming from behind the shower stall. He was *not* amused. Even in the midst of turmoil, my husband found ways to bring laughter to others.

I began making periodic visits to the sheriff's office to ask procedural questions and make requests, usually involving Les's glasses, contacts, or medication. As we got closer to trial, I needed to know if I could bring him regular clothes to wear in the courtroom, what the rules were, and how I would get them to him.

I also asked the sheriff if I could arrange for a local barber to come in and give him a haircut before appearing in court. By now, Les had shaved his beard, as he had no way of keeping it neat and trim. He was also wearing his glasses, as they wouldn't allow him to keep his contacts and solution. So the big, burly guy in jeans and a flannel shirt, who looked like he had just stepped out of a cabin in the woods of Colorado, was now clean-shaven and wearing glasses.

The prosecution would make a big deal out of what they called "his transformation" at trial, saying he was trying to look like a regular guy instead of the killer they wanted him to be—implying that killers were large men with beards, apparently.

The first time I showed up at the sheriff's office, the person at the front desk seemed surprised. I guess most people visiting someone in jail didn't often pop in to see the sheriff while they were there. I was always polite and professional, going back to my high school days in theater and putting on my best act. But I always felt uneasiness in the sheriff's presence. Not mine, his.

The sheriff's office was situated within a larger office with windows that separated him from the main area. Think *Law & Order SVU*, but bigger. He could view the deputies working at their desks and any visitors who might come into the department.

I remember on more than one occasion waiting to see him in the outer office where the deputies were while he had someone with him in his office. He sat there watching me instead of giving his whole attention to the person who was talking to him. In turn, I would sit, wait, and watch him while he watched me. It felt like a game. If I came in and talked to one of the deputies or the receptionist, he would always follow me with his eyes.

Les had several kidney stone incidents that had sent him to the hospital starting in his late twenties. While in Grayson County Jail, he was in so much pain from a kidney stone that they transferred him to the local hospital. He was treated in the ER, given medication, and eventually passed the stone. No one called me about the incident. I learned about it at my next visit.

A few weeks later, I received a bill from the local hospital for their services with Les's kidney stone. On my next trip to visit, I bypassed the front desk in the main office and walked straight into the sheriff's office without knocking. All eyes were on me as I breezed through the outer office and straight in. Obviously, no one had ever done that before. Especially an inmate's wife.

The sheriff immediately rose from his desk, his face turning bright red and his eyes squinting, tightening to the point where they looked like black dots about to jump out from beneath his glasses.

"I believe my husband was a guest of your facility at the time these procedures were done, and medications were given to him at the local hospital," I said as I slapped the bill on his desk.

He looked up at me, surprised by my intrusion, scowling as always. He continued to stare at me, not saying a word.

"By removing him from our home and thus losing his job as a result, we no longer have insurance. Therefore, as he was a guest of Grayson County, and in your custody at the time of the hospital's services, Grayson County will need to take care of this bill."

I turned and walked out, leaving the bill lying on his desk. He followed me with his glaring stare as I made my way through the maze of deputies and out the main door. I never heard from the hospital again.

It seemed he didn't like to be around me. Or maybe it was something else. He was dealing with what might be the biggest crime in his career. He had a man in his jail who claimed to be innocent and whose wife was not your typical jailhouse visitor. I asked questions and walked boldly into his space. As I learned more about the crime, more about the victims, and more about how business was done in some towns, I suspected there were people who needed Les to be guilty to keep the status quo.

Silken Webs

Those silken webs we often weave,
From thoughts of how we do perceive,
Serve only to trap and to deceive
Our minds from what we should believe.
Instead, our minds dwell in ecstasy,
Blocking out all sense of reality,
Feeding itself on pure fantasy,
Devoid of any hope of clarity.
Our shackled thoughts send out a plea,
But somewhere we must find the key
To unlock the hidden mystery
That will release our minds and set us free.
No longer a mystery we cannot share,
That key is simply but a prayer;
Our burdened thoughts we no longer bear—
They're now within another's care.

March 25, 1988

CHAPTER 10

Desperate for Answers

February 1984

Things could not have seemed more hopeless. I knew nothing about the judicial process, but it seemed all we had to go on were Les's word and our belief in his innocence. I became a regular fixture at the courthouse, and it wasn't just the sheriff who seemed to be uncomfortable around me. The county attorney would see me and turn the other way to avoid contact. Deputies avoided being in the same room with me. I couldn't believe I was so intimidating—unless it was something else. Guilt, maybe?

I received a call sometime in mid-February from someone who wanted to introduce me to a friend she thought could help us. This friend had a special gift and might be able to tell me things that would be helpful in the investigation. "What could it hurt?" she asked. I wasn't sure how the psychic named Ellen could help. As I talked to her on the phone, I had this sick feeling in the pit of my stomach. What she was proposing made me a bit nervous, like I was doing something I wasn't supposed to.

On my next visit to Les, I told him about this proposition so I could get his thoughts on the subject. I could see by his reaction he was clearly surprised. He, too, was hesitant about what was being proposed, but like me, we both felt desperate for the truth to be revealed—through investigation, a confession, even a good, solid lead to someone who knew the truth. Our entire fifteen-minute visit that day and the subsequent visit on Saturday were spent discussing this idea of consulting a psychic.

What we were asked to be a part of went beyond what our faith believed. In fact, deep inside, we both knew it was wrong, but something kept saying, "But *is* it?" So we cast our good judgment aside.

It was one of those times when we should have given it a lot of prayer—individually, but also together. Before I left our visit that Saturday, he agreed I should pursue this, just to see what she had to say. However, as I began to leave, he leaned in closer to the window and quietly voiced my own concern: "This doesn't feel right." I nodded slightly, my hands clasped in front of me, my left thumb making circles in the palm of my right hand. And so, we entered a very interesting yet disturbing period in our life. As if we didn't have enough of that already.

Ellen requested I bring a few personal items of Les's for our meeting at her house. I chose his senior class ring, his wallet, and a pocketknife. The latter two he normally carried daily. She was pleasant, well-dressed, and very sympathetic to our plight. I told her my husband and I were both Christians and a bit hesitant about this sort of thing. She said she understood our concerns, but she was a Christian as well, and her gifts came from God, leading her to help people. Hesitantly, I handed her his things.

Placing them in her hand, she continued to talk, telling me what a kind and generous man he was. She said he was holding some things back, but he didn't kill those men. I began to weep, wanting so much for her to tell me how this would all end.

We met on several occasions, and each time she would tell me more yet not enough. She was consulting with friends of hers at Duke University in North Carolina—experts who did this sort of thing all the time. In fact, she had someone she wanted to bring to Texas to visit the scene of the crime, hopefully recreating what actually happened that day. Again, we were hesitant, but we agreed to it and I arranged it with Klein.

A psychic, who supposedly helped in the Ted Bundy case, flew in from

Florida to attend a motions hearing and join us on a trip to view the crime scene that had previously been scheduled. He wanted to be in the courtroom as an onlooker, just to be near Les. After the hearing, deputies escorted us to view the crime scene, and he accompanied us to the ranch where the murders took place. The court allowed him to go with us, as Klein had listed him as an investigator. He told us many things he could not have known. Yet he didn't tell us anything that was really helpful. It was just enough to keep our interest and to think we might be on to something.

The sheriff's office turned over what was supposed to be discovery during this same period. Included in the material were the autopsy reports. In addition to describing the victims' wounds and how they were killed, the reports listed all the personal property found on the bodies and photocopies of items from their wallets, such as driver's licenses, credit cards, and any other personal effects. I had read every one of those reports more than once.

Ellen met with me one day with exciting news. She began telling me about her conversation with Philip. I was a bit confused, trying to figure out who she was talking about. Then I realized she was talking about Philip Good, one of the victims. He was dead! Once I got over the initial shock of her declaration, she informed me that this was a special gift she had.

She would take a notepad in the privacy of her home, sit quietly, and meditate. She would then write on the paper a question for the person she was trying to communicate with. The person would then answer her on the same page, using her as a conduit as she wrote their answers.

She showed me the yellow legal pad where there were several pages of writing. There was a short couple of sentences in the form of a question in her handwriting and then, just below hers, would be an answer in a very distinctive yet different handwriting.

Her writing was feminine; the other, masculine. In fact, it almost looked familiar. The conversation was rather benign at first, but as she began to ask questions regarding the murders, the masculine writing stated Les was not the murderer. I turned the pages, reading each question and answer. He was very vague as he described the hangar. When I came to the last page, I looked down where her "contact" had finished his last statement, and gasped. There at the very bottom of the page, he had signed his last statement with a singular "P."

It wasn't just any "P." It was very different. Very distinctive. I had seen it before. It was identical to the signature on Philip Good's driver's license, the one in the autopsy report. I couldn't believe it. I knew that signature. I had looked at it for days, even commented to Klein when we were reading the autopsy report how unusual Philip's "P" was in his signature.

If what she claimed was true, if she was really communicating with Philip, why was he not telling us exactly what had happened?

Ellen was overcome with excitement when I told her about the signature. She assured me she would attempt to contact him again, and perhaps this time he would tell us more. We had to be patient, she said. This took time. But we were on the right track.

In the meantime, her colleagues at Duke University in North Carolina were working on this case and asked for some of Les's things to be sent to them. They also wanted something from the crime scene. I told Ellen that getting something from the crime scene was not possible.

They had a session later that week with the few things belonging to Les and reported to Ellen that there were several men who were responsible for the murders, but Les wasn't one of them. Drugs were definitely involved and were the prime motive for the murders.

A few weeks later, Ellen told me it was time to move to the next step. She wanted to have a séance, and I needed to be there. A cold chill ran down my spine as I heard her request over the phone. I told her I wasn't comfortable with the idea, but she insisted it was important. We were so close to finding the truth, and this was the only way to know what really happened that day. We needed to speak to the men who were murdered. I told her I would think about it and get back to her. My heart was racing as I quickly hung up the phone. I sat there for a while, my hand still on the receiver, and watched as my hand shook uncontrollably. It was sometime before I could move.

I was terrified for several days after she and I spoke. I awoke one night from a terrible nightmare. I never had nightmares. I had seen the face of one of the victims. It was just floating in the air, looking at me. Another night, I saw one of the other victim's fathers. I felt as if I were being haunted. But I didn't believe in ghosts and hauntings. I had never experienced anything like it. I felt like it was akin to poking a hornet's nest. We had stirred something up. My imagination? Or perhaps there were spirits among us. I was familiar with the Spirit of God, but had I ever acknowledged there were also evil spirits that wanted to harm or distract us? I wondered, *Has our rush to find answers clouded our otherwise grounded faith?*

I went to the grocery store across the street from church the next Sunday night to get a few things for the week. As I walked in the door, there was a revolving rack near the entrance that had Christian books on it. I had seen it several times before, but on this particular night, a book in the middle of the rack—the cover a brilliant white, the title in a soft mauve color, written in beautiful cursive—read *The Beautiful Side of Evil.* The last word was in thick block letters of black, and there was a single red rose in the middle of the menacing word. I walked toward it, as it appeared the rose was glowing and beckoning, "Buy me."

I lifted the book off the rack and saw Johanna Michaelsen had written it, and the foreword was by Hal Lindsey. Everyone in my circle of friends knew who Hal Lindsey was. He was a very popular Christian author at the time, author of *The Late Great Planet Earth.* I turned the book over to read the back cover.

"Are all miracles from God, or is there a beautiful side of evil? The blind see, the deaf hear, and the lame walk. Is God always behind such miracles, or can there be another source?"

I bought it.

I began reading this powerful book. All the Scripture I had studied just weeks earlier and was confused about was in the author's story and explained. What we were doing was wrong! Deep down, I knew it. I had been blinded by an overwhelming desire for answers, but I was looking in the wrong place. God was revealing to me, through this woman's experiences, just how deceived I was.

I couldn't put the book down. One night, while reading in bed, I came to the end. *How could I have been so blind?* What we were doing was not from God. This was from Satan.

As this realization flooded through me, I felt an ominous presence in my room. The temperature seemed to drop, and I felt very cold. I began to shiver and knew there was an evil spirit present. I could feel the anger that he'd been found out and the lie had been revealed.

For just an instant, I became afraid, and then immediately I began to pray to God, asking for His protection and to remove the spirit from my presence. Like a fog quickly lifting as the sun comes up, the temperature in the room once more felt normal, and the feeling of anger all around me left, replaced by a sense of love and peace. I thanked God for revealing to me the lie we were following and for not leaving us alone. I turned out the light and fell into a peaceful sleep.

I called Ellen the following morning and told her there would be no séance and we were done with our sessions. She thought I was being foolish. I knew I was being wise. But more importantly, I was obeying God's Word.

And I never looked back.

Silent Words

You look into my eyes, and sweet words of love
Are silently expressed as you gently caress me with your gaze.
I want so much more, but I dare not look away,
Because, for now, this is all you can give.
In those brief moments, there is a tenderness that is only shared
Through memories of what once was and hopeful expectations
Of what will be.

April 20, 1984

CHAPTER 11

Do Your Homework

Les always took so much time researching before making a purchase. He would decide to buy something for me, himself, or for our home, and he would know everything about the item he was considering. He checked out all the references, warranties, and feedback he might be able to find, including *Consumer Reports* to pore over the pros and cons—a big task before the internet and online customer reviews.

He was so thorough in making decisions that sometimes we would be in the middle of an argument, and while I waited (impatiently) to hear what he had to say, he would ask for time to think about it and get back to me. It drove me crazy.

Looking back, it seems somewhat surreal we didn't take that same approach when picking an attorney or in choosing to go to trial as soon as we did. All we could see was innocent equals not guilty; not guilty equals a jury declaring so; and a jury declaring so equals get out of jail and go home.

Oh, our naivete.

We would have been better off waiting three years to go to trial. Instead, it was just three months. None of us knew how to prepare for a four-count capital murder trial. And we had no clue as to what the prosecution was doing to prepare. We certainly didn't know what Klein's defense plan was.

There were a lot of things I didn't know. And the more I found out, the more I wondered how well I really knew my husband. I would soon find out he was not at work, as I thought, on the afternoon of Wednesday, October 5, 1983, four days before the murders. He made his first trip to Grayson County that afternoon to look at the plane he was later accused of stealing, supposedly killing four people in the process.

He had rushed back home after looking at the plane, as we had an early evening appointment to have a family photo taken at Olan Mills Photography Studio. Each time I look at that photo, unaware of the events put in motion earlier, I feel a little nauseated. Yet I love the picture. It was the last one we had made as a family.

Les got up early on Saturday, October 8, 1983, and headed out in his light-blue Scout. My friend and business partner, Sharon, and I were going to have a garage sale at her house in a few weeks, and I was busy preparing for that.

We normally ate dinner around 6:00 P.M., so I told Les we were having hamburgers that night and asked that he be home before dark so he would have time to cook them on the grill. He said he would. And he did. He made it back home that evening in time to fire up the grill and cook hamburgers for the family.

I was standing in the kitchen prepping the food when I saw him through the window, pulling into the driveway. It was still light out, and I watched as he got out of the Scout and came into the house through the garage door. He walked into the kitchen, greeted me, and went to clean up and get the grill started. Just a typical Saturday night at our house.

I had no idea at the time how important it was that Les had arrived home before dark that day. But it was a vivid memory to me, as we had a conversation about it before he left, and he wouldn't have cooked hamburgers outside in the dark.

Les had told his story to Gayle prior to seeing any newspaper accounts of his arrest or of the investigation. Klein had been given a copy of Les's story, yet when he visited Les for the first time on January 23, 1984, four days after his arrest, he didn't ask Les to clarify any of the details or ask any questions about his story during his short, thirty-minute visit. They spoke only of the bail reduction hearing.

Instead of discussing the case with him, Klein told Les he was troubled by specific details of his story that didn't agree with some of the times reported in newspaper accounts of the murders. He was already depending on newspaper accounts for his information rather than listening to his own client or examining any evidence.

Klein held several impromptu press conferences the three times he was in Sherman before trial. Those were the only times that he saw or spoke to Les in preparation for trial as well, and the time he spent was short. After a brief visit with Les, following a hearing in early February, my heart sank as I read in the Sherman paper that Klein claimed, "My client has never been to Grayson County."

Klein, as well as many other people, knew that was a lie. He had read Les's account of that day so there would be no misunderstanding of what took place. He knew Les had been there. Yet Klein lied.

Klein didn't want Reverend Gayle Baucum around. He went so far as to ask our family if we could send him away on a sabbatical or vacation until after the trial was over. Baucum knew Les's story, knew what was going on, and was present at almost all the family gatherings. Klein was concerned about Les's story going public. We had agreed not to tell his story to the press or let it get out, because we knew Les had to be the one to tell it. And he needed to tell it on the witness stand.

Yet he was making it increasingly difficult, if not impossible, for Les to testify. Only one story was being told in the cafés and stores in Sherman, and Les was the murderer in that story. The longer it went on, the guiltier he looked. It terrified and infuriated me the way Les's case was being handled.

Time sheets indicate that Klein worked eighty-six hours on Les's case between January 20, 1984, and April 10, 1984. That's seventy-seven days from the time of his arrest until jury selection, making it just barely one hour a day. However, Klein billed 407 hours, and approximately 150 hours were billed for time spent at the trial.

We knew that Klein worked on numerous civil matters, tried two civil cases, and appeared regularly in court on thirteen criminal matters in the weeks before Les's trial. He had assured us at the contract signing and made a point to tell the press that Les's case would be his sole focus from the time he contracted with us through the time of trial.

He convinced me that if I helped him with the paralegal part of preparation, it would save a lot of billable hours. I thought that was what the contracted money was paying for. I agreed, as it would give me something to do to help and I would know what was going on.

I had no paralegal experience. I was detail-oriented and had been a secretary and administrative assistant during all the years I had worked, but the legal world was not part of my résumé. I decided, however, it was a good idea, so we set up a makeshift office in a small meeting room where I could work and sort through the documents we would receive.

After multiple requests to the state for discovery of investigative reports, depositions, autopsy reports, and evidence found at the scene, we finally got a call that they were ready to turn everything over to us. Klein told me that I should drive to Sherman to pick up the documents rather than send a courier, which Klein would bill me for. So I got in my little green VW Rabbit, and on March 19, 1984, I drove the hour and a half to Sherman, parked in front of the courthouse, and climbed the stairs to the sheriff's office to pick up the evidence.

I returned that afternoon with one box full of loose sheets of paper. There were no notebooks, no order to things—just papers thrown into a box. I couldn't believe this was all the evidence they had. I knew enough that a grant of discovery meant the prosecution had to turn over to the defense all the evidence they planned to use at trial. Unless the motion Klein had filed had been less than thorough in its request, we should have been given access to interviews with potential witnesses, crime scene pictures, crime scene evidence, lists of potential witnesses to call at trial, and any physical evidence that was gathered at the scene of the crime and at the search of our house, our cars, and Les's hair samples taken at the hospital. Instead, we had random call sheets with handwritten notes of people calling in sightings of ultralights the day of the murders. There was absolutely little of value in that box to help prepare for Les's trial.

Klein put me to work. I read all the documents, divided them into categories, made notes of things I thought were significant, tagged pages, and wrote questions I had on legal pads as I began to catalog the information. Klein wanted everything in notebooks behind dividers clearly labeled, making it easier for him to study. Once that was completed, I thought he and I would sit down and go through each binder as I showed him all the discrepancies that had been found. But that didn't happen. Instead, I worked all day in the office, and I rarely had a chance to even talk to him.

I never saw him look at the notebooks. There were times I referred to something I had noted on one of the reports, and his reaction was as if he didn't know anything about it. He would look at me with a dead stare and ask, "What are you talking about?" And then I would tell him, and he would then go back into his office.

One day as Klein walked through my work area, he told me he planned to have me at the defense table so if anything came up, I could tell him if it was in the notebooks and where to find it. All I heard was that I would be with my husband instead of sitting in the gallery of the courtroom with the other spectators. We would be together. As far as I knew, this was normal. I discovered later it wasn't. In fact, it was totally unheard of.

I wasn't sure why we were doing all this if he wasn't going to pay attention to the multiple alternative motives I had uncovered. After all, alternative motives and reasonable doubt were the cornerstone to Les's defense. There were a lot of other reasons some people might have wanted at least one or more of the victims dead.

Authorities received questionable phone calls during this time, pointing suspicion to other people and motives other than stealing a plane. Calls had been made to the sheriff's office with allegations of known drug-dealing from the murder site and sightings of trucks and ultralight airplanes coming and going, as well as other mysterious activities.

Included in the documents were autopsy reports for each victim. Some interesting things caught my eye as I read them, and I would point them out to Klein if I ever saw him. If I didn't, I would leave him a note. He would tell me that when we were finished cataloging, he would look at it. We had so little time; I felt like he needed to be looking at these discrepancies now rather than later.

On the autopsy report for Bob Tate, one of the victims and owner of the ultralight, the coroner noted that there was a business card in his shirt pocket. And yet there was no business card or photocopy of the card in the box of evidence. There were no notes in the officers' reports indicating any follow-up on their part to find the business card.

We knew Les had given Tate three thousand dollars cash as a down payment for the airplane, with his business card in a white business envelope. On the back of the card, Les had written the conditions of the sale, including the lessons and further payment. There was no mention of any money on any of the men, other than some small bills and change.

There was, however, a call-in report to the sheriff's office the day after the murders from Tate's wife, Bobbie, asking if they had found three thousand dollars on her husband's body. She was told no by one of the sheriff's deputies. She told the officer that her husband, Bob Tate, was meeting a buyer for the plane that afternoon at 4:00 P.M. and had called her after the meeting to say he sold the plane and was given three thousand dollars cash as a partial payment. That money was not listed on the coroner's report, but the card was.

Tate was asking $4,500 for the plane. How did she know he had three thousand dollars when the asking price was more? Her call indicated she had talked to her husband *after* the sale was made, and he told her how much the buyer gave him. Knowing how much he was asking for the plane, it would be logical that the two of them discussed the terms of the agreement, as she would likely ask him why he didn't get the whole amount. However, the money was not found. The card had made it through the autopsy but then disappeared.

It also validated Les's story. Tate had been alive between the time Les had left and when the murders had taken place. And he called his wife to tell her the transaction had been a success and he had been paid in cash. The plane had been sold, not stolen, and the buyer had already left.

Sometime in March, as our mid-April court date drew near, I suggested to Klein we might want to see what evidence the prosecution was going to use during trial, especially the evidence removed the night of the search of our house. He thought that was a good idea. Why had he not already asked the court or filed a motion to have access? I couldn't believe he actually thought the small box with the autopsy reports and random notes taken by officers was their complete discovery.

I was getting a lot more nervous about him being our legal representative. Klein told me he would make arrangements with the prosecution for the two of us to view the evidence. I then suggested that he might want Les to be there also to explain anything that we might have questions about. Again, he thought that was a great idea. Another red flag!

We stood in the middle of a room set up in the courthouse as Klein and Les talked while viewing the evidence from our house. None of it seemed all that damaging. This was only the second time since his arrest in January that Les had met or had a conversation with Klein, and it was taking place in an open room with deputies surrounding him. Klein told us he had a plan and that there wasn't enough evidence lying there in front of us to convict. He didn't share what his plan was.

At that time, we weren't aware of the experts the prosecution was planning on calling, the things we couldn't see, or the things they conveniently left out. There were no lists of witnesses they planned to call, and Les and I didn't know enough to ask about those possibilities. We assumed Klein knew all the questions to ask.

How could we have been so naive? The inevitable barreled toward us like a freight train with no engineer in sight. We couldn't stop it.

It's one thing to see in hindsight what might have been done differently. But at the time, we were doing the best we knew how. Throughout those three months, I believed Les would take the stand and tell his story and I would testify with corroborative information, showing enough reasonable doubt.

I pleaded with Klein to do some investigation, to follow up on the leads, to do *something* other than "prepare for trial." The only evidence I saw of him preparing for trial was when he brought in a private tailor to make three new, custom-tailored suits. He gave me a big grin as the tailor took his measurements and bragged, "I'm going to dazzle them with my custom suits and boots! Those country folk will be impressed by this big-town lawyer." Big-town lawyer? We were in small-town Texas, not Houston or Dallas.

There were numerous reports linking some of the victims to illegal drug activity. We could offer other motives for these murders by digging deeper into the little information we had. An investigator could follow up on the leads that had been called in to the sheriff's office immediately following the murders.

There were multiple notes in the discovery files of witnesses willing to testify to the identities of other suspects. Klein claimed that he followed up on these rumors but found no one willing at the time to make a statement. During subsequent appeals and affidavits from these witnesses, we discovered that Klein had never spoken to any of them.

First Week of April 1984, Sherman, Texas

Shari,

You would think that after not writing for so long, I should be able to turn out an extra-long letter—somehow I don't think this is going to be that way. I have given some thought to the events of last week and have determined that the tide has turned. I have the most wonderful feeling about the outcome of this trial. It's hard to explain, but when things seem to be going your way, and the cloud of doubt starts to clear, that's when you're the most vulnerable. If Satan thinks you are getting the upper hand, he will muddy the water some way, and I think that's what's happening now. If he can't attack you on the matter at hand, he will find an unrelated matter that will cause doubt. Don't let him divert your energy and faith from the trial at hand. If that's the best Satan has to offer one week before trial, then with God's help, we will prevail. I have asked, and you should too, that whatever the outcome, it will be His will.

I have enjoyed LeRoy Eims's book on prayer very much. Any books on the power of prayer have been a great help and inspiration to me lately, but you know what's funny? They only reflect and interpret what's in the Bible. I asked for books on prayer, and I had one all along.

Read Ecclesiastes 4:9–12 (NIV): "Two are better than one, because they have a good return for their labor: If either of them falls down, one can help the other up. But pity anyone who falls and has no one to help them up. Also, if two lie down together, they will keep warm. But how can one keep warm alone? Though one may be overpowered, two can defend themselves. A cord of three strands is not quickly broken."

You amaze me more and more as time goes along. I guess I really never stopped and thought about how strong a person you are. Maybe I listened to you too much when you kept telling me how weak a person you were. Who are you kidding? I've seen enough strength in you the last seventy-three days to make me realize that you can do anything you set your mind to. I'm tired of hearing how weak you are—that's only a poor excuse anymore. I'm putting you on notice that that excuse is to be used no longer. I love you very much and am growing impatient to get home and be with you and the kids.

I guess I'll end this "short" note and I'll see you tomorrow.

I don't know what will happen or if we will have any time to-gether. If we can't, here is a kiss from me now. I love you always.

—Les

(Don't forget: Prayer time 6:30 A.M. every day.)

On April 10, *voir dire*, the process of selecting a jury, began, and for two weeks, we sat in the courtroom watching and listening as each prospective juror was questioned. It was obvious by the questions Klein asked that he was posturing for Les not to testify. We told him several times that Les's testimony was crucial. He had to tell his story. Without Les testifying and allowing the jurors to hear from him, he would look guilty.

Klein lied the day after Les was arrested; he told the press his client had never been to Grayson County. Klein's statement made it almost impossible for Les to get on that stand—at least in his mind. Les wanted to take the stand and tell the jurors what had happened that day, and we believed we had enough evidence to prove reasonable doubt by bringing witnesses that could testify to questionable activity by at least one of the victims that there were other people who wanted him dead. Klein said he'd already told the press that Les wasn't ever in Grayson County and we were just going to go with that. It was as if Richard Klein would rather Les not testify than have the world learn that he had lied to the press.

He assured us that the questions posed to the prospective jurors were merely to see and hear their responses. He would preface his questioning of each prospective juror by telling them that any defendant accused of a crime had the right to testify or not testify on his behalf. He would then ask them if they understood that. He asked the jurors, if Les decided not to take the stand and testify, would they hold that against him? Would they think his not testifying was because he was guilty? It was like putting the idea into their heads.

He assured us that we would continue to discuss that option of Les testifying as the trial moved forward. He also assured us that he would not make the decision for Les *not* to testify without consulting him first. As far as we were concerned, we had no reason to believe that he would make that decision without consulting us first.

Each day I came to the courthouse, I saw people on the street staring as I walked from my car to the old building in the middle of the square. *What must it be like for Les when they bring him in?* A chill of fear often ran down my back. *Is my husband safe?*

The Navigator

Where are we going? Look around the bend.

We've only just begun; this isn't our journey's end.

The way may not be easy, the day may seem long.

The path may seem dark, as if each turn were wrong.

The canyon may be narrow, the water cold and deep.

The waves may break over us, but at the helm we keep,

For the Navigator has charted our course and carefully planned our way.

So we'll keep our eyes on Him, and in the boat we'll stay.

He'll lead us through the storm, for He's been there times before.

He'll take us through the current, till we're safely on the shore.

June 13, 1984

CHAPTER 12

A Deal with the Devil

April 23, 1984

On May 9, 1930, a maddened lynch mob burned the Grayson County Courthouse in an effort to get to a prisoner being held inside. The man had been placed in the courthouse vault for protection from the crowd. When the mob was refused custody, gasoline was thrown inside and the building burned. Attempts to extinguish the blaze were thwarted when the mob slashed the fire hoses. A new courthouse was built in 1936.

It was this courthouse, built during the Great Depression, that we entered on April 23, 1984. Even though we didn't know the history of the courthouse at the time, we did not feel welcome there. We were still concerned about being outsiders in a town where we were not sure we would find justice.

We had asked Klein to request a change of venue from the very beginning. Even local reporters had asked him at an impromptu press conference on January 23, the Monday after Les's arrest, if he would ask for a change. Klein replied, "The good people of Grayson County can be trusted to do the right thing." He continued to adhere to this philosophy.

The huge courtroom we had been ushered into was packed with spectators and the press. The old, musty courthouse housed much larger courtrooms than the newer ones in other counties built in recent decades. No cameras were allowed, but reporters from two local papers and television stations were present, along with several from the Dallas–Fort Worth area.

The activity around us was frenzied, yet it seemed as if we were in a vacuum, watching the scene unfold from inside the sphere of activity itself. Words and sounds blurred, people and things around us moved fast, but Les and I seemed to be in slow motion.

I felt at any moment I would awaken from this nightmare, reach over to touch my husband lying close to me as we slept, and then drift back into a peaceful sleep. That serene moment escaped me, leaving only memories of tender ones that had once been. Moments we might not ever share again.

I didn't have the luxury of thinking about that right now. My anxiety was palpable, and I could feel his as well while we sat, our hands clasped together, clinging to one another.

Everyone seemed surprised that I was sitting at the defense table next to Les. Klein had said he needed me nearby in case he had to look for something in the numerous notebooks that I had put together. Those notebooks were now stacked in front of us on the defense table. And so far, in my opinion, being by my husband's side was the only positive thing I had seen come out of the many motions he had filed with the court.

In his motion to the court for permission for me to sit at the table, Klein stated I was his assistant and investigator and he needed me with him. Thinking about it now, I wonder exactly why he wanted me there. He never once opened any of the notebooks, nor did he ask me for any recollection of the events or the subjects that came up in the trial that had been part of my investigation of the notes provided to us. It soon became clear to me that all the notes, autopsy reports, call-ins, and affidavits that I had pored over, cataloged, and highlighted were of no use at all at the trial. The row of notebooks was all for show. And they soon became a backroom joke to the opposition.

Just before the trial began, lead prosecutor Stephen Davidchik asked to speak with Klein in the judge's chambers. I assumed this was standard procedure prior to the beginning of a trial. They were gone for several minutes, and upon their return, Klein walked over to the defense table where Les and I were sitting.

"I just made a deal with the prosecution regarding evidence that was found in your home during the search," he said.

"What kind of evidence?" I asked, puzzled by what they might have that warranted some kind of "deal."

"What kind of deal?" Les asked, as if he were reading my mind. "If it was that important, why would we not have seen it when we were shown the evidence taken from the search?"

Klein cleared his throat. "Can I talk to you privately for a moment, Les?" He eyed me as the two of them stepped away toward the front of the courtroom, giving them more privacy.

Klein reached into his pocket, bringing out what appeared to be a stack of Polaroid photographs. He handed them to Les, and I watched as he looked at each one while Klein quietly spoke to him.

Les said something to Klein as he handed back the photographs. Les was calm but seemed somewhat agitated as he continued to talk to his attorney. Klein just shook his head, placed the photographs back in his pocket, and walked away.

"What was it?" I asked quietly when Les returned to my side at the defense table.

"Years ago," he began, while rubbing the bridge of his nose as if he had a headache he was trying to relieve, "when we had our business in Fort Collins, one of the employees had some rather racy pictures in the office of him and his girlfriend. I found them tucked away in a desk drawer. I didn't want anyone else to see them. We were about to shut down the office, getting rid of the desks and packing up things. So I threw them in his file in a desk drawer with the intention of giving them to him to get rid of. I should have just destroyed them, but I forgot about them."

He took a moment to study me, his eyebrows furrowed. "When we closed the office, I packed all the files and documents, payroll records—everything—and just moved it out of the office space. I took all the files home and stored them in the barn until I had time to go through all the stuff. I just never seemed to find the time. I didn't give it much thought, as we were looking for a new job and those files were the last thing on my mind."

I was confused. What did this have to do with Les or his charges? I looked at him, twisting my wedding ring around and around on my finger, waiting for him to say more. We were still in the courtroom, people were still in the gallery, and we were trying to appear calm and keep our voices low.

"Evidently, we moved all that stuff from Fort Collins to Grand Junction when I took the job with Thompson-Hayward. Then I guess we moved it all again to Arlington, because I never did go through and weed out the files to get rid of what I needed to keep and what I didn't. I had totally forgotten about those pictures."

"What does that have to do with us?" I asked, my voice cracking slightly as he lifted his eyes to look at me, taking my hands in both of his and softly rubbing them with his thumbs. He looked back down at our hands, studying them as if it were the first time he had seen them.

Looking back at me, he said, "You can't really tell who it is in the pictures, unless you knew the person in them, but it isn't me. The prosecution is claiming it's me. They're claiming I am with another woman in these pictures, and they will use them to try to make me look like I'm not the upstanding citizen I claim to be. Klein was told they wouldn't use them to try to smear my image or reputation, but only if we made a deal with them."

I stared at him for what seemed like a lifetime but was only a few seconds, taking in the words he had just said. I wanted so badly to throw my arms around him but knew I couldn't, so I moved in closer.

"What deal?" I whispered, as I felt my stomach churn. "And why didn't Klein confer with you before making some kind of deal?"

Les looked me straight in the eye, a hint of a sheen over them, and replied, "That's a good question. And one I don't have an answer for." He shook his head. "The prosecution agreed they wouldn't use the pictures against me, and in return, we wouldn't bring any testimony or witnesses that might cast an unflattering light on any of the victims."

"He can't make that deal!" I almost shouted, catching myself as everyone was watching us. "It's not you!" I almost cried out loud. "They need to know that. How could he agree to that without even talking to you? Why weren't you part of the meeting in the judge's chambers?"

I wanted to burst into tears right there.

"I don't have any answers for you," he said quietly, leaning over to kiss the top of both my hands, trying to calm me, calm himself, as we were sitting at the defense table in the middle of the courtroom filled with people.

County Attorney Stephen Davidchik had introduced a motion *in limine* just prior to the beginning of the trial. A motion *in limine* requests the judge to rule that certain testimony be excluded. The motion is always discussed outside the presence of the jury and decided by a judge.

The motion restricted Klein and any other defense witnesses from mentioning or asking any questions concerning the following topics:

First, any mention of any matter within the personal background of the victims, other than the dealing of the purchase and sale of ultralights, and their marital status. This included no mentioning of any allegations of illegal activities that may have been engaged in by the victims, or any alleged allegations of extramarital activities, unless the relevance was demonstrated to the court (i.e., judge).

Second, there would be no mention or reference to the defendant's alleged good character or reputation for being a peaceful and law-abiding citizen during the guilt stage of the trial. Such evidence was only admissible during the punishment stage.

Third, no mention of the defendant's alleged reputation for truth and veracity unless and until the defendant testified.

Klein didn't tell us at this time about the third point on the motion that demanded Les to testify if the defense planned to use Les's good reputation as part of a defense strategy.

Les and I were in total shock. Making that deal destroyed any hope of our presenting an alternative theory for the murders of those men. We could no longer bring evidence to produce reasonable doubt. And reasonable doubt had been our key defense. This was not good. And yet, we had no idea how to remedy it.

Les's whole defense was to show how at least one of the victims was allegedly involved in illegal activity and was more than likely killed over a drug deal gone badly. We had managed to find someone who had witnessed illegal activity by at least one of the victims and was willing to testify to that. Two of the victims were also former or current law enforcement officers, and if anyone dealing in drugs knew that, it would be a major motive to get rid of them.

This was insane. Without presenting the overwhelming evidence that had been uncovered to show what one of the victims was up to, including all his illegal involvements and criminal activity he was linked to, Les had no defense except his word, as well as testimony regarding his good character. Klein had always alluded to us that when it came time, we would discuss Les testifying. But now, Klein had put another nail in the coffin by agreeing to these ludicrous terms.

"Why was this evidence not shown to us when we went to view it just weeks before?" I asked Les. "If they found these pictures in a box in our garage when they searched the house, then they've clearly had them all along."

"They weren't logged in as evidence," Les replied. "There were no numbers on them. The county attorney obviously was holding them as a bargaining chip," he said as if he were putting a puzzle together. "Did you see Klein put them in *his* pocket? He didn't hand them back to Davidchik to be put back in evidence. It's like they played a game of poker in the judge's chamber, and Klein won the pictures."

I looked at him incredulously, taking in all that he was saying.

"What else do they have that we don't know about?" he wondered out loud.

I knew very little about the justice system, but I knew that withholding that piece of evidence in order to basically attempt to blackmail us at the last minute did not seem right. The purpose of discovery is to allow the defense to see what evidence the prosecution had to use in court against you.

Discovery, I thought, was to eliminate any surprises. This was certainly a surprise. And I, like Les, wondered if there would be any more.

I would learn later that law enforcement and prosecutors withholding exculpatory evidence was a Brady violation. In 1963, *Brady v. Maryland* was a landmark United States Supreme Court case that established the prosecution must turn over all evidence that might exonerate the defendant (exculpatory evidence) to the defense. In the decision, Supreme Court Judge William O. Davis wrote: "We now hold that the suppression by the prosecution of evidence favorable to an accused upon request violates due process where the evidence is material either to guilt or to punishment . . . . Society wins not only when the guilty are convicted, but when criminal trials are fair."

The prosecution knew at least one of the victims had things they didn't want us to bring up during this trial, as it would be damaging to their theory of Les killing them merely to steal the airplane. Other people had axes to grind with one of the victims we knew of. And their motivation was much more powerful than a $4,500 ultralight.

Had Klein consulted with Les regarding this deal the prosecution wanted to make, Les would have said no. The former employee could be subpoenaed to testify that those were his pictures, not Les's. The trial had not begun yet, and we had lost the first round.

The thought never occurred to either of us to say "Stop!" But I've thought about it since. Could we have stopped this trial before it went any further?

Could the defendant, Les, make his own motion to the judge requesting new counsel? Or have I watched too much TV all these years in between?

We wanted this to be over and for Les to come home, but more and more, it was looking like he was a sitting duck, just ready to be picked off. Sure, we would have lost any money that had already been paid to Klein, but why didn't we consider that an option? It would have delayed the case more and we would have had to start over with a new attorney, but the prosecution had already tipped their hand at this point, making it obvious where they were going with this. Someone (or ones) among the deceased had things no one wanted to be made public.

Honestly, in this scenario, I wonder if it would have saved us. I think the judge would have denied the motion. No matter the decision we made, firing Klein would have increased the risk of overturning the trial verdict on appeal. But we didn't think of that. And for the life of me (and for Les), I don't know why we didn't. We would today. But today, I'm a lot more enlightened than I was then.

I turned to Les and said, "There's still my testimony. I have the timeline of when you came home the night of the murders. That will prove to the jury you couldn't have killed them."

I could hear the hollow words as they came out of my mouth and knew that we were in way over our heads. We had no idea what we were doing, and the person we hired to navigate us through this was not helping.

"We'll have to convince Klein to call you to testify as well. There's no other way to win this if we don't," I said, doing everything I could to hold back the tears.

Caught in our own thoughts and our own fears, we sat, looking at each other, our faces blank. He looked older than he had three months ago. I suppose I did too. I could not imagine how things could get any worse, but in a matter of just a few minutes, it had. He squeezed my hand and gave me a slight smile, as much as he could muster.

And then the court was called to order.

From Darkness to Light

I love you more than words can say,
And it breaks my heart to see you this way.
Why can't the world see you as I do?
A kind and loving person, the real you.
The world around us is screaming, "Justice be done!"
But how can it be justice if you're not the one?
Satan tries to confuse me: "Maybe they're right."
But God gently leads me from darkness to light.
"Trust me, my child, your steps will I lead.
I'll not let you stumble; I'll provide every need."
Praise God, He's my Savior, my Shepherd, and my guide.
A comfort, a solace, a quiet place to hide.
He lifts me in His arms, till the troubled waters cease,
And fills me with His love, hope, joy, and eternal peace.

April 17, 1984

CHAPTER 13

Now Entering the Twilight Zone

The Trial — Day 1 — April 23, 1984

W e clung to the belief that innocent people did not get convicted for crimes they did not commit. Les was facing just that, and death could be waiting for him at the end. This was a concept we couldn't even imagine. We held strong to our faith that God would lead us through. Unfortunately, we were losing faith in the person we had chosen as our attorney. Klein seemed to be a bit bothered by the list of witnesses that the prosecution was going to call. Many of them he was seeing for the first time as the state handed him their finalized list just as the trial began.

"The judge read each of the four case numbers, each presented by the state of Texas versus Lester Leroy Bower Jr." He looked toward the prosecution table. "Is the state ready, Mr. Davidchik?"

"The state is ready, Your Honor, on all four counts," replied the county attorney.

The judge looked at the defense table. "Is the defendant ready, Mr. Klein?"

"The defendant is ready on all four counts, Your Honor."

And so it began.

We watched as the jurors entered the room and took their seats. I knew each one of them by name. I had pages of notes on them: which part of the county they lived in, if they were married, how many children they had, where they worked, what their houses looked like, and what kind of cars they drove. But I had no clue as to what they were thinking, who they really were, or how easily they might be convinced that Les might be guilty. I hadn't allowed myself to consider that option. These weren't our neighbors, our peers. These were strangers.

During the almost two weeks of jury selection, questioning, accepting, and eliminating potential jurors based on questions that had been meticulously asked of them, Klein had seemed more interested in finding out whether they would hold it against Les if he didn't testify. This caused many a discussion between the three of us during that whole process, as it was clearly evident to us and the prosecution that Klein was not going to put Les on the stand to defend himself.

"Now that we have all these restrictions placed on Les by the deal you made with the prosecution," I said to Klein, "Les *has* to testify. Why are you so adamantly against him taking the stand?"

Klein seemed agitated that I asked and said, "Letting Les testify is a bad move. His story does not match the time frame one of the victim's wives had given in an interview with one of the local reporters."

"That's the reason!" I said, throwing my hands in the air. "What if her timeline is off? We have testimony for his timeline that is ironclad, and maybe on cross-examination you can show the jury her discrepancies."

We believed Les would come across as guilty if he didn't testify. Klein had inferred on several occasions that Les was shy and not very articulate, which could not be further from the truth. He had even asked the potential jury panel not to hold that against him.

No one would ever get to hear his story either, and many questions would go unanswered. Our protests fell on deaf ears. Les and I thought the subject had not been entirely closed, believing there was still a chance Klein would change his mind and call Les to testify.

The documents we prepared before trial had enough witness statements that would show the jury ample evidence as to the character and activities of at least one of the victims. We had hoped with this evidence in hand that Klein would be able to present an alternative motive and multiple opportunities for someone else to murder those men. But now, Klein had made a deal with the state not to disparage the reputation of any of the victims, so that option had been taken off the table. Les not telling his story, not speaking for himself, in our opinion, was tantamount to suicide.

Les made the mistake of not being forthright in the beginning with the authorities as to his purchasing the aircraft, but he did not kill those men. And yes, he had several opportunities to remedy the situation but didn't. It still did not make him guilty of murdering four men. Klein had to convince a jury of that. Les and I had no idea how that would be accomplished. And we weren't sure Klein did either.

The jurors were called and came in, walking single file to the jury box, and took their seats. Some looked around the courtroom, perhaps to see if there was anyone there they knew. Others fidgeted with pen and paper or smoothed wrinkles out of their shirts. Searching each face, I tried to see any sign of their thoughts, their feelings. But I couldn't. A few looked over at the defense table, but none directly at Les, just a glance. The process of a capital murder trial began to unfold before our eyes.

Judge Vaughn turned to face the jury and began reciting the jury instructions to the panel. Once he finished, he addressed the county attorney and asked that he read the indictments to the jury. Mr. Sampson, the assistant county attorney, read all four of them, one at a time.

Les sat at the defense table, his hands folded in his lap, looking straight at Mr. Sampson as he read the charges. He looked just as he would have had he been going off to work this morning. Yet I still had not become accustomed to his clean-shaven face.

He was wearing his navy suit and a blue-and-white-striped shirt with a navy tie. I had ironed his clothes for the week at home the night before, made a list of which suits went with which shirts and ties, and dropped his wardrobe off at the jail early that morning. I wished the barber I had hired to come in to cut his hair had taken a little more off, but it was okay.

At the end of reading each indictment, Judge Vaughn turned to Les and asked, "How does the defendant plead to the indictment—guilty or not guilty?"

"Not guilty," Les replied to each one.

The judge called the witnesses who would be testifying during the trial to stand in front of his bench, and we were sworn in. He sent the witnesses to wait in the hallway outside the courtroom until it was time for them to testify. He allowed the widows of the victims and me to remain inside the courtroom. Opening statements were waived by the state, and they called their first witness, Grayson County Deputy Sheriff Robert Murry.

Murry, a tall, heavyset man with black-rimmed glasses, took the witness seat and began the task of painting a picture for the jurors of the scene that was found on the night of October 8, 1983, at the B&B Ranch in Denison, Texas, the location of the murders.

Building contractor Bob Tate and his wife, Bobbie, owned the property that included a modest airplane hangar and a house that Bob was in the process of building. Murry produced pictures taken during the investigation just hours after the discovery of the four bodies in the hangar. All the photographs were shown to the jurors and entered into evidence.

Klein cross-examined Murry with only twenty questions, most of which pertained to what brand of cigarettes were found at the scene and who smoked what. I wondered where Klein was going with this line of questioning. Les didn't smoke, and I didn't recall any pertinent information found in any of the reports regarding cigarettes.

Bobbie Tate, the widow of Bob Tate, was called as the next witness. I unconsciously exhaled a long breath as I watched the dark-haired woman walk past us to take the stand. I wasn't sure how emotional this would be for her. Her face was pinched as if she were in pain, and she looked almost frail. Les reached under the table and squeezed my hand to steady me. I could not imagine the grief and sorrow this woman was experiencing. I had felt loneliness and despair for the last three months as my husband was locked away in a small prison cell, miles away from his family. But she had lost her husband in a horrific way, buried him, and now was going to have to relive that horrible night all over again.

The county attorney asked Bobbie to tell the jurors what she recalled on October 8, 1983. She turned and looked at the jurors and began to speak.

"My son from a previous marriage, along with his wife and their daughter, had driven to our house in Denison that morning from the Dallas area to visit. We had lunch at our house, and then we drove out to the ranch. Bob showed them around the property where we would soon live once Bob finished the house. They also wanted to see the two planes Bob had in the hangar."

Mrs. Tate paused for a moment, looking down at her lap, and took a deep breath.

"Bob owned one of the planes and was trying to sell it. He told me that his friend, Philip Good, was bringing a prospective buyer to look at the plane around four P.M. Bob felt confident that the guy was going to buy the plane that day. The second plane in the hangar was owned by Philip but had recently been sold. The buyer hadn't come to pick it up yet.

"My family needed to get back home to Dallas, so they took me back to town about three thirty. Bob stayed at the ranch to finish some work on the house while he waited for Philip to join him with the buyer.

"I waited for Bob at the house in Denison and then got concerned about him when he had not arrived home by six P.M. At seven thirty, I got in my car and started back to the ranch to see what was keeping him.

"When I got closer to the ranch, I came to an intersection by the ranch and I saw Bob's son, Bobby Glenn, and some of his friends at a four-way stop there." She nodded toward Bobby Glenn, who was sitting in the courtroom. Everyone turned to look to see where he was. I had seen him before around the courthouse but didn't know that was him. He had dark hair and was in his early twenties, perhaps.

"Bobby Glenn told me they had just left the ranch. He had hoped to show his friends the hangar and the planes. Bobby Glenn saw Bob's truck and a couple of other vehicles when they pulled up to the ranch but did not find anyone on the property. All the doors were locked so they assumed Bob and some of his friends had gone to town and would be back later."

Bobbie became a little more animated as she continued. "I was upset, alarmed—telling him his dad would never go off with someone else and leave his truck. I told Bobby Glenn we had to go back to the ranch together and check things out. I kept telling him something was not right."

She paused to gather her emotions and then said, "When we arrived at the ranch, I saw Bob's truck along with the other vehicles. I became more concerned that something was wrong. I was almost hysterical at this point and kept yelling that there was something terribly wrong. The boys looked in some of the windows, but it was dark and they didn't see anyone.

"I remembered that Bob kept the keys to the hangar in his truck, so I ran to get them to unlock the east door. I opened the door, turned on the lights, and saw a body lying on the floor. I didn't know who it was, so I started screaming. My stepson began pulling me by the arm, trying to drag me back out the door. I fought him, trying to go back in, and I was yelling to him that we had to find his dad, that something terrible had happened. 'No!' Bobby Glenn yelled. 'We have to call the police!'"

She went on to explain that she and her stepson continued to argue about what to do until Bobby Glenn physically put her in his car and drove to the nearest house to call the police.

The prosecution had finished their questions for Mrs. Tate and passed her to Klein for cross-examination. Most of Klein's questions were simply confirming the things she had just testified about.

Finally, he asked her what Philip Good had told her husband about the prospective buyer for the plane.

Tate: Philip had shown the plane to a man on Wednesday, and he seemed to be interested in it, Bob told me that night.

Klein: How much was your husband asking for the plane?

Tate: Forty-five hundred dollars.

And then Klein was done.

I knew more about Bobbie Tate than what he had just uncovered. And I knew a whole lot more about her husband based on the information that was sitting in front of us in those notebooks.

Bob Tate was a questionable individual. There were numerous pages in those notebooks of multiple call-ins to the sheriff's office just days after the killings from people stating that Tate had been involved in drugs and other illegal activities. Other callers had reported that they had seen drug buys and money exchanges between Tate and others—some unknown, others they could identify.

One of those people called and talked to Klein prior to the trial, telling him he had run drug money for Tate. But Klein didn't ask Mrs. Tate about any of that. He had made a deal with the state, so his hands were tied. This particular victim had a myriad of reasons why someone might want to do him harm, and it seemed obvious that there were people who didn't want his indiscretions brought up in public.

I was beginning to think that there might be more people than we knew who were somehow tied to one or more of the victims and didn't want that information known. I also couldn't help but wonder if some of those people might be in the courtroom. Or people who might normally be called to testify in criminal cases but were conspicuously absent. If you have something to hide, it's best not to make yourself a target by being called as a witness and opening yourself up to questioning.

Was that Klein's plan? He knew Les's story. Did he not believe him? If he would've talked to Les for more than twenty minutes at a time, which he didn't, he would've seen that my husband's story was logical. He hadn't even spent enough time with him to get to know him as a person.

We had put all our trust, as well as a great deal of money, into a defense attorney who was supposed to be looking out for our best interest. As we sat there, halfway through the first day of a four-count capital murder trial, it was crystal clear that our advocate did not trust his client's ability to convince the jury he was innocent, despite a timeline that made it impossible for him to be the killer.

Gary Jackson, chief criminal investigator with the Grayson County Sheriff's Department, was the next witness called. Mr. Jackson testified that he, along with several other sheriff's officers, arrived at the scene around nine on the night of the murders. When they entered the hangar from the east door, they saw a body lying facedown just to the right.

They walked across the hangar toward the west end of the building, where they found several pieces of carpet that had been piled up in rolls. Upon closer examination, they discovered three more bodies rolled up inside the carpet, with other loose pieces of carpet on top of the roll.

In addition, several .22 hulls, or shell casings, were found scattered around the hangar, as well as pieces of small nylon rope used on ultralights. Other items, including blood, were found around the bodies and on a card table near where the bodies were hidden.

I remember thinking, *Les never left shell casings anywhere.* He was a reloader and always retrieved his shells. Anyone who knew him knew that. But the jury didn't. And probably wouldn't. *Will such a conservative habit like that of my husband's make a difference in a juror's mind?*

The assistant county attorney, Sampson, opened his questioning by asking Officer Jackson, "To your knowledge, were any fingerprints raised or lifted out there that day from the hangar identifiable with anyone other than the four victims?"

Officer Jackson: They were not.

Mr. Sampson: Pass the witness.

Other than the four victims? Les's prints were not found at the crime scene. That's very good news.

Once again, Klein proceeded with his cross-examination by merely going over what Jackson had just stated, asking innocuous questions of the witness that seemed to be of no value.

The state called Dallas County Chief Medical Officer Charles Petty, who did the autopsies on the four victims from the hangar. Dr. Petty began by describing the wounds of the four victims, using Styrofoam mannequin heads and knitting needles to show the trajectory of the bullets.

Bob Tate had been shot twice in the head at close range. One of those shots was a contact wound, meaning the muzzle of the gun had been on his skin when the weapon had been fired. Killings done in that manner were commonly known as "execution style," usually reserved for a gang- or drug-related murder. There were no exit wounds.

Petty was asked if there was anything about the wound that would indicate the gun used had been altered. He responded by saying the amount of soot on the skin would lead him to believe the gun was probably equipped with some sort of extension of the barrel, possibly a silencer.

The same type and number of wounds were found on two of the other victims, Philip Good and Jerry Brown. These three men had been found rolled up in carpet and covered near the west end of the hangar.

There were no indications that any of them had been bound. Because they were all three killed in an execution-style manner—on their knees, gun to their heads—it was hard to believe that at least one of them would not have tried to flee the scene, or the three of them would try to overcome one shooter. One man could not have killed the three of them alone.

As one person in our group said at a recess, "There would have been elbows and asses running like crazy if it were me, three against one. I can't imagine anyone just standing there, one guy with a gun, and someone not running for their life. It had to be more than one person."

He was right. Even one gun is intimidating, but at least you might have a chance to get away under those circumstances. It seemed logical for the victims to have been outnumbered and that more than one gun had been pointed at them for them to be murdered in that manner.

But Ronald Mayes's wounds were different. His body was visible just inside the east door on the other side of the hangar from the other three. He was killed by five gunshot wounds. One bullet had entered on the outside of his right arm and had proceeded through the arm, exiting and then entering the chest opposite the point of entry.

A second bullet had entered in the back of his chest and a third bullet had entered just below and inside the second, making a "complex of gunshot wounds," according to the coroner, on the right side of his body. These three shots were from long range, as if he had come through the door and surprised the shooter. With the pattern of trajectories, it appeared he had entered the door, witnessed what was happening, and turned to his left to run back out the door as he was shot three times.

Two other shots were found, one just in front of the left ear and the other on the left side of the neck near the base. These two shots were at close range and were contact wounds similar to the other three victims' wounds. Ron Mayes had been shot five times. The last two shots were to make sure he did not survive. All four men had been shot in a typical execution style used by professionals.

Dr. Petty said he had concluded the weapon used was a .22 caliber. Eleven bullets had been removed from the four bodies. He also stated that each victim would have succumbed to the one contact wound. Any further shots were superfluous.

Again, Klein's cross-examination seemed lacking. He asked what the wounds would have looked like from an inch away rather than as a contact wound. What if it were six inches, how would it be different? I saw no reason either of those questions was helpful.

Klein asked the doctor if he had determined the time of death. Dr. Petty said he couldn't determine an exact time of death unless there was a witness who could verify the actual time.

Klein passed the witness.

The state called Larry Fletcher, a firearms examiner with the Dallas County Southwestern Institute of Forensic Science. Mr. Fletcher was in his early forties and dressed in a light-brown suit. Ronald Sievert, an assistant United States district attorney who had been assigned to the investigation and trial by the FBI, conducted questioning on this witness.

US Assistant District Attorney Sievert was interested in the bullets and the caliber of weapon that was used in the murders. Fletcher had determined there were three firearms that could be the murder weapon: an AR-7 .22 caliber rifle, a Ruger .22 caliber semiautomatic pistol, or a High Standard .22 caliber semiautomatic pistol. A semiautomatic fires one shot when the trigger is pulled. An automatic weapon fires continuously until the trigger is released.

Sievert: From your examination, could you make any determination as to what type of weapon you feel those bullets may have been fired from?

Fletcher: Yes, by identifying the bullet and the land and groove impressions and looking at the general characteristic of the bullets, there are three firearms that would be possible in firing this type of bullet. An AR-7 .22 caliber rifle, a Ruger .22 caliber semiautomatic pistol, or a High Standard .22 caliber semiautomatic pistol.

Sievert: In your estimation of the .22 casings, did you notice anything on the lands and grooves that came to your attention?

Fletcher: The lands and grooves markings were measured to find out their measurements. Also, there were markings placed on the bullet after the bullet had traveled down the barrel, which would lead me to believe that there was some type of device at the end of the barrel in which the bullet must have passed through after it had traveled down the barrel.

Sievert: Would these markings on the bullets be consistent with the use of a silencer?

Fletcher: Yes, sir.

Sievert: If you would, take a look at these casings that you examined during recess and let me know if you were able to determine what type of ammunition was used.

Fletcher: The head stamp, or the marking, the manufacturer's marking, on the cartridge case is Julio Fiocchi.

Court Reporter: Would you spell that, please?

Fletcher stumbled with the spelling until he got it correct on his third try.

Sievert: I noticed when the court reporter asked you to spell this type of bullet, you had some trouble. In the course of your nine years as a firearms examiner, have you ever encountered Julio Fiocchi ammunition before?

Fletcher: Not before this case, no, sir.

Sievert: This is the first time?

Fletcher: It is.

Sievert: Indicating that it is a rather unique type of ammunition?

Fletcher: To me it is, yes, sir.

Sievert: During the course of your investigation, were you called upon to examine various weapons that were sent to you to determine if maybe those weapons had fired the bullets you had?

Fletcher: Yes, sir.

Sievert: Would you please take a look at those so we can go over what type of guns you have checked?

Fletcher: There was a .22 caliber Model E pistol, serial number ABO3546, with some ammunition also submitted.

Sievert: Okay. And do you know where that came from?

Fletcher: No, sir, I do not.

Sievert: That did not test out as being the weapon?

Fletcher: It could not be associated with any of the autopsy bullets or cartridge casings.

Sievert: Do you have any record of any other weapons that you may have tested?

Fletcher: The only record I have is some spent cartridge cases that were submitted.

Sievert: And do they compare?

Fletcher: No. None of the eleven cartridges that were submitted matched the weapons I had been given.

Sievert: Once again, this was Julio Fiocchi ammunition?

Fletcher: Yes, sir.

Sievert: Your Honor, I yield the witness.

Judge: Very well. Mr. Klein, you may cross-examine this witness.

Klein: Thank you, Your Honor.

Klein stepped toward the witness stand and began.

Klein: Mr. Fletcher, could you look back over your records and see if you were submitted a .22 caliber Ruger pistol with the serial number 13-63451?

Fletcher: There is a .22 caliber Ruger pistol that was submitted originally with the eleven spent cartridge casings. The serial number 13-63451 and with two live rounds.

Klein: Did you test fire that pistol?

Fletcher: Yes, sir.

Klein: And with what conclusion?

Fletcher: The K2 pistol I tested cannot be associated with any of the K4 spent cartridges, which are the eleven cartridge casings found at the scene.

Klein: Did you compare the bullets that you fired from the gun submitted to you by the sheriff to see if the projectiles were the same as the ones used in this murder?

Fletcher: I did, sir.

Klein: Did the cartridges found at the scene have different lands and grooves than those that would have been fired from the pistol you tested?

Fletcher: The lands and grooves were different. The measurements on the lands and grooves were different than the one taken from the autopsy.

Klein: May I assume, then, that all .22 Ruger pistols don't have the same kind of lands and grooves?

Fletcher: I believe there is a little bit of difference on each one of them.

Klein: Because of the differences and comparing it to the pistol you tested, did you call Sheriff Driscoll and tell him that the pistol used in the murders has to be an older model than the one you're looking at? And that it had to have a locking mechanism to hold eleven rounds?

Fletcher: I remember a conversation with Sheriff Driscoll, yes, sir.

Klein: When you examined the pistol that was given to you to test—the one with the eleven cartridge cases—did you determine if it was able to hold eleven rounds?

Fletcher: The magazine only holds ten.

Klein: Did it have a locking mechanism?

Fletcher: No, sir, it did not. I do not recall that it did.

Klein: Is this statement correct: "In order to hold eleven rounds, the Ruger pistol used in these murders must have been manufactured prior to the advent of the locking-slide mechanism to hold eleven rounds"?

Fletcher: I believe I had a conversation with Sheriff Driscoll such as that.

Klein: Is that statement correct, sir?

Fletcher: That is a possibility, yes, sir.

Klein: Where would you have to go to find out for sure?

Fletcher: You could look it up in some books or call the factory.

Klein: Would you have done that?

Fletcher: Would I have done that? No, I did not do that at the time, no, sir.

Klein: What would enable you to make a statement like that to the sheriff?

Fletcher: Because I have been through the Ruger school.

Klein: So the pistol you had is one that you were familiar with, and you told the sheriff that to hold eleven rounds, it had to be an older pistol than the one that you were looking at, prior to the advent of the locking-slide mechanism, right?

Fletcher: That's a possibility, yes.

Klein: Were you asked to check with the Ruger people and find out the date of issuance or any other dates of Ruger pistols with . . . ?

Fletcher: No, sir, I did not.

Klein: Would it be relatively easy to check with Ruger about that?

Fletcher: That's possible. But I normally do not do things like that, because I am not a certified police officer, nor am I in any federal agency. So my powers of calling certain types of records are beyond my control, sir.

Klein: You mean, it's not your job?

Fletcher: No, I didn't say that.

Klein: You can't do it?

Fletcher: I'm saying that some manufacturers don't open their records to just everybody.

> **Klein:** I'm not trying to be technical with you, and I don't believe there is any dispute that the serial number I am talking about is from a pistol that was previously owned by the Tates. Now can you tell the jury, did you or did you not tell Sheriff Driscoll, after examining this pistol, that the pistol he is looking for must be an older model than this one here that you were given to test?
>
> **Fletcher:** I may have said that.
>
> **Klein:** So it is your belief that the gun used in this crime had to be an older model than Bob Tate's pistol?
>
> **Fletcher:** Yes, the weapon used in the murders would have to be older, made prior to the advent of the locking mechanism, in order to hold eleven rounds.

We expected the prosecution was going to show that Les had owned a Ruger .22 caliber pistol by producing the receipt of purchase they had found at our house. Klein knew Les no longer had possession of his gun, but he didn't even want to talk about it. Les was the only one who could tell the jury where it was. But Klein didn't want Les talking to the jury either.

We were fortunate to have so many friends and family members at the trial in Sherman, Texas, in April 1984. Les's Aunt Evelyn and Uncle Tom Staples from Huntsville, Alabama, were there every day. Aunt Evie sat through both the jury selection and the trial, taking detailed shorthand notes of each.

Klein asked Evelyn to step outside the courtroom and make a phone call to the Ruger company to see if she could find the manufacture date of Les's Ruger .22 caliber pistol. Les was certain his pistol, which he no longer had in his possession, did not meet the requirements of the murder weapon, just as Tate's had not.

She made the call. Ruger was very helpful and gave her the information just from the serial numbers she provided them. Then she returned to the courtroom during a recess and handed Klein the information he had asked for. Klein never called her to the stand. He did not use the information that she had easily found.

June 12, 2000
Federal Hearing Appeal
for Lester Leroy Bower Jr. on
Ineffectiveness of Counsel of Richard Klein

Anthony Roth, one of Les's appellate attorneys from Morgan Lewis in Washington, DC, called Evelyn Staples to the witness stand at the ineffective of counsel hearing we had requested against Klein.

He established Evelyn's relationship with Les as being his mother's sister. He asked her if she had attended Les's original trial in Sherman in April 1984, and if so, which parts. She told the judge she and her husband had attended the entire trial, including jury selection.

Anthony inquired if she was asked to do anything for the defense during the trial in 1984. She said Klein had asked her to do some typing of subpoenas, and then later on, during the trial, she was asked to make a phone call.

Evelyn was passed a note by Klein asking her to contact the Ruger company concerning two guns, one belonging to Mr. Tate and the other belonging to Les Bower. She was given the name of the Ruger company and the address but had to call information to get the phone number.

She made the call from a pay phone in the hall of the courthouse and was able to talk to someone at Ruger. She had been instructed, via the note, to ask two things. The first was the ship dates for the Tate gun and for the Bower gun. She was also to ask the prefixes of the Tate gun and the Bower gun, as well as inquire as to which one had been made first and if either of those guns had a square firing pin. The casings on the eleven shells from the murder scene came from a .22 Ruger with a square firing pin.

She learned from her contact at Ruger that Bob Tate's gun was shipped to him on March 16, 1976, and Les Bower's gun was shipped to him on May 26, 1981. Both of these guns, according to the Ruger representative, had round firing pins. Neither of them would be a match to the gun that was used in the murders.

Roth walked with his hands clasped behind him as he questioned Staples.

Roth: Were these questions—that you understood to be important enough to the defense of Les Bower—to be asked in the middle of trial for you to do an investigation?

Staples: Yes. Yes.

Roth: And you understood that this was very important information for the defense?

Staples: Yes, sir, I did.

Roth: Once you made that call, what did you do with that information?

Staples: I went back into the courtroom and handed it to the desk, to the table.

Roth: When you say "the desk" and "the table," do you mean the defense counsel table?

Staples: Yes, yes, sir.

Roth: Did Mr. Klein ever ask you any questions about the information you'd provided?

Staples: No, sir, he did not.

Roth: Did you receive any requests to try to follow up on that information?

Staples: No, sir, I did not.

Roth: During any time that you were at the trial, did you ever hear anybody discussing the information you had obtained?

Staples: I did not.

Roth: Did Mr. Klein ask you about testifying regarding the information you had obtained?

Staples: He did not.

Obviously, the testimony of Mr. Fletcher that "I am saying that some manufacturers don't open up their records to just everybody" was incorrect, as the Ruger company gave Evelyn all the information she'd requested.

Evelyn's findings that she reported to Klein were that Les's gun was newer than Tate's gun. In addition, Ruger confirmed to her that the straight line marking left on the ammunition used in the murder would not be consistent with the marking, had that ammunition been fired from Les's gun, which had a round firing pin.

The prosecution knew Les's gun couldn't be the murder weapon because of the date it was shipped to Les; it was a brand-new gun. They wanted to put the thought and picture in the jury's minds of Les owning, at one time, the same caliber pistol that was used in the murders, hoping they wouldn't bother with all the details of firing pins and manufacture dates. Klein knew it too, but he never used the information he had to put the truth in the jury's minds.

It had been a long day. But it was only the first day. Les and I had sat scribbling notes to each other and to Klein throughout the day. Occasionally, one or the other would reach over and take the other's hand. We savored the time we had together for those few minutes, the touch of our fingers woven together, where they were meant to be. It was a common, everyday gesture that had been absent for the past three months.

As the jury filed out of the courtroom, we took a long look at one another, knowing that any minute the deputies would come swooping down on us and whisk him out the door.

I softly asked, "Do I need to pick up your suit or any of your other clothes and have something cleaned tonight?"

"No, I'm good. You have everything lined up for me on your sheet of paper you sent in with my clothes for the week," he said, smiling while he rolled his eyes just a bit.

I know he appreciated my efforts, but he was also half mocking me for my meticulous planning, tagging, and color-coordinating the list of what he should wear each day to court.

I was sure the guards thought I was crazy when they saw the clothes bags I brought in for him the weekend before the trial started. But I didn't care. It wasn't that Les couldn't dress himself; he just often relied on me to help him with what shirt looked best with which coat and tie.

There was so little I could do to help him. I could at least help him look his best. He had learned early in our relationship that wearing a striped shirt with plaid pants was just not suitable. Why mess with a plan we had set in place for the past sixteen years?

No one knew, but I had his jeans, his favorite shirt, and his boots in a bag in my car parked outside the courthouse. After all, when this was all over and he got to walk out of here, he'd have something comfortable to wear on the ride back home.

I'll Always Love You

No one has ever loved anyone as much as I do.
No one has ever felt the passion that I feel for you.
My heart still skips a beat when you walk through the door.
You can search, but you won't find anyone who loves you more.
Love is a combination of joy and of pain.
Love relishes the sunshine but grows in the rain.
I've tried to stop loving you. I wish that I could.
My life would be easier, if only I would.
But my love stands forever, like a giant redwood tree.
My love is much deeper than the depths of the sea.
No one has ever loved anyone as much as I do.
No matter what happens, I'll always love you.

May 19, 1984

CHAPTER 14

The Rare Ammunition

The Trial — Day 2 — April 24, 1984

O n Tuesday, I walked into the courtroom and found Les already sitting at the defense table, waiting for me to arrive. His chair was turned sideways so he could see me when I came into the room. The courtroom was beginning to fill with spectators, and our families were seated just behind us. I was so thankful I didn't have to sit in that area. It would have been torture to be so close yet so far away.

I sat down next to him, leaned over, and gave him a light kiss on the cheek. We had been warned about public displays of affection. We were pushing the envelope by holding hands under the table.

Once the judge took care of all his formalities for the beginning of day two, he brought the jury in and was ready to begin.

The prosecution started by calling Ms. Lou Troupe, a staff assistant and custodian of records from Southwestern Bell telephone company. Ms. Troupe was middle-aged and neatly dressed in a beige suit. Assistant County Attorney Kellis Sampson began the questioning.

Sampson: All right. Do you have under your care, custody, and control the records which I believe y'all refer to as terminating number records?

Troupe: Yes.

Sampson: What is a terminating number?

Troupe: A terminating number is a record of certain calls placed from a particular area code placed to a specific number.

Sampson: Would you explain to the court how this works?

Troupe: Okay, our records have listed every number that's placed from the 214 or 817 area code. These calls are placed directly, by credit card or third number. That's about it.

Sampson: Ms. Troupe, to whom was the telephone number 214-892-0852 listed to in September and October of 1983?

Troupe: In September and October of 1983, that telephone number was listed to Philip and Marlene Good in Sherman, Texas.

This cross-examination went on for some time with Ms. Troupe giving examples of calls made and how official her records were.

Sampson: Ms. Troupe, let's look at the billing periods of September 15 through October 15, 1983. All right. Now, during that October billing period, how many long-distance calls were made to telephone number 892-0852?

Troupe: There were four calls. Two credit card calls placed from credit card number 214-075-5454. And there was a direct dial

> call from telephone number 214-638-8037, and another direct
> dial from 214-744-6254.
>
> **Sampson:** Ms. Troupe, can you tell the court who the owner of
> that credit card was that made those calls?
>
> **Troupe:** That credit card number is listed to Thompson-Hayward
> Chemical Company in Dallas, Texas.
>
> **Sampson:** And Ms. Troupe, to whom is telephone number 214-
> 638-8037 listed?
>
> **Troupe:** That number is also listed to Thompson-Hayward
> Chemical Company in Dallas.

Sampson released the witness to Klein for cross-examination. Klein
cross-examined Ms. Troupe for some time, asking her why the credit card
numbers were only seven digits; most credit card numbers had more digits
than that. After fifteen minutes or more of going back and forth and pulling
his own phone credit card out to show her his had more numbers on it, the
judge put an end to the questioning. Ms. Troupe was dismissed.

The point of the prosecution bringing in the record keeper from the
telephone company was to show the jury that someone from Thompson-
Hayward Chemical Company in Dallas had called Philip Good's home three
times between September 15 and October 15, 1983.

Klein's cross-examination appeared to try to make her look incompetent
because his credit card had more numbers on it. It was almost embarrassing.
And it totally did nothing to help our cause.

FBI Agent Jim Knights was called to the stand and testified he had
questioned Les on January 9, 1984, at Les's office in Dallas. He had gathered
from his conversation that Les had an interest in ultralight planes. Knights
said Les told him he was, in fact, the one who had made the telephone calls

to the Good residence and inquired about the plane Philip Good had listed for sale.

FBI Agent Niles Duke, at the request of Agent Knights, appeared at Les's office on January 11, 1984, with follow-up questions regarding his phone calls to Philip Good in September and October of 1983. Duke stated Les had seen an ad in the *Glider Rider Magazine*, an ultralight enthusiast magazine, and he called about the ad because it said something about a two-seater. Les was concerned about his weight, and he wanted an aircraft that would support him. An aircraft that could accommodate two people seemed adequate, so he called to inquire about the one Good had advertised.

Duke testified Les said he had called Good's house twice. The first time he called, he talked to Mrs. Good, as her husband was not available. The second time he called, he was able to speak to Mr. Good.

The questioning continued, and Duke testified that the conversation between Philip Good and Les was about Les's body size and the type of plane he would need to accommodate his weight. Good informed him that any type of modification to a two-seater plane, which was what he had just recently advertised and sold, would require Les to get a pilot's license.

Duke asked Les if he would come to the Dallas office and take a polygraph. Les declined. It was mid-January 1984, and Les had spoken to two FBI agents, both of whom had shown up at his workplace unannounced. Now he had been asked to come to the Dallas FBI office to do a polygraph. After Les told them no one more time, Duke called and asked Les if he would come to the office and just talk to Agent Tiegen, the polygrapher, about how the polygraph worked. Les reluctantly agreed.

Tiegen testified the interview he had with Les was on Friday, January 13, 1984, at the FBI office in Dallas. Agent Duke was present as well. Agent Jim Blanton joined the interview near the end.

Tiegen said they covered most of the same information that the other FBI agents had previously. He told Les the purpose of his interview was an attempt to locate and identify the potential buyer for the ultralight that was missing. Their hope was, if they could identify this potential customer, they might have someone who may have witnessed something that could help them solve the crime.

Klein asked Tiegen if Les had been read his rights during any of those interviews. Tiegen made it clear that Les was not a person of interest at the time; therefore, there was no reason to Mirandize him. That particular interview, however, lasted almost four hours. When Les got home that afternoon, I could tell he was exhausted. He told me how long he had been at the FBI office in Dallas.

We had planned a weekend trip to Gayle and Pat Baucum's house in Callisburg, just outside of Gainesville, Texas. It was obvious Les was very stressed; he was clenching the steering wheel and didn't say much on the drive. The girls were in the back seat, so we didn't want to talk in front of them. I could see his furrowed brow and knew he was processing the whole afternoon, and he said he wished he hadn't agreed to go to the FBI office. He was worried and a bit angry at the way they had ganged up on him. Going to the country was a good idea. Hopefully, he would get some rest, talk to Gayle, do some hunting, and relax.

Once we had finished dinner with our family in Callisburg, it wasn't long until there was a knock at the front door of my aunt and uncle's home. Two Texas rangers—one, Weldon Lucas and the other, Charlie Fleming— had followed us that night. When Gayle opened the door, they told him they wanted to talk to me.

A surge of hot anger welled up in me as I told Lucas they had no right to follow us there. Never removing their trademark Texas ranger hats, they both sat down at the dining table, which divided the kitchen and the living room. Gayle and I sat down as well while Pat took the kids to their bedrooms. Les sat down in the living room. Lucas began berating me for not cooperating with them.

"You don't know what's going on with your husband," he said to me from across the table. "I'm just looking out for your best interest," he added, leaning toward me, his face softening with what he hoped I would perceive as concern. He then lowered his voice, speaking to me as if he were my friend.

"I left my card in your mailbox, asking you to call me. I wouldn't have made this trip if you had just returned my phone calls." He was turning the inconvenience on me rather than him.

Les silently sat in the living room, his back to the kitchen, obviously fuming, something I had never seen. Lucas pointed his finger toward Les and said, "Look at him. He's just sitting there, letting you take all the heat."

"You asked to speak to me, not him," I reminded Lucas through gritted teeth.

Lucas continued, saying my husband was not telling me everything. "I don't want you or your girls to get hurt," he said.

That was when my anger had reached the boiling point. Somehow, despite my frayed nerves and a fire of contempt burning within me, I refrained from yelling at him. I reminded Lucas, once more, he had come to talk to *me*, not my husband, and that this conversation was over. I stood up, walked to the door, and opened it wide, indicating they were no longer welcome. The two rangers stood, turned to Les with a look of disgust, and then marched out the door.

We were all pretty shook up. I could not stop thinking about the fact that they had followed us for an hour and a half. *What other times had they followed us? Or me? Or Les?* Given that Tiegen would later testify that Les was not a person of interest at that time seemed to contradict their behavior.

Texas Ranger Weldon Lucas was the next witness to be called by the prosecution after the lunch break. Lucas headed up the investigation of the murders in conjunction with the Grayson County Sheriff's Department and the FBI. I never understood why the FBI was involved and never got an answer when I asked any of the agents. They were "cooperating at the request of the local authorities" was all they would say.

Lucas's testimony began with his account of the night of January 20, 1984, when he and the other officers conducted the search of our home on Quail Lane in Arlington.

He had obtained a search warrant from a Tarrant County judge based on a visit he and another Texas ranger had made to our home the week before the arrest. They had come to see if I was home so they could talk to me.

After finding no one there, they peered into the garage through the windows that were positioned about six feet above the ground and saw aluminum tubing in the garage they believed to be from an ultralight aircraft. (Although none of the rangers were close to six feet tall, a subsequent motion to quash this obviously illegal search was denied by the court.)

With that information and the phone calls made to one of the victims, Lucas was able to get a search warrant. He then gathered about twenty-three law enforcement officers from various agencies to serve the warrant and the subsequent search.

Lucas's initial testimony was an account of the evidence that was seized during the search. He testified to the various magazines and catalogs that were found. On the list were a Cabela's catalog and a Paladin Press US Army Special Forces catalog. Lucas emphasized the numerous books that could be ordered, some of which were about survival techniques and "how to kill."

No mention was made of the other hunting and camping equipment that was available in these catalogs. The state emphasized specific words. *Killing. Survival. Bomb-building.* Not *outdoor leisure* and *recreation*, which were the majority of items available in the catalogs.

They did not find any books during the search on how to kill people. They found pages in a catalog where one might order an actual book on "how to kill." The references were strictly to what "could have" been ordered, but they wanted the jurors to think they found actual books at our house on that subject. The prosecution wanted the jury to hear the titles to put the thought in their minds that Les was ordering and reading books on how to kill people.

On Klein's cross-examination of Lucas, he tried to elicit a more detailed description of some of these catalogs and what other things were offered by this company, such as flashlights, boots, canteens, and camping equipment. He did it by asking Lucas in a staccato method, "Did they sell lanterns? Did they sell tents? Did they sell sleeping bags?"

Spectators in the courtroom would later express that they, too, had one or both of those publications in their homes and never knew books like that were available in the catalogs. That's because the majority of these catalog customers were campers, hikers, fishermen, hunters, and other sportsmen, not hired or trained killers. And none of those books was found in the search.

It was at this point I realized how choreographed a trial was. The right testimony, word, or phrase at the right time painted a picture in the jurors' minds that was often hard, if not impossible, to erase.

Some of those advertisements to purchase "how to kill" books were directed to military customers and even mercenaries. But the prosecution implied Les had those books and not that they were books that could be ordered.

Just because someone might have a hardware store catalog in their possession, and the catalog contains multiple items, such as fertilizer and chemicals and all the other items to make a bomb, does having that catalog mean you are a bomber?

In our minds, it was irrelevant, as we knew Les did not murder those four men. To the prosecution, it was one of many innuendos that would insinuate that Les was a person who studied and read articles on how to kill people. All they had to do was put a thought in place, a question in someone's mind.

Their presentation of the evidence was being carefully manipulated in a manner to guide the jurors to believe what the prosecution wanted them to believe and to vote what they wanted them to vote. It didn't matter if some of the testimony was twisted to suit them or if exculpatory evidence (to clear from alleged fault or guilt) was left out of the testimony.

I had never been to a trial, but I questioned why Klein didn't do a more thorough job of trying to erase that picture or thought from their minds. A perfunctory list of benign items available for purchase in those publications was not enough to take the picture out of the jurors' minds of Les focusing on "killing books."

We believed it was the defense's job to unravel their story and to create doubt in the jurors' minds as to Les's guilt, presenting arguments and testimony to contradict the packaged version that was being presented by the prosecution.

We were not seeing that happen with Klein's cross-examination of the witnesses. It was apparent he was not prepared for their testimony, and it showed as such during his cross-examination. It was also apparent Klein had not been given a full witness list. Les and I had not seen one. There had been no preparation with Les concerning many of the subjects that continually came up in testimony. Klein had not asked Les any questions in preparation for the things the prosecution was bringing up.

Not only did Les and I question Klein every day as to why he didn't do this or that, but many of our family and friends questioned him as well. He continued to assure us he had everything under control. But he definitely didn't have this under control. Or he had another agenda we weren't aware of. The nightmare just kept getting worse.

June 12–16, 2000
Federal Hearing Appeal on Ineffectiveness of Counsel of Richard Klein in April 1984 Trial of Lester Leroy Bower Jr.

In 1989, Les obtained a new appellate team to investigate and work on his appeals in the higher courts in an effort to get him a hearing, a new trial, or anything to get the truth of what happened at the B&B Ranch on the night of October 8, 1983, on the record and to win Les's freedom. I was not aware until this time that you couldn't file a motion in federal court for such relief unless one of your constitutional rights had been violated.

After much hard work and investigation, what we referred to as the Bower Dream Team—Peter Buscemi, Grace Speights, and Anthony Roth—was granted a hearing based on a motion filed in federal court that

Les had been denied his rights, according to the Sixth Amendment of the Constitution, which guaranteed citizens the right to not only a speedy trial, but also to an effective representative to argue their case before the courts (i.e., an effective attorney).

FBI Agent Jim Blanton hadn't been called to testify at the original trial in 1984 even though he was a lead investigator. He was called during the federal hearing to testify on his investigation and findings that were used to not only arrest Les but were used against him in the trial in 1984.

At the federal hearing held in Sherman, Texas, in June 2000, Federal Judge Richard Schell called out FBI Agent Jim Blanton, questioning him on the veracity of not only what he had claimed to be damning evidence found during the search but also the testimony of Texas Ranger Weldon Lucas.

Judge Richard Schell asked Agent Blanton what else they found in the search as far as literature. Blanton replied that they found pamphlets from Paladin Press, one in particular on how to kill a man. Judge Schell asked Blanton to repeat himself, as Schell seemed surprised by the title and asked Blanton what it was about.

Blanton: It was a— What did it come from? It was a publication that—

Schell: On how to kill people?

Blanton: It was literature on how to kill people. Another pamphlet had to do with how to rig explosives. That was in there— how to make explosive devices.

June 2000
Re-cross-examination of James Blanton,
FBI Agent, by Peter Buscemi,
Defense Counsel for Lester Leroy Bower

Buscemi: Okay. Mr. Blanton, you made a number of mistakes in testifying in response to the court's questions, did you not?

Blanton: I'm not aware of any.

Buscemi: Okay. You never found a book in Mr. Bower's home that was called *How to Kill a Man*, did you, sir?

Blanton: It was *How to Kill*.

Buscemi: You found a book called *How to Kill*?

Blanton: There was a publication.

Buscemi: There was a publication with that title?

Blanton: Yes, sir, something that dealt with that matter.

Buscemi: Something that dealt with that matter?

Blanton: A publication.

Buscemi: Isn't it true, sir, that what you found in Mr. Bower's home was a catalog from Paladin Press, and that one of the items, of many dozens of items listed in the Paladin Press catalog, was a book called *How to Kill*, but there was no *book* called *How to Kill* at Mr. Bower's house? Isn't that a fact?

Schell: Did you hear the question?

Blanton: I heard the question. I remember seeing—having—literature in his possession that referred to "how to kill."

Buscemi: Mr. Blanton, is it your testimony that what I just said is incorrect and that you found at Mr. Bower's house not a catalog listing a book entitled *How to Kill*, but the actual volume with that title?

Blanton: I may have misspoken, if I said an actual book entitled *How to Kill*. There was a book that had that information or had that statement in there—*How to Kill*.

The testimony went back and forth between Mr. Buscemi and Mr. Blanton regarding the various titles of books available to order from Paladin Press.

Buscemi: So the references to *How to Kill* are the titles of books that can be ordered in these two Paladin Press catalogs?

Schell: That's a catalog! Are those catalogs in the state's evidence? I guess they are.

Buscemi: Yes, 54-B and 54-C.

Schell: So whatever literature there was that mentioned "how to kill" would be in the record?

Buscemi: I believe so, Your Honor.

Schell: Okay, Mr. Blanton, I've asked for a couple of exhibits. Were you planning to leave now?

Blanton: I was thinking about it, but whatever the court desires.

Schell: Could you stay a little bit longer in case I have some more questions for you?

Blanton: Sure.

Schell: Okay. If you could wait outside, I would appreciate it.

Blanton: Sure. Thank you.

Schell: Okay. We'll go ahead and break for lunch. It's eleven thirty. Let's break until twelve forty-five.

Everyone returned to the courtroom by 12:45 P.M. to begin the afternoon session.

Schell had Blanton come back in and told him that, before the court went to a new witness, he wanted him to take the stand once more.

Schell: I had one of my clerks go to the county courthouse across the street where evidence from trials are stored. I had him bring back the exhibits regarding the man-killing books that you testified about. I wanted to see them for myself. And I wanted to ask you if these were the manuals that you were recalling—(*Judge Schell held up the catalogs that were used as evidence in Les's 1984 trial, showing them to Blanton*)—when you testified earlier. I have here Exhibits 54-A, B, C, D, and E, specifically Exhibits 54-B and 54-C. I want you to take a look at those and tell me if that's what you're remembering when you testified about books on how to kill.

Blanton: These are the books I recall. It's been seventeen years, but—

Schell: All right. You've turned to a particular page here, you mean?

Blanton: Well, I just opened them up there to the sections, where it talked about *How to Kill, Volume—*

Schell: Yeah.

Blanton: And it's Paladin Press Publications. That's what I'm— Those are the books I'm referring to.

Schell: Yeah, okay. But what we actually have are catalogs that list various books, right?

Blanton: Lists them—

Schell: That's what this is.

Blanton: Yes, sir. But if you read on the—

Schell: And some of the books are on how to kill.

Blanton: Right. And it tells various things if you read in there.

Schell: Uh-huh. It describes the pamphlets, or whatever it is they're selling here, eighty-page— There's one that has eighty pages, another one with seventy-one pages. So it gives a paragraph description of each of these pamphlets on how to kill.

Blanton: Right. Those are the books I'm referring to, Your Honor. If I misled the court, I— Those are the books I'm talking about.

Schell: Okay. Any other questions?

Blanton was excused.

It was obvious from the questions asked of Blanton that Judge Schell saw there were no books found in our house entitled *How to Kill*, as Blanton and Ranger Lucas so vividly portrayed for both the trial jury and the federal judge. Judge Schell basically called Blanton out on it. But Blanton's arrogance would not allow him to back down, as he continued to portray the evidence as damning just as it had been in 1984.

We were elated. But this was a hearing on whether Klein had or had not properly represented Les in his trial in 1984, providing him with effective representation by counsel. Judge Schell's ruling would be on that issue—not on the issue of whether the Texas ranger and the FBI agent misrepresented the evidence to the jury.

April 24, 1984
State of Texas vs. Lester Leroy Bower Jr.
Original Trial – Day 2

As the judge called for a lunch break on Tuesday, April 24, 1984, the second day of the original trial, I saw Klein having what seemed to be a serious, if not heated, conversation with my dad in a corner in the hallway. A few minutes later, I saw my dad say something to my mother and walk out of the courthouse. I had no idea what that conversation was about. I didn't ask. I went back to being with Les.

When we signed the contract with Klein, our families were able to get together around $35,000 as a down payment to him. I never knew for sure where it all came from, but I was pretty sure that second mortgages were taken and several people—my parents, his parents' friends, and other family members—may have dipped into retirement funds. Three months had gone by since Les's arrest, and I didn't know what, if anything, had been done regarding Klein's fee.

Many years later, I asked my dad what that conversation was all about in the courtroom that second day. He said Klein told him he didn't think he could continue to represent Les unless he got some more money. He couldn't concentrate on the trial because we still owed him the balance. Klein told him if he didn't have any more money by the end of the day, he would resign as Les's attorney. So Dad left and drove back home to try to get some more money, while the rest of us sat and listened to testimony, not knowing what was going on behind-the-scenes. Dad was able to double what he had already paid, but I had no idea how he had done it.

I can't help but wonder what might have happened if Dad had told him no. I'm sure he didn't want to tell Les or me what Klein had said, fearing it would upset us. But maybe, just maybe, that might not have been a bad idea.

Mr. Sandy Brygidier, owner of Bingham LTD Gun Parts in Norcross, Georgia, was the next witness called by the prosecution.

It was time for the prosecution to bring out the elephant in the room: the so-called rare ammunition that was used to kill the victims.

Assistant US District Attorney Ron Sievert conducted the questioning of Mr. Brygidier, first asking him if his company sold .22 subsonic Fiocchi ammunition. And Mr. Brygidier seemed to sit up a bit taller with pride and declared in a clear, booming voice, "Yes, sir, we do. In fact, sir, we are the only seller of that ammunition in the United States." He looked around the courtroom and at each table as if this was quite an honor.

Sievert: Is this ammunition generally sold over the counter, like your average gun store or what?

Brygidier: No, it's not. It's a specialty item, usually ordered for use in suppressed weapons because of the nature of the rounds, the velocity of the rounds. It's usually ordered by dealers who either have customers or they themselves have suppressed weapons.

Sievert went on to ask Brygidier what the overall market percentage of all the .22 bullets sold in the United States would be Fiocchi ammunition. Brygidier said it would be very miniscule; in fact, it probably couldn't be measured, as it was an extremely small percentage.

Sievert then produced State's Exhibit 111 and asked Brygidier if he could tell him what it was. Brygidier told him it was an order, or rather a copy of an invoice of an order, that was shipped on February 12, 1982, to Lester L. Bower Jr. in Grand Junction, Colorado, for three boxes of Fiocchi .22 long rifle, subsonic hollow-point ammunition.

Sievert then yielded the witness to the defense for cross-examination. Klein asked one question: If the ammunition in question was advertised as being an excellent ammunition for small-game hunting. Brygidier acknowledged that, yes, it could be used for hunting. But then, Sievert interrupted Klein's questioning, despite the fact that this would normally not be permitted during a trial. He asked if the rounds were rare, and Brygidier agreed that they were not very commonplace. Klein then continued with his questioning.

Klein: Well, did you examine those figures before you came here to court to testify about different distributorships throughout the United States?

Brygidier: Well, I was involved with the record search that was provided to the FBI. I am the custodian of the records.

Klein: Do the records reflect that during this period of time indicated there were thirty-two hundred rounds sold in the state of Texas?

Brygidier: Possibly. I don't have the records in front of me. I can't speculate, so I don't know.

Klein: Well, it's not speculation. It says, "Richard Brown, Anchorage, Alaska, two boxes of—"

Brygidier: If that's what it says, yes, sir, that would be right.

Klein: Then it doesn't sound unreasonable to you that it is thirty-two hundred rounds sold in Texas?

Brygidier: No, but it's not a large quantity.

Klein: Is it true you purchased two one-hundred-thousand-round lots in December?

Brygidier: Well, yes.

Klein: Pass the witness.

The press continued to use the term "rare ammunition," as had been given to the press by the prosecution. It continued to come up every time a reporter wrote about the case, as most had not heard the testimony at the trial that debunked the idea of it being rare at all. It was a label that stuck, and still cannot be removed.

The term was used in the courtroom often in front of the jury even after Brygidier's testimony, especially in closing arguments by the prosecution, reminding the jurors that Les was one of "the few people" who had purchased Fiocchi .22 ammunition, the brand and caliber that was used in the murders.

The documents that Brygidier and many others that were used during the trial had not been provided to Klein as part of discovery. If the prosecution was going to use the documents Brygidier had carefully complied, they had to give the defense a copy. But they gave it to us that morning before they called Brygidier to the stand. We also discovered that the FBI had this information as early as December 1983, just a month prior to Les's arrest.

None of the findings of any investigations going on behind-the-scenes through various federal and state agencies involved in taking this case to trial were shown to the defense prior to trial. Our appellate team found even more undisclosed exculpatory information post-conviction and sentencing that the defense should have had access to under the law. It was blatantly withholding evidence and should have been addressed as a Brady violation with the granting of a new trial.

June 12–16, 2000
Federal Hearing Appeal on
Ineffectiveness of Counsel of Richard Klein
in April 1984 Trial of Lester Leroy Bower Jr.

Grace Speights, one of Les's appellate attorneys, called Les's sister, Denise Knippa, at the federal ineffective assistance of counsel hearing in June 2000 regarding the testimony of the so-called rare ammunition.

Grace asked Denise if she had had any discussions with Mr. Klein during the trial.

Denise told the court that, about midweek during the original trial during a recess, Klein asked her if she would make a tally list. He had a list of purchasers of Julio Fiocchi ammunition. The state had presented that Julio Fiocchi was rare ammunition, but Klein asked her to go through the list of purchasers to determine how many people had ever purchased this ammunition.

She found the ammunition was not rare at all. The list contained individuals who had purchased the ammunition, as well as distributors, or anyone else who could sell it. Some purchases were listed by someone's name, or it might have been listed as a company. It was difficult to know exactly how many people had purchased the ammunition; but obviously, there were a lot of people who had. The sales from the distributors, of course, meant it went out to a lot more people from there. People who weren't necessarily listed at all. Distributors might sell at gun shows, and there would be no record of who had purchased the ammunition.

Grace walked the floor with confidence as she continued her questioning.

Speights: Did you advise Mr. Klein of the results of your tally?

Knippa: Yes. I gave him a tally sheet that showed what I just told you.

Speights: Did Mr. Klein ever present this information at trial?

Knippa: No. He never did. I really expected him to. But he never did anything with that information once I handed it back to him.

Speights: Why did you expect that Mr. Klein would present that information at trial?

Knippa: Well, I guess I just assumed, because he asked for me to make a tally list to show that the ammunition wasn't that rare.

The issue of the "rare ammunition" kept rearing its ugly head, not only during the trial but during each appeal. Reporters kept the myth alive, continuing to claim that this ammunition was rare, despite the fact that it wasn't. It was the first question I was asked by either the press or just friends and acquaintances: "How do you explain the rare ammunition?"

Throughout the appeal process, our appellate team filed multiple lawsuits under the Freedom of Information Act (FOIA) to obtain the FBI files that had not been disclosed to the defense during the original trial.

FOIA is described as the law that keeps citizens in the know about their government. Federal agencies are required to disclose any information requested under FOIA unless it falls under one of nine exemptions, which protect interests such as personal privacy, national security, and law enforcement. Our situation did not fall under any of the exemptions. But in order to obtain information using FOIA, you have to file a request with the agency you want information from. In this case, the federal agency was the FBI.

Each time we filed FOIA requests with the FBI, it was a long process. Eventually, they would produce the records we requested. The first time we received the documents requested, the information was so redacted that it was worthless.

Each request over the years resulted in a better and more legible work product. As a result, we were able to put together valuable information to use in our appeals.

Though the federal government was very involved in the prosecution of this case in 1984 and the state claimed to have an "open-file policy" of providing complete investigative files to the defense, only four documents regarding the availability of Fiocchi subsonic ammunition were produced.

The prosecution repeatedly presented testimony at trial that Fiocchi subsonic ammunition was virtually unknown in the United States and available only through Bingham, Mr. Brygidier's company in Georgia. Mr. Brygidier's testimony was obviously misleading, if not fabricated.

On day two of the original trial, we were handed for the first time Brygidier's list of sales for the period of February 5, 1981, through October 1, 1983. The list that Denise Bower had tallied for Klein contained 261 invoices for the sale of 152,600 rounds of Fiocchi .22 caliber subsonic ammunition to individuals and dealers all across the United States. All of these and other FBI documents should have been disclosed to us when our motion for discovery was granted—several weeks before the beginning of the trial.

Many of the purchases were made by gun shops, pawnshops, or licensed gun dealers who, in turn, sold them to other people. It didn't matter in what state or who had purchased it. Most of the rounds were resold over the counter or at gun shows and to individual buyers whose names would not be known without digging deeper into the records of each individual or company who had purchased this ammunition from Bingham Arms during this time. Records showed that Fiocchi subsonic ammunition was being sold at gun shows in Texas, but the prosecution did not disclose information about its sale at a Dallas gun show before or during the time of the murders.

In their closing arguments, the prosecution repeatedly told the jurors that this ammunition was important to establishing Les's guilt. This ammunition was such "rare and unusual ammunition that state and federal firearms examiners had not seen it in all their years of experience." They continued to remind the jurors that Mr. Bower had ordered it twice.

Klein realized the importance of getting an accurate count of ammunition sales during that time period, because he enlisted Denise Bower to do the tally for him, which she did. And then he did nothing with the information. He stuck it in a file in his briefcase.

"Why didn't he use them?" Les asked him.

I asked Klein the same question.

We never got an answer.

Dreams

Sometimes I dream that you are here with me.
And yet it's been so long, it can only be a dream.
Sometimes the dream is sweet and warm and safe,
Or was that not a dream? I can't tell the difference.
Sometimes I dream that I wake up with you
And you are there. But then I wake, and you aren't.
Sometimes I wish that dreams came true,
So I dare to dream and make my wish.

May 15, 1984

CHAPTER 15

Juggling the Truth

The Trial — Day 3 — April 25, 1984

I was worried about Les, wondering how he was holding up. We barely had time to say goodbye, as he was whisked away each day when court adjourned. The deputies would return him to his cell, stripping him of his street clothes and giving back his orange jumpsuit he had become so accustomed to over the last three months.

I knew he was replaying every person's testimony in his head as he sat on the edge of his bunk in his cell. He was going over the things he wished had been brought up, the opportunities he felt we lost when Klein didn't object or cross-examine when we thought he should. I knew all this, because I thought the same thing.

Our confidence was dwindling. But we still believed in his innocence. Our hope was that, when the prosecution rested, the defense could remedy many of the things that had been said. It was difficult to enjoy a hot meal with our family and friends at a local restaurant, knowing only blocks away Les was all alone, eating who knew what. I couldn't imagine the loneliness he felt, knowing the people he loved the most were gathered together somewhere near, comforting one another while he sat in a dreary cell.

On day three, Lori Grennan of American Aerolights, an ultralight manufacturer in Albuquerque, New Mexico, verified through purchase orders and receipts that the ultralight in question was purchased by R.G. Flight Company, sold to Philip Good, for $3,584 on August 31, 1982, from American Aerolights. And Good then sold it to a retail customer, Bob Tate, for $3,625.

On cross-examination, Klein determined from Ms. Grennan that some-one having knowledge of that model plane could easily take it down in about twenty to thirty minutes. A novice with little or no knowledge of disassem-bling a plane for transporting would take more than an hour, perhaps an hour and a half, to complete the task.

This was one of the few things I felt Klein had tapped into. The time spent taking the plane apart was important to Les's timeline. If the sellers, knowing how to take the plane apart, had taken it down themselves and loaded it for a buyer, it would fit within Les's timeline of how long he was at the hangar. If the sellers—Tate, Good, and their friend Brown who was with them—were murdered and someone who had never taken a plane apart at-tempted to do so, then it would have taken almost two hours to disassemble. If Les had been that person, he would not have been able to make it home at the time he did.

I noticed Klein reading over the list of witnesses that the prosecution was calling for that day. This list was provided to both the defense and the pros-ecution each morning. He seemed a bit rattled when he saw the list of po-tential witnesses. He pointed to a name, asking us if we knew who Marjorie Carr of Taylor's Tomato Patch was. We had never heard of her and had no idea who she was or what part she played in the prosecution of this case.

The past three months had been full of surprises, and this was just one more. Again, I realized we had not been shown all the evidence they had against Les. Nor did we have a complete list of potential witnesses.

Later, when our appellate attorneys were preparing for hearings, they would find FBI documents, investigative reports, interviews, and crucial documents that had not been provided to us pretrial but had been in the hands of the DA's office as early as November and December 1983, before they even knew about Les.

Despite my lack of knowledge of all things judicial, I knew that Les had a constitutional right to have access to, or at least the knowledge of, what or who was going to be used in the prosecution of a case against him so his attorney could prepare himself for any witness or evidence that might be used in court. Now it appeared we had been blindsided by the prosecution with a bait-and-switch game of showing us the most benign documents they had, hoping no one would question the absence of witness lists, names of possible expert witnesses, and pertinent letters, emails, and other communication from organizations that were helping with the investigation.

Marjorie Carr did a whole lot more damage than we could ever imagine. She identified herself as the person who ran Taylor's Tomato Patch in Sherman. She had worked there off and on for the past fifteen years but had taken over the responsibility of running it in the last two years. Her father, Clarence Taylor, had established the fruit and vegetable stand in the 1950s.

Mrs. Carr knew Philip Good, as he was the son of her friend, Stella Good. He had been a customer at the fruit stand for many years. When asked if she knew the defendant, Lester Bower, she said that she recognized him. She claimed to have seen him sometime in the latter part of September 1983 when he came in with Philip Good and wanted to purchase some navel oranges. When asked by the prosecution if it could possibly have been sometime in October (which would better fit their timeline), Mrs. Carr was adamant that it was September. She was asked if she saw him in the courtroom today, and she said yes as she pointed out Les. We were stunned. Les had never been to Taylor's Tomato Patch. Carr's testimony was not true—a lie or a mistake of identity.

There seemed to be a faint audible "swish" through the courtroom, as I saw not only spectators, but I saw jurors as well quietly discussing Carr identifying Les as having been in Sherman in September. Klein sat quietly at the desk flipping through papers, acting as if it were no big thing.

We had been furious with Klein when we read his statement in the paper on February 3. I confronted him, telling him he knew it was not true and it would make Les look bad when he testified at trial and told his own story of what had taken place that day. Klein had given an interview to the press just days after Les's arrest, stating that his client, Lester Bower, had never been to Sherman. Klein knew that was not true, as he grandstanded for the press on the steps of the courthouse, taking in all the attention of the local cameras and reporters. He had been told just days before the press conference that Les had gone to Sherman to look at the ultralight and meet with Philip Good, and then he returned three days later and purchased the ultralight from Bob Tate at his ranch.

Klein told me then, in early February, less than a week after Les had been arrested, that he didn't think it was a good idea for Les to testify; plus, the prosecution couldn't prove that he had ever been there.

Klein approached the bench to cross-examine Mrs. Carr.

Klein: Mrs. Carr, you didn't know there was evidence in the newspapers that my client hadn't been in Grayson County until you reported it in February?

Carr: State the question again.

Klein: You said you didn't come forward because you didn't think there was any— You couldn't help any?

Carr: When they arrested him and it appeared in the newspapers, it stated that he knew Philip Good, and that's the reason I didn't come forward, because I just assumed he knew Philip.

Klein: Are you telling the jury that you didn't see anything in the newspapers to the effect that he was claiming he hadn't been in this county until February 3?

Carr: Not until later. As I told my husband that morning— He wanted me to notify the authorities right away.

Klein: Why didn't you?

Carr: Because I assumed they had already connected him by what the newspaper said with Philip Good.

Klein: And you didn't know anything further until February?

Carr: Until your article came out, saying that he had never been through Sherman.

Klein: Mrs. Carr, you are the only person—and the only evidence—who links my client to this county. Now, are you willing to swear under oath, positively, to this jury—

Carr: Yes, sir.

Klein seemed to be chastising the only witness who claimed to be able to place Les in Sherman, while at the same time trying to place responsibility of the lie (about never being there) on Les rather than himself. His handling of her was a mess. Marjorie Carr would forever be referred to in subsequent appeal discussions as the "Fruit Stand Lady."

Later that day, after Carr's testimony, three FBI agents sat on the front row in the courtroom, laughing and juggling oranges in full view of the jury. I watched, shocked at the audacity of the act and that no one, particularly Klein, was doing anything about it. I brought it to his attention, at which time he raised an objection, and the judge ordered them to stop and remove the oranges from the courtroom.

After a recess for lunch on the third day, the prosecution called Marlene Good, the widow of Philip Good. She was asked about the phone calls to Philip from a prospective buyer for the airplane. She indicated that the buyer had phoned the house on two different occasions, once talking to her and another time to her husband.

She testified that Philip had made an appointment to meet with the buyer on Wednesday, October 5 to see the plane and returned home, telling her he thought he had it sold. Philip had made a second appointment with the buyer for Saturday, October 8, but Marlene didn't know the name of the man, only that he was from Dallas. The state rested its case after three days of testimony, and the jury was excused for the night.

As our family and friends gathered together, we began to talk to Klein about who he was going to call the next day. He hadn't decided yet. He had no plan. It was time for the defense to bring in a rebuttal, but Klein had no plan. I convinced him we needed to call Jim Widmier in Fort Collins and Billy Moore in Denver to come testify on Les's behalf. I called both of them, and they agreed to get on the next plane to Dallas.

Billy was Les's manager with Thompson-Hayward in Colorado for years and would be an excellent character witness. They spent a lot of time together and were friends as well as coworkers.

Jim was Les's best friend and hunting buddy in Fort Collins. He could testify about the dangers of the mountains and the rigorous hunting trips they took and set the scene for my testimony later in the day.

Jim knew where Les's Ruger was, but he wouldn't be able to tell the jury because Les told him where it was. Testifying as to its whereabouts would be considered hearsay. That was why Les needed to testify. No one else could tell the jury how he lost his gun or tell them what happened on the day of the murders. Only Les could. He was our best witness—our only witness who could tell the real story.

Anguished Heart

Anguished heart, when will at last you break these bonds that tie?
Pain is so deep, so tight within—it feels as if I'll die.
Yet walk I must, my head erect, as if there were no pain.
But now I know these bags I bear will no way help me gain.
To rid the hands clenched 'round my throat, the hands that wish me ill,
I pray, dear Lord, take them away, dear Lord, please break my will.
But clouded are these eyes of mine, somehow I cannot see
The person you intended, Lord, when you created me.

July 30, 1990

CHAPTER 16

It's Our Turn

The Trial — Day 4 — April 26, 1984

I t was our turn. I was excited and terrified. There were so many questions still unanswered.

The picture the state had presented looked bad for Les, but there was still so much the jury didn't know. We now had the opportunity to make it clear to the jury that Les did not kill those men. We had to show them he couldn't have killed them. He was home, cooking hamburgers around the time they were being murdered. The question was, how would the defense be able to present it?

Klein called Sheriff Jack Driscoll. Driscoll hadn't been a state's witness for some reason, but Klein decided to call him as the defense's first. I wasn't sure why, as Driscoll was definitely a hostile witness.

Klein proceeded to riddle Driscoll with short, meaningless questions regarding the investigation, taking the jury on a wild goose chase of sorts with innuendos and allegations, using the call reports, the deputies' investigations, and notes that were scribbled and housed in the notebooks that sat unused all week on the defense table. He was like a pinball machine, bouncing random thoughts and bits of subjects that seemed to mean nothing at all or have any bearing on the case. Driscoll's answers were succinct and dry, leading nowhere.

Most of Klein's questions to the sheriff were focused on whether he had followed up on several leads that had been called in or uncovered during the months after the murders. Klein looked like a rookie with no playbook, no plan. Just shooting from the hip. Did Driscoll investigate every lead? No, he didn't. I knew why he was asking, and Driscoll knew as well. But did the jurors?

He was trying to create alternative theories out of the air. There were plenty out there to present. We found lots of reasons other people might have wanted at least one of the victims dead, but his shotgun approach was not getting the job done. Not enough had been presented. Not enough was asked and answered in order to help the jury connect the dots and show them exactly where Klein was going with all these random and confusing questions. The deal that Klein made prior to the start of the trial—agreeing not to disparage the reputation of any of the deceased—was handcuffing him from presenting alternative motives for murdering any of the victims.

The motive was drugs. The killers were professionals. And a lot of innocent people had been caught in the middle. It was like playing charades without having all the information you needed to get your clues across to those trying to get the answer. No matter how much Klein tried to get the jurors to understand what he was acting out, they couldn't get it. Because they didn't know the whole story. The *real* story.

Klein's second witness was Irene Flaherty, a reporter with the then *Denison Herald*. He questioned her at length about a time-of-death conversation she had with the sheriff the night of the murders. She reported that, the day after the murders, Driscoll had told her the bodies were "still warm" upon discovery, indicating the murders had been committed very recently based on body temperature. Driscoll denied saying that, despite the fact that Flaherty's teenage grandson was following her around the crime scene, recording all her conversations, including those with Driscoll, while she was interviewing.

Again, the questions were asked and reasked, seeming to bore the jurors rather than inform or enlighten them. After several minutes and failure to elicit anything useful to the defense from Flaherty, Klein passed the witness.

Davidchik, the county attorney, stood, looked toward Klein in a puzzled manner, and asked in a snarky tone, "Is that it? That's all you've got?" He even lifted his hands in the air, grandstanding for the jury to show how unimportant he felt that information was. It was a classic, psychological courtroom move for one attorney, trying to show the jury the other attorney had nothing.

"Yes, that's all," Klein replied.

Davidchik turned and gave a comical smirk directed at the courtroom, shrugging his shoulders upward and shaking his head as he turned to the judge. "Your Honor," he said, "I have no further questions for this witness." He then sat down, still shaking his head as he leaned toward his colleagues at the prosecution table, and they all mumbled to each other and silently laughed.

The rest of the witnesses were Gary Dawson, Les's best friend in high school; Sandra Dusek, our neighbor at our apartments while in College Station; Leone Seebo, a good friend and counselor at the Housing and Counseling Center at Mesa College in Grand Junction; and finally, Bill Moore, Les's sales manager and good friend from Denver. They all testified on behalf of Les's character as longtime friends and coworkers.

Unfortunately, they could not testify to any specifics of the crime itself or shed light on an alibi or a solid reason why Les could not be the killer. Davidchik was quick to point this out to the jury, making it clear when each one took the witness stand that they could not testify to anything other than the fact that Les was a man of "impeccable character." And he made that statement mockingly each time he said it.

Les and I were so thankful for each one of them. So lucky to have such devoted friends. Yet it was a futile attempt. Each one was telling the truth. Les was the best friend anyone could have. He was loyal, helpful, and fair; he lived a life directed by a strong moral compass and his devotion to God. But all the friends he had in the world couldn't save him just with those platitudes.

When Les was arrested, our friends from all over the country, throughout various places we had lived and worked, came together in support of him to vouch for his character and do whatever needed to be done to help in any way they could. I sat there and listened to each one of them, then looked around me and wondered how many people in that room had as many friends as Les did. Friends who would drop everything they were doing to fly from every corner of the country to support him.

Jim Widmier, Les's friend and owner of Arrow Dynamics in Fort Collins, would go above and beyond. Jim would go as far as risking his life to help Les.

We always believed that Les needed to testify, especially since the state had made it clear that he owned a .22 Ruger pistol, leading the jury to believe it was the murder weapon. We still hoped that, when the end of the defense time came around, Les and I could insist that Klein let him testify. If not, there were other ways to make sure the jury knew the murder weapon couldn't have been his gun. We knew Widmier could help corroborate my testimony that Les no longer owned the .22 and why.

Richard Klein did not meet with Jim to go over his testimony or walk him through what he was going to ask him. He met him for the first time in the hallway outside the courtroom on Friday, the last day of the trial, just before he called him as a defense witness. There was no strategy, no discussions.

Jim Widmier took the stand, and after asking him the preliminaries of his name, where he lived, and what he did for a living, Klein asked Jim when he arrived in Sherman.

Widmier: This morning, or this afternoon.

Klein: Did you come down here voluntarily, on a phone call?

Widmier: Yes, sir, I did.

Jim then established he had known Les since 1975 when Les came to his place of business, Aerodynamics, an archery shop in Fort Collins. Les became good friends with him and with the other members of the Archery Club. They went on multiple hunting trips together. He testified to Les's outstanding character and how well the community respected him.

Klein: Okay. Now, I didn't have much of a chance to talk to you, but one thing I want to be sure that you understand: You can't say what anybody else told you, so I am asking things only of your own personal knowledge. Okay?

Widmier: Okay.

Klein then asked Jim to talk about Les's permit to hunt mountain goats during the 1982 hunting season.

Jim told the court, in order to hunt mountain goats in Colorado, each section of the state had a limited number of permits, and there would be a drawing for each section. Les wanted to hunt in the San Juan mountain range in southwestern Colorado between Durango and Silverton. He was thrilled when his name was drawn for one of the three permits in that area.

Klein: Can you describe the type of terrain, please?

Widmier: Rugged. You're talking— In fact, they nicknamed it the Switzerland of the United States. It's rugged. Your elevations are probably anywhere from ninety-five hundred to eleven thousand feet. It's above timberline.

Klein: Do you recall the date of archery season there in the fall of 1982?

Widmier: Not offhand. Usually it starts in August or September.

Klein: Okay. Do you recall whether or not Les went hunting up there?

Widmier: Yes, sir, he did.

Klein: Did Les go by himself?

Widmier: Yes, sir.

Klein: But you don't know for sure when he came back?

Widmier: No, I sure don't. The guy that hunts mountain goats in that area—he's pretty tough.

Jim went on to say that, when he heard Les was arrested and there was some question about his gun, he had planned to go up to the place where Les was hunting in 1982, but it was impossible to get there at that time of year.

Widmier: First of all, due to the steepness, there is the risk of avalanches. It's a high avalanche area. There is no way I would go in there right now. Second, Colorado is close to 157 percent above normal snowfall right now. It will be at least July fourth or the middle of August before you can get in there this year.

Klein: And what was your purpose of wanting to go in there?

Widmier: To retrieve a camp.

Klein: What kind of camp?

Widmier: It was a camp that Les had set up around Silax Lake, back in the San Juan's. He had stashed it there. He got in a lightning storm, and fearing for his life, he got the heck out of there.

Davidchik: Your Honor, I have agreed to let Klein bring some character witnesses here, but I don't see the relevance of any of this that will be of any benefit to the agreement we have. We object to it on the ground of relevance, Your Honor.

Klein: Your Honor, I believe if I might ask one more question, that will conclude my questioning and also show relevance.

Court: All right.

Klein: Was one of the purposes for your wanting to go retrieve a camp to find a Ruger pistol?

Widmier: Yes, sir.

Klein: Pass the witness.

Davidchik: Did you say a Ruger pistol? *(Davidchik did not mishear Jim. He was merely restating it in a very loud voice to make sure the jury heard those two words:* Ruger pistol.*)*

Widmier: Yes.

Davidchik: And it *snowed* up in some mountains where *nobody* can get to it, is that right?

Widmier: You better believe it.

Davidchik: Okay . . .

Widmier: Honest. Elevation is around eleven thousand feet.

Davidchik: I get the picture. It is almost impenetrable?

Widmier: Yes, sir.

Davidchik: Thank you very much, sir. Pass the witness.

Davidchik had as much as waved Jim off, scoffing at the fact that no one could go up there.

Jim had told the jury where Les's gun was but couldn't tell them why it was there, only that it couldn't be retrieved at this time due to weather conditions. He couldn't tell Les's story, as the state would object that it was hearsay.

It was April in Texas, and everyone in Sherman was enjoying the warm spring weather. Chances were good that no one on that jury had ever experienced the winters and rugged conditions of the Colorado high country and could not understand why anyone would need to leave a perfectly good camp buried up there, especially a pistol, and not be able to retrieve it at any time they wanted. It was almost impossible for them to imagine that scenario.

I had a churning feeling in my stomach as I looked around the courtroom. Something had just gone very, very wrong. The whole thing sounded ridiculous. If I didn't know the story and didn't know Les or Jim, I would think they were crazy to expect anyone to believe this. The jurors probably didn't even understand what they had just heard.

Not long after Les's arrest, Jim and I had discussed the possibility of someone going into the Lake Silax area to search for Les's camp. Forest rangers advised against it, as it was too dangerous due to the weather conditions between January and April 1984. It would be months before anyone could get in there to try to find that gun.

I asked Les to write out detailed directions to his camp, hoping someone would be able to get up there. He did so in early February, after his arrest, and I gave them to Jim.

Les Bower's Directions to Lake Silax — February 1984

The area around Storm King Mountain is a pretty place, but it can be a real pain in the butt to get into. The problem of getting to Lake Silax is a twofold problem. Number one is getting to the trailhead below Kite Lake. Number two is getting from the trailhead to Lake Silax.

Let's take number one first. There are two ways to get to Kite Lake. One way is to go to Silverton, then northeast to Howardsville, then up Cunningham Creek and on to Stoney Pass. Over Stoney Pass, down along the headwaters of the Rio Grande River to Bear Creek, and then west up Bear Creek to the trailhead below Kite Lake. This route is the best and quickest. The road is real good up to Stoney Pass, but on the backside going down to Bear Creek, there are several areas where the road washes badly, or there can even be rockslides from flash floods coming down off the steep mountains. You will cross several creeks, a couple of bogs, a full-fledge river, and travel some spectacular four-wheel drive trails. This is the best way, and you can't pull horse trailers in over these roads.

The second way to Kite Lake can be used if the road over Stoney Pass is impassable or the road on the backside of the pass is washed out. From Creed, you come about fifteen miles northwest of town on the road that goes to Lake City. You will be traveling along the Rio Grande River. When you come to the turnoff to travel up the Rio Grande, you will turn left off the main road and follow the signs to Rio Grande Reservoir and Lost Creek Campgrounds. At the west end of the reservoir is Lost Creek Campground. From this point to Kite Lake is twelve miles. Travel up along the Rio Grande till you come to Bear Creek. Turn left down through a bad bog, across the river, and onto the trailhead. Again, this is four-wheel drive country, and this way is impossible to pull a horse trailer up this route. This route has some steep, very rough sections but can be traveled.

To get horses into this area, you either ride them in, or you might be very lucky and have some very specialized equipment that can handle these roads. I ran into John Denver up at Kite Lake at his camp, and he had horses, but an outfitter had *driven them up the road from around Rio Grande Reservoir. I think you should drop your idea of taking horses on this trip. I would wait till the snow is gone and the roads are clear so you can drive up to the trailhead at the lake. If the road is clear and the weather is good, you can drive from Silverton to Kite Lake in one hour and fifteen minutes if you know where you're going.*

Now that you are at the trailhead below Kite Lake (Lake Bear townsite), you strap on a pack and start walking. There are no trail markers (there weren't any two years ago), but the trail is clear going to Hunchback Pass. It will take you about one hour to walk from the cars to Hunchback Pass. From Hunchback, you can look down to the valley toward the Guardian mountain range.

Down at Stormy Gulch, you will turn west up Trinity Creek toward Storm King. This trail is not marked on the topographical map, but it is there on the south side of the Trinity. This turnoff wasn't marked when I was there, and I went past it. When you come to this turnoff, there will be a small clearing or park off the trail on your right (west) where there are some campsites for hikers right next to the river. This can be a sloppy trail if it rains, but the trail is real clear and you won't have trouble following it.

Travel up the Trinity to a slide area between Storm King and Mount Silax. Leave any extra gear here and climb the mountain with as little gear as possible. You'll need both hands free. On the west side of the slide area is an area of grass. Start your climb on the steep grass area, traversing back and forth across the face till you come to the boulder field. Be careful when you walk on these rocks, as one slip on an unsteady rock could be bad news. At the end of the boulder field, you will have to cross a glacier where your footing should be good, but be careful. Past the glacier are more boulders, and then you're in the basin where Lake Silax is. Walk directly toward the lake and about 15 to 20 yards this side of the lake, and you will come to the one and only campsite. Someone dug out a small area large enough for one two-man tent to fit in. It was the only one there, and I'm sure when you consider how much time it took to make it, I'm sure it's still the only one. From this campsite, look directly at the center of the lake and look 90 degrees to your left, and out away from you, maybe 15 yards, will be a square pile of rocks about 3' by 8' and about 2' to 3' high. If you step down into the pit where you pitch the tent, you should be able to look out across the ground level and see the cache. If you have to camp overnight, camp in the valley and not at Silax. You'll see why. Don't make the climb from the valley to Silax in an electrical storm.

If I were you, I would go in one day and back out the next. Take gear for overnight. Take rain gear. You won't need climbing gear. You might as well take the route in that I took. I saw no better. Take your camera because you won't be in as beautiful a place for a long time. The time it will take you to get from the trailhead to Lake Silax will depend on the weather, how good of shape you're in, and your ability to follow the trails. It should take you about six hours to go in. You can go in and out in one day, but you'll be dead, and you've built in no time if something goes wrong.

The following is a list of items I remember leaving at the cache:

Brown two-man tent
H_2O purification canister
Foam rubber pad 3' x 6' x 4'
Sheath knife (skinning knife)

Plastic washbasin

Red/silver space blanket

Tripod (for spotting scope)

Game bags

Small Hank Roberts-type stove

Trash bags

Several gas bottles for stove

Candles/matches/rope

Cooking pots and pans

Tent pegs

Knife, fork, spoon

1 set of camo

Several packages of freeze-dried food

Socks/underwear

Two water bottles

1 Ruger RST-6 pistol/loads

—*Les*

June 12–16, 2000
Federal Hearing Appeal on
Ineffectiveness of Counsel of Richard Klein
in April 1984 Trial of Lester Leroy Bower Jr.

Jim Widmier would be called again sixteen years later to testify on Les's behalf during the evidentiary hearing in federal court on our claim of ineffective assistance of counsel. This time, he had finally been able to make the trip Les had mapped out for him to search for his camp.

Anthony Roth, one of Les's appellate attorneys, questioned Jim about the testimony he gave in the original 1984 trial. Jim told the court how Klein had not prepared him for his testimony but merely told him to "follow his lead."

Anthony walked Jim through his testimony about not being able to go into the mountains to try to locate Les's camp between the time Les was arrested and the time of the trial.

Jim and three other men followed Les's map and instructions in the summer of 1984, just months after his conviction, locating parts of Les's cache exactly where he had told Jim to look for it.

Widmier: We found parts and pieces of the cache. From what we saw, it appeared pikas, which are probably about half the size of a rat, had gotten into the cache and chewed up most of the soft items.

Anthony asked Jim to tell the court what items from Les's list they *did* find at his September 1982 campsite. They were able to find parts of a propane bottle for a cook stove, a knife and a spoon, and pieces of a red-and-silver space blanket—all of which were on his list.

Roth: Did you find a gun?

Widmier: No, we did not.

Roth: Are you sure that was the cache that Les described?

Widmier: It had to be the cache. One of the items that he had on the list was a red-and-silver space blanket, and we did find parts and pieces of that.

Roth: Based on your observation of that site in 1984, what did you conclude concerning the items in the cache and what might have happened to them?

Widmier: A cache is actually items that are buried under rocks that are going to weigh anywhere from one to ten pounds or more. He would have buried everything about two feet below the surface using these rocks. I think what happened was the pikas got into the cache and weaseled around the rocks, bringing up most of the chewable items like your foam pad, your space blanket—things like that. Then the light stuff from the cache would be on the surface. I think someone saw it, started looking around, and found the rest of the cache, taking the more valuable items such as his gun, knife, tripod, and such.

Roth: Could you describe for us what it was like to trek into that cache?

Widmier: I have a lot of respect for Les for going in there. Les had given us directions on how to get there. The first thing that you had to do was drive about thirteen miles on a rough Jeep trail to get in there. We had to ford the headwaters of the Rio Grande River. I had a 1984 S-10 Blazer, and when I got through, the water was up to the floorboards in the Blazer. My wife didn't want me taking it because it was a new vehicle. The license plate was supposed to be straight down, but it was bent upward once we got through the river. It was a nasty area. We drove in the night before, and we set up camp, sleeping under tents that night because it was raining. The next day, we headed up. I had been running six miles a day, so I thought I was in fairly decent shape. The first mile was a thousand yards uphill over Hunchback Pass. The next two miles were two thousand feet downhill. Then we went two more miles, two thousand feet back up the hill to Lake Silax where the cache was. That was the roughest trip that I had ever made.

Roth: How long did it take you to get in and get out?

Widmier: We started that morning about five. We got out of there probably about nine thirty that night—five miles in and five miles out.

Roth: In your testimony at Les's trial, was there anything that you thought the local Texas jury didn't understand regarding what you were speaking about?

Widmier: The trial was in April. When we got here, it's 98 degrees out, nice and hot. I start talking about not being able to get into that area because of snow, and you could see the people snicker like there can't be snow in Colorado at this time of year. I think Colorado was 150 percent above normal precipitation in that area, so there had to be snow drifts that would be sixteen feet deep in some areas.

Roth: In the years you've lived in Colorado and thinking back to the early 1980s, had you had an opportunity to hike, hunt, and camp around remote areas?

Widmier: I had, yes.

Roth: In connection with conversations you had with people—your customers and outdoorsmen who would come into your business—were you aware of the existence of caches in the mountains?

Widmier: There's a lot. We do it all the time. Sometimes you can't carry all the stuff in one time so you're going to have to hide it. We do it with tree stands. We'll carry stuff in one day and then sort of cache them, hide them to where we can use them later on.

April 24, 1984
Original Trial, Sherman, Texas

Joe Halifax, one of our Texas A&M friends Les still hunted with, was called to the stand to talk about some of the misconceptions regarding an Allen wrench that had been taken from our house during the search. The prosecution had made a big deal about finding this wrench in Les's briefcase. They staged a demonstration using his Allen wrench to attach a silencer to a pistol. The wrench fit perfectly. The attachment went smoothly. The thing they didn't tell the jury was the silencer was a random one they brought in, along with a random pistol, to use for their demonstration. Les didn't own a silencer, and one was not found during the search. The prosecution believed that a "suppression device" of some kind had been used and tried to connect the Allen wrench to such a device.

Oftentimes, things that are shown rather than said make a more lasting impact on one's brain. Continually stating that the Allen wrench had been found in Les's possession, the prosecution inserted a visual thought to the jurors, leading them to believe that the silencer—which had not been found in the search and did not belong to Les—was the silencer that was used in the murders. The demonstration also connected Les's Allen wrench to the silencer and the pistol, never saying they were not his, but placing the image that something of his *could* connect the two parts of what they had already deemed the murder weapon.

Joe was asked if he owned an Allen wrench and what type of things he used it for. He testified that he adjusted carburetors with it, used it on his reloading press when he was reloading ammunition, and tightened various other things. It was a common-size wrench that he used often.

Davidchik on cross-examination asked Halifax if he happened to have his Allen wrench with him today.

"Not in my pocket," Joe replied to the county attorney.

He then asked Joe if he had it in his briefcase. Joe answered him that he did not believe he had one in his briefcase, at which time the DA said, "That's all. Thank you very much, sir."

The judge called for a short recess before calling the next witness. Recesses are always hectic, as everyone is trying to get a drink, go to the restroom, or grab a smoke. It's always a time when you have the defense side and the prosecution side roaming the hallways and running into one another. A lot of interesting conversations have taken place and have been overheard during trial breaks.

Evidently, Assistant County Attorney Kellis Sampson and Les's brother-in-law, Mike, had found themselves in the same area on many breaks and shared several benign conversations throughout the trial. The prosecution had already rested, and at this break, Mike and Sampson found themselves once more chatting when Sampson said to Mike, "I don't think the amount of evidence we have will be enough to convict him."

I heard this story quite sometime after the trial and was shocked that he would make a comment regarding the case, especially one of that nature. If he didn't think there was enough evidence, then what happened? Did Klein do as bad a job as we all thought he was doing? Or was the jury weak enough to buy in to the evidence they had presented?

Whatever May Happen

Whatever may happen, wherever we go,
There's only one thing you need to know:
I've loved you always from the very start
And I'll love you forever, with all of my heart.
So I lift up my heart, so filled with love,
And offer it to God, in His heaven above.
To guard safe within His loving hand,
Until together, one day we'll stand.
Whether here on earth or heaven above,
God blesses us both and blesses our love.

February 27, 2000

CHAPTER 17

The Defense Rests

April 26, 1984

I remember hearing my name called from what seemed a long way off. I was seated at the defense table, so it couldn't have been that far away when the bailiff called me. I looked forward to finally being able to tell our side, yet I dreaded having to be grilled by the prosecution.

I thought Jim's testimony had been powerful in setting the scene to show why Les's gun couldn't be the murder weapon. Jim had found Les's cache, and everything of value had been stolen. It was totally logical, but it would have been so much better coming from Les. I would now have to be the one to make the jury see why Les could not have killed those men. The responsibility seemed overwhelming. *Would they believe me?* Anyone who knew me knew I wouldn't lie.

But the jurors didn't know me.

I reached the jury box and took the three steps up to enter and sit down in the ancient chair that had been holding witnesses for over half a century. I looked over at Les and smiled slightly at him, releasing a silent breath.

I was asked to state my name and my relationship to the defendant, who was obviously my husband, but I had to tell them. I looked at the jury box and made eye contact with each one of them while I talked. I continued by telling the jury where we lived, how many children we had, their names and ages. I tried to smile as I spoke, despite the churning going on inside my stomach.

Klein asked me if my parents were in the courtroom, and I told him they were. He asked about Les's family and if they were there, and I told him they were; like my parents, they had been there all week.

Klein asked me about Les's contacts. I told him the sheriff informed me the night he was arrested he wouldn't be able to wear them, as there was no way to keep them safe. He would have to wear his glasses.

He also asked me if I had made arrangements to have his hair cut and his beard kept neat. I told him that the sheriff had allowed me to trim his beard twice, but the second time, he informed me I wouldn't be able to do it anymore.

Since the county wasn't going to allow his contacts or some way to maintain his beard without it becoming unruly, Les decided to just wear his glasses and shave rather than look like a ZZ Top band member. There were a few smiles from the jurors, and I felt that I had made my point that he was not trying to look different for the jury.

Klein asked me if I remembered the prosecution introducing the rubber boots into evidence and if I was familiar with those boots. I told him I was. When he asked me what size boots they were, I told him they were a size thirteen and Les wore a ten-and-a-half shoe or boot.

Klein: Would you tell the jury where Les got the boots and what he used them for?

Bower: Les had a summer job working at the Baskin-Robbins ice cream plant in College Station. He worked in the freezer section, so he was given a very large, heavily layered coat with a fur-lined hood and that pair of rubber boots. The only ones they had at the time were too big for him and required him to wear layers of socks to keep the boots on his feet. He had to wear about five or six pairs just to keep them on. But that many socks also kept his feet much warmer than just one pair.

Klein: Was Les allowed to keep the boots when he left the plant?

Bower: He was. But because they were so big, he only wore them in the coldest of temperatures, because they would be too hot otherwise.

Klein: Do you know what the temperature was on October 8, 1983, and what time the sun set?

Bower: The high was 80 degrees, and the sun set at 7:07 that evening, according to the records at the *Fort Worth Star-Telegram.*

Klein: Have you ever seen Les wear those rubber boots, other than at Baskin-Robbins?

Bower: Yes, when we lived in Fort Collins. We lived on thirty acres out on a ranch. I recall several times the snow was very deep, and he would wear them then. We had horses and goats, and part of the property had barbed wire, especially near the stalls and corrals. The only time I remember him wearing them was when we were working in the snow and mending fences or shoveling snow. Those boots had been packed away for over three years, as we hadn't been on the ranch since then. We had a large box just filled with snowmobile boots, cross-country ski boots—things you don't use often.

Klein: Can you recall any time that Les or someone else might have gotten blood on the boots?

Bower: Keeping barbed-wire fence up on a ranch almost always ends up with someone getting a cut or puncture from the wire. It could have been any time.

Klein: Does Les like oranges?

Bower: No, he doesn't. He would pick some other fruit.

Klein: Does he go to farmers markets?

Bower: No, that's not something he likes to do.

Klein reminded me the FBI said Les told Good he wanted to build his own ultralight. Was that something that he would normally do?

"Yes," I answered. "Making things himself was one of the things he liked to do best. He was always making something or rebuilding one thing or another. Just rearranging storage boxes in the garage, repacking them, and making the garage cleaner was something he liked to do."

I told him about the hutch he built for me when we were first married. He built a cardboard room inside our bedroom where he kept the item he was creating inside so I couldn't see it. He would work on it when I was at work and when he was in between classes.

Before I got home, he would close the cardboard door to the little room and lock it so I couldn't see what he was doing. I would find wood shavings and wood dust in my flowerpots and in odd places he had missed when he would clean up. It was driving me crazy, wondering what he was building inside that little room. It turned out to be a very nice china cabinet that he gave me for Christmas.

One year, he made a grandfather clock for me for Christmas. We had a storage room in the garage at that time, so he didn't have to go to such lengths to keep it hidden from me. It was beautiful. We still have it in our living room.

He started making goose-down vests, jackets, and sleeping bags that he sewed baffles into and then filled with goose down. He also made tents and backpacks. The living room would be filled with remnants of goose down all over the floor that had escaped when he was stuffing the baffles he had sewn into the outerwear. After he used my sewing machine, I would always need to have it repaired because he used some heavy-duty material. He also recovered two of our couches over the years, and the work he did was perfect. He always had to be working on or building something.

Klein continued his questioning.

Klein: Right after the state discussed finding Mr. Tate's blood on the table, they pointed to what had been indicated as human blood on a large blue bag marked as Exhibit 66, insinuating this had something to do with the murders, possibly a bag to carry an ultralight in. Do you know what state's Exhibit 66 is?

Bower: Yes, I know what it is. It's a cortex liner for a sleeping bag. It's too small to use as a carrying case for an ultralight. You put your sleeping bag in it to keep the sleeping bag warmer—like a double layer of insulation. It's used when you're backpacking or carrying a lighter camp because it's small and can be rolled up and carried in a backpack. You can use it instead of a tent. My husband made it when we lived in Fort Collins, probably sometime around 1976 to 1978.

Klein: Do you have any idea where that tiny drop of blood came from?

Bower: No, and I doubt he does either. The bag came up missing in Grand Junction after a large group took a weekend whitewater-rafting trip. When you have twenty to thirty people coming back from an outdoor trip like that, and you are all dragging your gear around, it can get pretty confusing. It went missing for three or four weeks. Someone thought it belonged to the Mesa Outdoor Program, and several people checked it out of Mesa's inventory and took it on river trips, camping trips, and all over western Colorado before we finally found it.

Klein: So you have no idea where that tiny drop of blood came from?

Bower: No. It could have been someone cutting up something to throw in a pot for dinner, cutting a rope to tie something down, a scrape on a rock—anything. The drop is too small to have been any kind of significant cut.

Klein: When was the last time you saw his .22 Ruger pistol?

Bower: It was in August of 1982.

Klein: What was going on during August of 1982 that would make you recall that so clearly?

Bower: That's when Les had his big hunt for goats high up in the mountains.

Klein: And do you know whether or not he took that pistol with him when he went up to hunt the mountain goats?

Bower: Yes, he did.

Klein: Was that a bowhunting trip, primarily?

Bower: Yes.

Klein: When he came down from the mountain, do you know whether he had the pistol on him?

Bower: No, he did not.

Klein: Now again, without going into anything that Les might have said, where or what did you do after he came down?

Bower: He came home unexpectedly. He was supposed to be gone for several days, and he came home without his gear.

Klein: Without his what?

Bower: His gear. His backpack. He took a fifty-five-pound or sixty-pound backpack with everything he needed in the pack. He drove partway up, but then he had to hike in to where the goats were, above the tree line. He was traveling by foot into the Guardian Peak area that Mr. Widmier described earlier. I knew he was in trouble when he walked through the door. I had witnessed the symptoms of a kidney stone attack three years prior when I had to take him to the hospital, and I knew that was his problem. He would not be able to bring his pack down with that much pain, so he left everything buried up in the mountains. It was something he had done before, knowing he would be going back up.

Klein: When did you move from your house in Grand Junction, and to where?

Bower: To Arlington, Texas, in late June of 1983.

Klein: And when was the aborted mountain goat-hunting trip?

Bower: September or August of 1982. By the time he had recovered from the kidney stone attack, Guardian Peak was deep in snow and he knew it would be July or August of 1983 before he could get back up there. The story of his aborted hunt was all he could talk about with his friends and hunting buddies.

Klein asked me to tell the jury about the move from Colorado to Texas in 1983.

Les was starting work in Dallas on June 1, 1983, but the girls and I weren't going to move until July, because I was still working. Les and I flew to Dallas in June to find a place to live, and then I returned to Grand Junction to get us ready to move.

One of the football coaches at Mesa, Ray Biggs, drove us to the airport in Grand Junction. Ray had pulled up to the plane, as it was a small commuter taking us to Denver where we would change planes for Dallas. Several friends had joined us as we were about to board from the tarmac. Les was saying his goodbyes to our friends who had come to see him off. He told Ray and some of the other Outdoor Program friends he didn't know when he'd be able to get back and asked if they could put together a trip up to Guardian to get his stuff, which included his .22 Ruger. He had planned to go himself that summer, but the move to Texas interrupted his plans. Everyone knew about it; it was the talk all over Mesa College: "Who wants to go find Bower's cache?" But not just anyone could make that rugged trip.

Klein: How much luggage did you take with you on that trip to Dallas, and who packed it?

Bower: I packed both our bags for the trip to Dallas. I didn't need much, as I was coming back in a few days. I packed all of Les's suits and clothes he would need for a longer stay. He would be staying with my parents until we got into a house. I included all of his camera equipment. I didn't pack any guns, and Les had no other luggage than what I had packed for us.

Klein: Tell us about the actual move from Grand Junction to Dallas.

Bower: I returned to Grand Junction and began to get ready for the moving company. We had a twenty-three-foot travel trailer, and because it was our responsibility to move any firearms we had, I put all the guns in the trailer. Some were in cases, and the rest I wrapped in blankets. The trailer was designed with two twin beds, one on each side of the trailer. Each bed had a large storage area underneath. I put the guns under the beds two days before the movers came. There were four or five rifles, a couple of shotguns and black-powder rifles, and one pistol.

Klein: What kind of pistol was it?

Bower: A .44.

Klein: Do you know the type of pistol?

Bower: Yes, because he had left it with me before.

Klein: What do you mean by "left it"?

Bower: Left it for me when he was traveling or on hunting trips and away for several days.

Klein: Do you know how to shoot it?

Bower: Yes, I do. He taught me when we were at A&M.

Klein: Did he instruct you on how to fire the weapon?

Bower: Yes, he did.

Klein asked me to testify as to the events of the night of January 20, 1984, when the search warrant was served and Les was arrested. I recounted that night to the jurors in great detail, including the officer's behavior in our bedroom, how long they were there that night, and how I was both frightened and upset by them.

Klein: Let's go to another night. Do you recall the day of October 8, 1983?

Bower: Yes. Les got up early the morning of October 8, 1983. It was bow season, and he was going somewhere in East Texas to bowhunt. He left around six thirty. My friend Sharon and I were having a garage sale later that month, and I was going through boxes and marking items to sell. I told Les we were going to have hamburgers for dinner and asked if he would be home in time to cook them on the grill. He said he would. We usually ate around six or six thirty, so I was watching for him as I prepared the ingredients for dinner. I could see the driveway and front walk from the kitchen through a window in the laundry room just off the kitchen. He drove up around six thirty. The sun was still up, and he didn't have his headlights on. He came into the kitchen, greeted me, and washed his hands. Then I sent him out with a platter of hamburgers to put on the grill.

Klein: Was there anything unusual in his behavior?

Bower: No.

Klein: Did he appear to be in good or bad spirits?

Bower: He was in good spirits. Very good spirits.

Klein: Do you love your husband?

Bower: Yes, I do.

Klein: Would you lie for him?

Bower: No.

Klein: Please tell the jury your thoughts concerning your husband and whether or not you would lie to free him.

Bower: Yes, I do love my husband. If, for one minute, I ever thought he had committed this crime, I wouldn't have driven

190 miles round trip twice a week to visit him in jail. I wouldn't have assisted Mr. Klein if I thought he was guilty or even capable of this crime. Under no circumstances would I get up here and lie for him.

Klein: Thank you, Mrs. Bower. I pass the witness.

I looked down at my hands in my lap, straightened my skirt, and looked back up at Les. He gave me a smile and a wink, telling me I was doing a good job. Now I had to deal with County Attorney Davidchik.

Davidchik: I take it from the graphic description you have given us of the search of your home in Arlington on January 20, 1984, that it was quite an unhappy and unpleasant thing for you to go through.

Bower: Yes, it was.

Davidchik: I would assume that you would acknowledge it is probably less unhappy and less unpleasant for somebody to come to your front door at that hour and tell you that your husband had been murdered?

I didn't know what to expect from Davidchik, but it had not been that particular question. I didn't let it rattle me, nor did I hesitate as I looked over at the families of the four men who had been brutally killed on Saturday, October 8, 1983, and answered his question.

Bower: Yes, I would.

And so the cross-examination began, Davidchik hammering away at me with various questions in an attempt to trip me up on one detail or another. He went over almost all the testimony of the other prosecution's witnesses, asking me if I was aware of this or that statement.

Davidchik continued with his questions, most of them about various parts of the plane that I saw or didn't see at the house and whether we had discussed them. I told him that I had seen some of it but was not happy with his latest project of building an ultralight, so I didn't pay that much attention to it.

He asked me why. I told him that this was one project I didn't want him to get into, the building of an ultralight, and especially the flying of one. "It was dangerous," I told him.

His questions mirrored some of what Klein had already asked me, and then he peppered me with a staccato of questions, one after another, regarding what Les was wearing that day, if I had seen a propeller or an engine, where his briefcase was kept, and if I packed that as well for the move. How often did he reload shells, when was the last time I had seen the reloader?

All these things were thrown at me as if he were trying to elicit different answers than those I had given before. My answers were usually one or two words and answered without hesitation. His attempts to rattle me failed, and I was surprised that I remained as calm as I did. I was in the witness box for three hours.

Davidchik: Thank you, Mrs. Bower. That's all the questions I have for this witness.

Klein: I have no further questions, Your Honor.

Court: All right. You may step down.

Klein: The defense rests, Your Honor.

The defense rests? Klein spoke those three words before I stepped out of the box. I was so shocked that I stopped and looked up before my foot even touched the steps. I think even the prosecution was surprised. Les and I looked at him and then at each other.

I rushed to the defense table where I could see Les had already started asking Klein questions; understandably, he was not happy. I could see some of our family members sitting in the gallery behind us standing up, leaning across the rail and trying to ask their own questions.

He had lost his mind. Klein shut the defense down with those three little words. It was not enough.

Warriors

I watched as the crash came, listened as the impact hit.
Mightily, without warning, my world fell apart.
I took bandages and tried to hold it together,
To mend it somehow, make it whole once more.
But again and again, the blows took their toll.
The disappointments, the nos, the setbacks, the defeats.
I watched as it crumbled, piece by piece,
Falling all around me, big, ugly pieces strewn about my feet.
A constant reminder of my defeat.
I am stripped naked of my protection.
My armor lays useless by my side.
I have exhausted the desire to fight.
This warrior really is a child.

August 25, 1987

CHAPTER 18

One Last Goodbye

April 26, 1984

The defense had called eleven witnesses and rested before lunch on Thursday, April 25. It could hardly be called a defense. No viable alternative to Les being the murderer had been presented, nor had any reasonable doubt been shown to the jury. Klein had failed miserably as far as we were concerned.

Once he returned to the defense table, Les and I were all over him without causing a scene. Our parents were ready to have words with him as well, yet there was really no point in it, and our decorum would only make things worse. *Worse? How could it get worse?* I thought. We admonished Klein for not checking with us before he made the decision to rest. All he had to say was, "Your Honor, might I have a minute with my client?" Instead, he decided to rest! No discussion, no vote—just throw in the towel and say we're done.

Les and I had little time to talk about it before the bailiffs came and took him away. We didn't know what to do. We felt betrayed. And all Klein would say was, "We still have closing arguments. I'll be able to get the jury with our closing arguments."

It bothered me every night when Les had to go back to his cell alone. I had choices to be with other people and find comfort or answers from our families, but that night, I thought I might want to be alone as well. I just wished we could be alone together. Even if it was in a visitation booth.

We returned at 9:00 A.M. on Friday, April 26 for closing arguments. After reading the charges and giving the jury their instructions, the judge took a five-minute recess and then instructed the bailiff to lock the doors. No one was allowed in or out during the closing arguments.

Assistant County Attorney Sampson gave the state's opening summation, arguing for a guilty verdict. When he concluded, Klein gave the defense summation in favor of a not guilty verdict. In the guilt/innocence stage of the trial, the state gets to have a closing summation, and County Attorney Davidchik was the last to speak with his closing summation.

After hearing from both sides, the judge directed the bailiff to take the jury to lunch and recessed the court until 2:30. When the jurors returned from lunch, they were given more instructions, then sent to the jury room to elect a foreman and begin deliberations. It was after 3:00 P.M. when the jurors left the courtroom.

Some of the spectators left, but Les and I remained sitting at the defense table, holding hands, speaking to one another occasionally, still very much in shock. Friends and family members sat in the benches nearby, and we could hear soft whispers as some talked among themselves.

We would look at each other now and then, speechless. There seemed nothing more to say. I didn't know how to encourage him, and I suppose neither did he. It looked bad. It was too short. But somewhere inside me, I just couldn't believe the jurors would think he was a murderer, despite all the questions that had been left unanswered. I hadn't prepared myself for that. I wondered if Les had. I was so numb. I had been annoyed at Klein throughout the trial. Now I was very angry at the man sitting at the end of the table. Klein had betrayed us. He had made everything worse.

We had been sitting there less than two hours when the bailiff informed us the jurors would be returning to the courtroom. That didn't seem like a good sign. It was too quick. Just like the trial, not enough time had been taken. But maybe it was quick because they all agreed he wasn't guilty. What if that was it? What if they knew he didn't kill them, and they all agreed? We could go home!

Les squeezed my hand just a little tighter, and I felt nauseated as I tried to breathe normally. The anxiety we felt had become a way of life for us over the last three months, and I wasn't sure we would ever breathe normally again.

Klein said to us, "A short deliberation is not usually good. See if any of them look at you when they come in. If they don't, we're in trouble." *We're in trouble?* We all stood as the jurors filed in, and none of them looked in our direction. However, one of the jurors turned to someone in the gallery, smiled, and nodded. I turned to see Bobby Glenn Tate sitting in the middle of the courtroom, a huge smile on his face as he nodded back to the juror.

The jury handed down four guilty verdicts.

Les stood while we listened to each verdict as they read them individually. Hearing the first one, I couldn't believe it and thought, *The next one will be different.* But it wasn't. They were all the same.

There was a rustling of movement, an audible cry from one of the widows, and sounds of joy coming from the section where the victims' families were sitting. My mind could not comprehend what was happening.

When they finished reading the verdicts, Les sat down, and I continued to sit at the defense table, unable to speak or move. I reached over and put my arms around him, and we softly cried into each other's necks, trying to understand how this had all happened.

I felt as if we were the only two people in the room as we pulled away and looked at one another, tears running down our faces. I reached over and wrapped our hands together so tightly I couldn't feel where his stopped and mine began. The adrenaline had slowly drained from our bodies. The shock of the guilty verdicts consumed us.

I could feel the presence of our grieving friends and family behind us, but I felt as if he and I were in a bubble, alone in a world of our own pain and sorrow. I saw they were talking, their mouths were moving, some were crying, but I didn't hear what they said. It was as if I were underwater.

And it wasn't over. We had to go through the punishment phase of the trial, and the prosecution and defense had agreed to hear it on Saturday rather than postpone it until the next week. *Why was everyone in such a hurry?*

Sheriff's deputies suddenly appeared to escort Les out of the courtroom, taking him back to his cell to spend another night alone. My plan had been to take him home. I wanted him as far away from Sherman, Texas, as we could be, allowing us to finally fall apart in each other's arms after the months of separation, anxiety, and grief we had endured. I watched his back, his wrists handcuffed in front of him, as he walked out of the courtroom once again. He turned and looked over his shoulder at me one more time. I had never felt so helpless in my life.

I remember someone coming up next to me and taking my arm, leading me out of the courthouse. I was in a daze, not really knowing where I was or where I was going, so I just followed them. I had people who loved us surrounding me. But Les? He was alone. I couldn't bear that thought. No matter how bad things had appeared in the last three months, we didn't expect to hear those verdicts. We believed that if you were innocent, this wouldn't happen.

Innocent people don't get guilty verdicts, right? Right?

Somehow, I found myself back at the hotel. Klein suggested that we all meet out by the pool to have a family meeting. The pool was the largest gathering area at the hotel with ample seating for all of us.

He told us what to expect the next day. The jurors needed to hear favorable testimony as to Les's character. They would be answering questions regarding punishment based on his being a threat to society. Conveying to the jurors his good character and his reputation as a friend and member of the community was crucial.

Klein looked around at everyone, sizing them up as to who should testify, and decided on five people to call to testify the next day. All of them were female, mostly family members. None of them knew what they were supposed to do. Several asked him what they were supposed to say, what they were not supposed to say. All he told them was he would lead them through the questions.

"Just be honest," he said, "and speak from your hearts." Everyone seemed to be confused, but no discussions were held about what they were to say.

"Just follow my lead" was the only instruction he gave.

Klein pulled me aside to a corner of the swimming pool area where there were some large bushes. He guided us behind them with his left hand. His right hand held a drink, obviously not his first one that evening. He leaned in close to me, causing the warm and humid April air to feel even more stifling as the smell of alcohol from his breath wafted toward me.

"You know, Shari," he said, looking around to make sure there was no one else there, "I always thought he did it." Taking another drink from his nearly empty glass, he waited for a response from me.

I looked at him, staring at his bloodshot eyes in disbelief. There were no words. My state of shock from the events of the day turned to contempt, and my blood boiled with anger at this declaration. Yet I was rendered speechless.

"I'll tell you what I can do for you," he continued, leaning in closer in a conspiratorial manner so that only he and I could hear what he was proposing.

"For twenty-five thousand dollars and the rest of my fee you owe me, I'll do the appeal for you."

Unable to believe what he was saying, I continued staring at him. His tone was as if he was doing me a favor, and I should be grateful that he was there for me. I glared at him, still unable to speak. Shocked at the audacity of it all, I simply walked away.

I had no idea what to do except show up in the courtroom the next morning beside my husband as we faced another horrific day. It made me physically ill to look at Klein as he talked about things that I didn't understand. Appeals, further trials. The only thing I knew for sure was that whatever happened after today, Richard Klein would not be a part of it.

He better pull a rabbit out of his hat, I thought. *Or produce a miracle somehow by making a strong argument.*

Les was either going to prison for the rest of his life, or he would be executed. And as far as I was concerned, Klein had helped put him in this position. *Is he really that bad? Or is he playing for the other team?* So far, he had done nothing to help our cause. In fact, he had only made it worse.

None of us knew that the annual Spring Carnival was scheduled for this particular Saturday in April. As we arrived at the courthouse that morning for the jury to make their decision, it was in full force on the courthouse lawn and square. *What is wrong with these people?* I thought. *Don't they know a man's life lies in the balance just inside those doors? Don't they care?*

People were eating cotton candy. Carnies called out, "Come take a chance! Spin the wheel! Do you feel lucky? Will you win or will you lose?" *Are they talking about the games? Or about us?*

Kids walked around in balloon hats and carried bags of popcorn. Others rode Ferris wheels or bumper cars while we were fighting for Les's life. It was a pathetic sight to see us pushing our way through the crowd and climbing the stairs to get into the courthouse, as if we, too, were rolling the dice to see what was in store.

Life in Sherman, Texas, was moving on while ours was falling apart. Our life and the surreal events taking place for the last three months suddenly morphed into a carnival, and we were part of the sideshow for all the ticket holders to see.

Les was brought in and sat down next to me as he did each day. His face was drawn and tired, older-looking than his thirty-six years. I could tell he hadn't slept much the night before. I knew how he felt, yet I didn't. He reached over and took my hands in his as we both looked down, our hands locked together, as if we were taking a mental picture to remember. I loved his hands. They were large, with squared fingers, and wrapped perfectly around mine.

Memories of him holding my hand in church, not only when we first started dating, but also during the eighteen years after, came pouring in. His hands were strong enough to take down a linebacker, yet gentle enough to reach for mine to help me out of a car. These were the hands that reached out to take his newborn daughters in his arms for the first time and then later lead them through the fields, picking wildflowers as they each held on to just one finger.

He took both mine in his, rubbing his thumbs across the back of my hands as we sat face-to-face, his slow, deliberate movements reminding me of so many other times. He looked up into my eyes—his blue, mine brown—and gently squeezed my hands as he struggled to smile at me. Slowly, he pulled them toward his face and laid a kiss in the palm of each one. We fought the tears that threatened to spill. No words were spoken. This was one of those times when words were not needed.

Les continued to hold my hands as we sat through the next few hours while our attorney poorly attempted to convince the jury Les was not a murderer, bringing witnesses to testify to his good character.

The second-floor windows of the courtroom had been opened to let the cool April breeze in. Birds sang while the din of chatter continued on the lawn. An Elvis impersonator sang "Jailhouse Rock" as a band played, and the music and laughter drifted into the room. I thought it couldn't get any worse.

I was wrong.

Curious bystanders wandered in and out of the courtroom; children with painted faces and balloons tied around their hands walked up and down the aisles. We had become one of the sideshows. The judge finally asked the bailiff to close the windows and instructed everyone to be respectful of the proceedings going on by taking their seats.

We listened once more as the prosecution painted him out to be a ruthless, cold-blooded killer with no remorse. *How can you have remorse for something you didn't do?* They made their closing arguments, and we made ours. It was such a pathetic attempt to try to save a man's life.

The judge sent the jurors out once more to deliberate and answer two questions. If a jury finds a defendant guilty of capital murder in the state of Texas, during the punishment phase of the trial, they must answer two questions.

The first is whether there exists a probability the defendant would commit criminal acts of violence that would constitute a "continuing threat to society."

The second is whether, taking into consideration the circumstances of the offense, the defendant's character and background, and the personal moral culpability of the defendant, there exists sufficient mitigating circumstances to warrant a sentence of life imprisonment rather than a death sentence.

In order for a death sentence to be imposed, the jury must answer the first question *yes* and the second question *no*. Otherwise, the sentence is life in prison.

I turned to Les as we sat there, once more waiting for the jurors to return. He looked at me, still holding my hands in his.

"You know what they are going to do, don't you?" I asked him.

"Yes," he said, pausing for a moment, his beautiful blue eyes never leaving mine. "They wouldn't find me guilty of such a horrendous crime and not give me the death penalty."

And that's exactly what they did.

The ink wasn't even dry on the judge's signature when Klein turned to Les and me, still sitting at the defense table, trying to wrap our heads around what had just happened.

"You know," Klein said to us, "it's probably better that you got the death penalty rather than life in prison," he said casually. We stared at him in disbelief. "You get an automatic appeal with the death penalty, but you aren't eligible for parole for twenty years if you get life." He smiled at us, as if he'd just given us a gift. Then he walked over to shake hands with the prosecution.

Ironically, in 2004 at one of our visitations, Les brought that up to me in our conversation. "Just think," he said, mockingly, "if I had gotten life, I might be getting out this year, if the parole board agreed."

The only worthwhile thing our attorney did was ask the judge to agree to allow us some time with Les before they took him away for the last time.

I would not learn until later that Klein was anxious to leave as well. He and his wife had plans to fly to Mexico that evening from the Dallas–Fort Worth (DFW) airport. He told my dad they were going on a "much-needed vacation." He asked Dad if he would drive his car back to his house for him while they went straight to the DFW airport from Sherman. He packed his stash of liquor in the back seat of his luxury car, put some ice in a cup, handed it to my dad, and said, "Here, have one for the road on me."

I would look back later and wonder, did Klein buy tickets for a flight out of the country for the same day he was scheduled to make closing arguments for his capital murder client? How would you know when a trial was going to end? Or were he and his wife just hoping they could get tickets at the airport? What about clothes? Do you show up at a capital murder trial as the defense attorney with your beach towel and a swimsuit, ready to go on vacation? Let that sink in a minute. I would think only someone who knows what is going to happen and when can make plans like that.

As my sister Kelli and her husband, Tracy, left the courthouse where they visited Les for the last time where they could hug him and tell him goodbye, they returned to the hotel to get their things and go home. They encountered Klein and his wife, as they, too, were leaving. Klein walked over to Kelli and said, "Well, the operation was a success, but we lost the patient." Kelli and Tracy were shocked and disgusted by such an outrageous comment. They walked past them toward the hotel without a response. Kelli looked over at Klein's wife as they passed and saw that even she was surprised by her husband's comment.

It's not normal for a capital murder trial, especially with multiple victims, to have such a short trial. The state made a sweet deal for them on the first day that pretty much shut down the defense. And then they finished their part in three days. The defense put their case on in less than eight hours, and then the two sides, with the exception of the defendant, decided to do the punishment phase on a Saturday. If that makes me sound like a conspiracy theorist, then you are probably right. But I'm not alone in my theory.

During the time that Les had been in Grayson County Jail, he was on the fourth floor of the old courthouse—or what Les referred to as "The Penthouse." The county built a new jail while he was there, and they had recently moved all the prisoners to the new facility. The fourth floor was now unoccupied. Only a few cells and peeling paint remained.

The judge gave us four hours for visitation on the empty fourth floor that had recently served as Les's jail. Two of those hours he could spend with his extended family and friends who were there. The last two hours he could spend alone with the girls and me.

Where are the girls? I thought. I thought someone had gone to get them the night before, or maybe it was that morning. I couldn't remember. Where had they been all this time? What a terrible mother I was! I didn't know where my children were.

He stood in the middle of what seemed like a hundred people. Each of them, tears filling their eyes, came to him, said something, embraced him, prayed with him, and cried with him. I stood close by as he held one or both of the girls who had been brought to see their daddy by their uncle Mike. It was the first time Les had seen them since he had been arrested. He picked them both up and covered their faces with his sweet daddy kisses.

Two hours flew by quickly, and the deputies ushered everyone out except for our two small girls and me. Our youngest child, Hollie, only eight years old, stood there, bewildered and afraid, not knowing what exactly was going on. As the others left, Hollie looked up at Les, still clinging to his hand, and asked, "Daddy, are you coming home with us now?"

Les squatted down to meet her eyes and, trying not to cry, said, "Not today, baby, not today."

Leslea, our oldest, had recently turned twelve. I wasn't sure what her level of understanding was, but I knew Leslea. She knew a lot more than her sister did. Leslea was resourceful, quick to figure things out, and had even confronted me with newspapers from the trash in her attempt to find out what was going on. She did not accept the "Daddy was gone for a little while" answers she got from the adults around her. I had tried to protect them both from the ugliness, the pain, the sorrow, but she would not allow me to keep her in the dark. I didn't even understand it all. How could she?

He spoke to both of them, holding one in each arm, kissing their cheeks and embracing them, drinking in the sweet smell of his children. He spoke of nothing in particular, but everything that mattered. I'm not sure what all was said, nor did it matter.

We realized that we were all four in the same room together for the first time in a very long time. And none of us could even imagine it might also be the last time. He had no idea that, when his three girls were finally escorted out that door, he would never feel his arms around any of us again, his hands in ours, or a kiss upon our brows. Had we known, we might not have been able to bear it.

Such anguish and heartbreak, uncertainty and disbelief, grasping for one last moment as we stood in front of rusty bars and empty cells, filled with years of terrible memories for so many others. The musty room reeked with years of sweat and bitter tears and now found a home on the faces of our little family, huddled together, not knowing what lay ahead or what would become of us.

I remembered our first kiss. Such anticipation and wonder as two teenagers, just getting to know one another, fumbling at a doorstep, anticipating exciting things yet to come.

And I certainly remembered our last one. The memory that will be forever burned within my heart is that last kiss. We stood there, our children clinging to our side, looking up at us with fear and questions in their eyes, tears streaming down their little cheeks. He took me in his arms and kissed me one last time. I had known him since I was sixteen years old. There had been a lot of kisses in those eighteen years, but none had ever been as passionate, so heartfelt, and so excruciatingly painful as that last kiss. I felt as if my heart were being ripped in two, and every ounce of blood had been drained from my body. I can still remember it today and will forever.

Now I Lay Me Down Awake

Now I lay me down awake.
I pray the Lord my soul to take.
Sometimes this life and all the care
Seems so much more than I can bear.
Yet as I pray, "Lord, take me home,"
I know that I am not alone.
And as I'm bathed in blessed peace,
I find in God such sweet release
From all the burdens, pain, and sorrow,
And in their place, hope for tomorrow.
Knowing that I am His to keep,
I find instead such peaceful sleep.

March 6, 1990

CHAPTER 19

The Woman with No Name

April 12, 1989

"You don't know me," she said softly. "Are you Lester Bower's wife?"

I almost hung up. An article about us and how we had coped the last five years had appeared in the *Fort Worth Star-Telegram* two days before. My first thought was that she was going to tell me what an awful person my husband was. I had received a few of those calls over the years, usually after publicity, but, fortunately, not often.

"Yes," I answered. "Who is this?"

There was a brief silence on the line, and I heard her crying as she tried to speak.

"He didn't kill those people. I didn't know anyone had been arrested, or I would have called sooner, but your husband didn't do it."

"I know he didn't do it," I replied, running my fingers through my hair as I looked for someplace to sit down. "Who is this?" My stomach began to roll as if I were being tossed by a wave. I had waited and prayed for a phone call like this, but what if it was a joke? I sat down on a barstool, afraid I might fall. "Why are you calling?"

"My boyfriend helped kill those people," she said just barely above a whisper. I held my breath for what seemed like forever.

"Your boyfriend?" I asked, my voice whispering to meet hers.

"They threatened to kill me and my kids if I said anything, so I left the state. I just came back . . . I thought it was okay to come back!" she cried out. "Then I saw the article in the paper, and I knew I had to call and tell you."

My mind began racing and my heart pounding. "Who are *they*?" I asked. "Who are *you*?" I tried not to scream. I grabbed a glass of water. My throat was dry.

"I can't tell you. They'll kill me if they find out. I just wanted you to know. I wanted you to have peace, knowing that he didn't kill them, that he's not a killer."

Clutching the landline phone to my ear, fearing she might hang up, I slowly walked around the breakfast bar from my living room into the kitchen. The long cord curled and uncurled as it followed behind me.

My hands were shaking as I turned off the dishwasher and the stove, moving the pan away from the heat. I could barely hear her, as she spoke so softly, crying as she tried to tell me my husband was not a murderer. I needed to understand every word she said. I needed to keep her talking.

Sitting down on a kitchen chair, I drew in a deep breath to calm myself and quietly asked once more, "Please tell me your name?"

The woman, who would soon become known to the public as Witness #1, did not want to tell me who she was. She was terrified the men who actually committed the murders would find out she had called me and would try to kill her or her family.

They had told her on more than one occasion they would do exactly that if she ever told anyone. But her conscience got the better of her when she saw the paper and learned that an innocent man had not only been arrested for a crime he didn't commit but had been found guilty and was scheduled to die because of it.

"I couldn't live with myself if I didn't tell you," she said.

She was so upset. I still wasn't sure if she was telling the truth or not. She could be someone who just wanted some attention, someone who followed stories and wanted to insinuate themselves into the picture. How could

I be sure?

"How did you find me?" I asked.

"I called Scott Nishimura, the reporter at the paper who wrote the article," she replied. "He gave me your phone number."

"Have you told anyone else about this?" I asked.

"Only my sister," she said. "I left the state soon after all this happened and moved to Arkansas. I had to get my children out of here, or they were going to kill me. I thought maybe it was safe now to come back home, so I did, just a few weeks ago. And then I saw the article in the paper. I couldn't believe it. I had no idea. I became hysterical, and that's when I told my sister. She said I needed to tell someone." She began to cry again, and I listened to her as she did.

My mind was racing as I tried not to get ahead of myself. Thoughts of throwing myself in Les's arms as they opened the prison doors and released him flooded through my mind. I jumped from excitement to fear and back to thoughts of him coming home.

First, I had to get a hold of my own emotions. I listened to her, jotted down some notes, and thought of ways to get her to talk. She wanted me to *know* Les was innocent. She thought that would give me peace of mind. I wanted to know *who* it was that killed them in order to set Les free.

"When I saw the paper, I was so upset that I didn't know before." She sniffled into the phone. "If I had, I would have come to you sooner. I could have helped him, helped you. I am so sorry. Please forgive me, I didn't know. I ran away to protect my family and I had no idea. You have to believe me."

"I do believe you. You can trust me. Please tell me your name?" I asked again, trying to get her to identify herself.

"I can't tell you," she said. "It's not safe."

"Give me your phone number," I asked calmly, "in case we get disconnected."

"No. You don't understand," she replied, on the verge of hysterics. "I have children. They will find me. I can't take that risk."

I began to ask her questions, prodding her to tell me more than I was telling her. I needed to know if she was telling the truth. I had to hear her story. For some reason, I knew she was telling the truth.

She started telling me how the four men were murdered that October evening in 1983. She knew things that had never been printed in the newspapers, things that no one would know, unless they had firsthand knowledge of the crime. Things we still had not revealed, as we were working on appeals.

It was not long before I knew that she was for real. She knew who killed those men.

Now I just had to convince her to trust me.

I asked her several times, almost pleading with her, to tell me who she was, but she was too afraid.

"This information won't help us," I said to her, "unless we know who you are."

"I don't want to talk to the cops," she said. "I just wanted you to know. This has to be awful for you and for him. I'm so sorry. I could have helped him. I had no idea. If I hadn't read this article in the paper, if I was still out of state, I would never have known. I'm so sorry."

"I'm not asking you to talk to the police. I don't want that either. I have a better idea, and I promise no one will find out who you are." I was trying to get her to trust me.

In 1988, a bright, young associate at Morgan Lewis law firm in Washington, DC, by the name of Grace Speights had just returned from maternity leave. She and another equally talented associate, Anthony Roth, were talking about doing a pro bono case, possibly a death penalty. One of the senior associates, Peter Buscemi, had done some pro bono cases, including capital murder cases before, presenting arguments before the Supreme Court. Grace and Anthony decided to talk to Peter about the possibility of them doing one together.

Peter told them how much work would be involved but agreed to take the lead when they found one they wanted to work. They asked Peter how long a capital appeal would take, and he told them maybe eight or ten years. Never in their wildest dreams did they think the project they would eventually take on would go on for twenty-five years, a quarter of a century. Not long after that, the Bower Case, as it soon began to be referred to in the Washington office, was well-known to all the attorneys.

After meeting with Les and agreeing to take his case, all three attorneys flew to Dallas to meet his family individually. I drove to the hotel at DFW and met them, glad to have someone to take the lead for whatever needed to be done next. They immediately got to work and started filing motions with the Supreme Court to get the appeal process going. They provided enough information to the court to get a stay of execution so they could dive deeper into the case, and began doing more investigating. They would work on Les's case in their spare time while working on their regular cases.

I told her about Les's new attorney team and how hard they were working to get him a new trial. I said we were so relieved to have them as our team now. I assured her they were good people and would keep her identity secure.

"Just let me have your phone number so they can call you."

She was quiet for a moment, hopefully considering what I said.

It took a forty-minute phone call to finally convince her. She gave me her phone number but not her name.

"I'll call them right now," I said to her. "Hopefully, I can find one of them still at the office. Thank you so much for calling." I tried to reassure her she had done the right thing. "It will be all right. You will be safe with them. I promise."

I didn't want to hang up the phone, worried I would never hear from her again. I was afraid she would have second thoughts and disappear once more. All she wanted to do was tell me Les was innocent, assuage her guilt and remorse with a phone call. I was afraid she would decide to go back into hiding and we would never be able to discover who the killers really were.

It was almost 7:00 P.M. in DC. I immediately called Peter's phone number at the Morgan Lewis office, praying that he or his secretary would answer the phone. The switchboard operator answered and informed me the offices were closed.

"I need to speak to Peter Buscemi," I said. I had practically yelled it.

I had to be calm. This was a huge corporate office, not a criminal attorney leased space. They probably were not accustomed to hysterical clients calling at night. And then again, maybe they were.

She tried his number, getting no response.

"I'm sorry, ma'am, he has left for the day. Would you like to leave a message?"

"This is an emergency. See if you can locate Anthony Roth or Grace Speights. I need to talk to one of them or someone in their office, please."

"Let me put you on hold and see what I can do."

Minutes ticked by as I waited with dead air on the other end, praying that someone would still be there.

"Grace Speights."

I took a gulp of air and spilled everything I could while keeping my emotions in control. As I relayed the account of my recent conversation, Grace asked, "Shari, do you think she is legitimate or just someone who is calling because of the article in the paper? How do we know she's not someone just trying to get attention?"

"Grace," I said, "she knows things she shouldn't know!"

There was a brief silence on the end of the line.

"Give me her number. I'll get back to you on this. Don't say anything to anyone about this until we've talked again."

I agreed, and we ended the call.

I sat there on the barstool, the crumpled piece of paper in my hand with a lone phone number scribbled on it but no name. I stared at it, still processing what just happened. My heart raced as I thought of the possibilities this revelation might bring. The adrenaline, which had kept me calm and clearheaded, began to subside within me, and I could feel my body begin to shake as the reality of it all sank in.

Tears welled up in my eyes and slowly ran down my cheeks. Now that I was alone with my thoughts, the drama subsided with each beat of my heart, and I felt myself coming back to normal. *What is normal? Is this my new normal?*

It seemed easier for me to be in super adrenaline mode than to be normal. I had turned this over and over to God to take care of, and now I turned it over to someone who legally knew what to do. I did not have to be strong and take care of the situation and try to fix it. *But fixing is what I do best. So if I'm not trying to fix it, what am I supposed to do?* I did what I always did. I came down from my high and began weeping uncontrollably until I was spent.

I thought of Les, 275 miles away, not knowing any of this. *Do I dare to hope? I can't write him and tell him. What happens next? Could this be the beginning of the end of this nightmare?* There were so many questions and no answers.

I don't know how long I sat there in silence, not knowing what to do next. My dishes were unwashed, the dinner uncooked, and little did I know our world would turn upside down once more as things took a dramatic turn.

During the next few hours, one of the attorneys talked to the woman on the phone and arranged a meeting with her. As a result of that conversation, Peter reached out to someone he knew in the justice department in Washington for a referral to a private detective in the Dallas–Fort Worth area. The contact in justice picked up the phone and called an attorney friend of his in Dallas. The attorney played golf every week with a bunch of buddies; one of them happened to be Roy Taylor, a former military man and private investigator.

Within a few days, Roy Taylor met Peter Buscemi and Mindy Hatton, another attorney with Morgan Lewis, at the Dallas–Fort Worth airport, and the three of them headed out to talk to the woman who called to tell me Les had not killed those men.

I still had no idea what her name was.

Faith

My God is a faithful God who has promised in His time
To deliver me from evil, because I am His and He is mine.
To God I pray for my deliverance from a life so full of pain
And ask that He take me home with Him—
That would not be loss, but gain.
Yet God may choose that I not go, but rather that I stay
So that I might have faith in Him and walk closer every day.
But faith isn't just something I ask for and receive.
Faith is a moment-by-moment trust in God
For the things I hope and believe.

May 19, 1984

CHAPTER 20

Witness #1

April 1989

Our newly retained private investigator, Roy Taylor, picked up Les's attorneys, Peter Buscemi and Mindy Hatton, who flew into Dallas not long after I received the call from the woman who had information about the killings. Roy was driving them to their first meeting with the woman who called me just days before. This would be the beginning of an investigation to identify the men who had committed the hangar killings and uncover what happened at the B&B Ranch in Denison, Texas, on October 8, 1983.

She agreed to the meeting because she said she couldn't live with herself if she didn't tell someone the truth. An innocent man could die for something he didn't do. Yet she was so afraid the people she had once lived with—the ones who had committed the murders—would find her and carry out their promise to kill her if she ever told anyone. Beginning that day, we would refer to her as Witness #1 in order to keep her safe.

Roy asked Witness #1 to tell them how she knew these guys and what she knew about the killings of the four men at the hangar in Denison.

She began by telling them that she and her friend went on a trip to Lake Texoma and while they were there, she met a man named Larry. Her friend had already taken up with Larry's friend Rick, so they spent the weekend with them.

After the weekend, the girls ended up moving in with the guys in a house in Mesquite, Texas. Later, they got kicked out of the house and moved with the guys to Lexington, Oklahoma, where she said the guys could do some work there with some friends by the name of Ches and Bear. They cooked meth and ran drugs; it was a pretty wild group.

On October 8, 1983, Witness #1 took a bus from Lexington to go visit her mother in Hillsboro, Texas, arriving at about 2:00 A.M. on Sunday morning, October 9, 1983. When she arrived, she was surprised to find Larry waiting for her outside her mother's house in his car. He had been out with Rick and some of his buddies when she decided to go see her mother and her kids in Hillsboro. She certainly didn't expect to see him there. He was very nervous and told her they had to return to Lexington in the morning because there had been some trouble. They grabbed some sleep and then left the next morning.

Larry told her to take the long way to Lexington in order to avoid Sherman. He fell asleep, and she ignored his request to go around Sherman, as it was faster. He woke up and saw they were driving through Sherman and began to freak out, yelling and screaming at her for not following his instructions. He huddled in the backseat floor as they drove through Sherman, telling her not to get pulled over. She said he was hysterical and scared to death.

Once he calmed down and they were out of Sherman, he told her that he and his friends had killed four people the night before. Larry, Rick, Ches, and a man called Bear had made a drug run to Denison and were meeting the seller at his hangar outside of town. When they got there, the seller was not alone. The drug deal went bad when they found out one of the guys at the hangar was a sheriff's deputy and another one was a former cop. So they had to kill all of them. She said Larry and his friends, Rick, Ches, and Bear, had been the ones who killed the four men in Sherman, not Les.

During the following weeks, Witness #1 overheard Ches and Larry talking about the killings when they would drink together. Larry would have recurring nightmares, where he saw the victim's eyes staring at him inside a big tin building as they each were shot. It was driving him crazy. All the men carried guns, and several weapons were always around their house. She gave physical descriptions of all four men and the house where they lived.

Peter asked Roy if he could check out her story and see if any or all of the four men she said did the killings could be located. Roy took Peter and Mindy back to the airport and would now officially be working the Bower Case.

The Lake Texoma Lodge and Resort confirmed Witness #1's story. The two women had rented a cottage during July 1983 and spent their time there with two unknown men. Roy found Ricky's mother, and she gave him his legal name. She didn't mind giving Roy the information, as her son had been in lots of trouble, and she didn't want to have anything to do with him. She didn't know where he was and didn't care.

Roy found Witness #1's friend living in Mesquite, Texas. The friend confirmed that "Ricky" had lived with her in 1983 and that his friend Larry had also lived at her house. Witness #1's friend was reluctant to answer many of Roy's questions.

Checking with the Oklahoma Department of Corrections, Roy discovered Ricky was an inmate in one of their prisons. Ricky had been convicted of manufacturing a controlled dangerous substance on December 30, 1987, and was given a two-and-a-half-year sentence.

Next, Roy interviewed Kingston Police Chief Dale Cissell. Chief Cissell said that he and Ricky had gone to Kingston High School together and that Ricky ran around with Larry and another friend. He agreed to contact Roy if he saw him in town.

Through the end of November, Roy continued to try to locate the four men who had been named by Witness #1. Early in December 1989, he took Witness #1 and a companion of hers on a trip to Oklahoma to help him locate several of the places she had mentioned she had lived in during her earlier interview.

She was able to confirm all the locations where these men had worked and lived during the time of the murders. They spent over seven hours in the car, and she had plenty of time to talk about her experiences while living with Linda and Ches. Roy took this opportunity to ask more specific questions about the men. It was on this trip that Roy became convinced she was telling the truth.

On January 19, 1990, Roy found Linda in the Cleveland County Jail in Norman, Oklahoma. If she would talk and confirm Witness #1's information, the case against the four men named by her would be much stronger.

Roy ran a background check on Ches. The booking sheet showed he had been arrested for assault with a deadly weapon. He had been convicted of conspiracy to distribute a controlled substance, concealing stolen property, escaping from a penitentiary, and carrying a firearm after a felony conviction. He was in the McLeod Correctional Center in Farris, Oklahoma.

In January 1990, Mindy Hatton, the attorney who accompanied Peter Buscemi on the first investigative trip, flew in from DC to accompany Roy with his interview with Linda. They arrived at the county jail in Norman, but Roy was not allowed to sit in on the interview as a private investigator. Mindy could interview her, as she was an attorney investigating a case. Linda confirmed with Mindy that Ches had worked for her father and that Larry and "some girl" had shared the two-story white house with them for a time.

Linda denied that Ches had any weapons or that he was involved with the dope business. When Mindy asked about the killings, she clammed up and said nothing more. Mindy was convinced Linda was lying, but she confirmed much of what Witness #1 had told them.

Mindy and Roy proceeded south to a manufacturing plant where they found Linda's father, the owner. He confirmed that Ches and Larry had worked for him, saying Ches was from a rough family and at one time tried to sell him a pistol he knew had been stolen. He said his daughter had a dope habit and confirmed that Ches also used dope. When asked if he thought Ches was capable of murder, he said yes without hesitation.

Mindy and Roy traveled farther south across the Red River into Texas, where they contacted an ex-sheriff's deputy employed by the Grayson County Sheriff's Department during the investigation of the

October 8, 1983, murders.

The former sheriff's deputy was convinced that Les had been used as a scapegoat to cover up victim Bob Tate's involvement in the drug business. He believed someone in the sheriff's office had looked the other way, possibly taking payoffs to allow drug dealers to move their product from Oklahoma to the Dallas–Fort Worth area through Grayson County.

On March 14, 1990, Roy accepted an invitation from Sheriff Arnold Isenberg of Johnson County to come to Tishomingo, Oklahoma, to discuss Brett, also known as "Bear." Isenberg said Bear, Ricky, Larry, and a guy known as "Tramp" were real close. They ran together in the Kingston area when Isenberg was a sheriff's deputy in Madill, Oklahoma. Isenberg said that he had arrested several of the running buddies, some currently serving sentences in the Oklahoma Department of Corrections.

While talking with Sheriff Isenberg, Roy asked if Bear was capable of murder. Isenberg did not hesitate before answering, "Without a doubt!" He then asked the same question about Ricky. He said, "Yes."

"What about Larry?" Roy asked.

Isenberg's answer was, "If he had to."

Roy found that Bear had met his wife at a club she worked at in Cartwright, Oklahoma, before 1983. Cartwright is a small town, just on the Oklahoma side of the Denison Dam, on Lake Texoma. The club was the local place to buy dope in the early '80s.

Testimony from some of the club owners in Cartwright was instrumental in the conviction of the sheriff of Bryan County, Oklahoma, of racketeering. They testified that they regularly gave him money to stay clear of Cartwright, which is a very small place with no local police.

This type of activity seemed to be standard procedure, as other allegations by former law enforcement ran rampant while Roy continued his investigation. There would be more witnesses who would come forward to corroborate that similar activity was going on in many counties along southern Oklahoma and northern Texas.

Sheriff Isenberg directed Roy to the location of a house that Bear had rented. According to Witness #1, Bear dropped a bottle of ether, causing a flash fire that destroyed the house completely. Isenberg had seen the site just after the fire and reported the scene was covered in broken lab glass, indicating it was a meth lab.

As Roy and Isenberg drove back to Tishomingo, he showed Isenberg the clippings of newspaper articles about the case. When Isenberg saw the picture of Les in the papers with a full beard, he said that Bower and Bear looked almost like twin brothers. It was possible Marjorie Carr, the Tomato Patch prosecution witness, could have seen Bear with Philip Good in her fruit stand instead of Les.

Roy learned that Bear and his wife lived in Lone Grove, Oklahoma, just west of Ardmore. Peter Buscemi wanted Roy to get a picture, so Roy packed his camera and headed north on the morning of March 28, 1990.

Bear had started a company called Sooner Insulation. Roy stopped at a convenience store in Ardmore to ask if the owner knew Bear and where he might find him. A friend of Bear's happened to walk in as Roy was inquiring and told him Bear was working on a job in the new business park south of Ardmore. Roy took off for the location to try to get some pictures of Bear.

Using an alias, Roy introduced himself to the owner when he arrived at the jobsite, saying he was from Dallas and his company had sent him to investigate the possibility of building a distribution center in Ardmore.

A man matching Bear's description came out, pulling off his hat to reveal long, dark hair. His full beard was frosted with insulation that had blown on him rather than the walls. Roy told him how funny his beard looked with the insulation on it and asked if he could take a picture of it. Roy was amazed that he was able to get several pictures of him and his wife without any problem.

Roy continued to contact witnesses and interview them. One of the most interesting was a lady from Denison, Texas. She and her daughter had driven past the Tate Ranch at 6:00 P.M. on October 8, 1983, the evening of the murders, and saw a bearded man standing beside a tan car talking to another man in a blue or black Blazer. She said the man with the beard was dressed in a cowboy hat and wore boots. The men and the cars were on the road in front of the B&B Ranch.

He would get a similar description of the same men and cars at the B&B Ranch from another woman, who somehow got lost on the county roads that same day and pulled into the drive at the ranch at 5:38 P.M. to turn around. She saw the same man in the cowboy hat along with four or five others on the drive up toward the hangar.

Both these women said that it was dusk when they made their sightings. If all three were giving correct information, then the person seen at the B&B Ranch by the two women couldn't have been Les, as he arrived home before dark. Roy believed it was Bear that the two witnesses saw.

On April 18, 1990, Roy went to Sherman, Texas, to meet another sheriff's deputy from 1983 for a breakfast interview. Roy asked many questions at their meeting with little result. He definitely got the impression the deputy was not convinced the whole truth about the murders had come out but was reluctant to go public with some of his thoughts or knowledge about the situation.

Once Roy returned to Dallas, he received a personal call from the Grayson County sheriff, telling him in a very unfriendly tone that if he wanted to talk to any of his officers in the future, call and ask him. Roy had obviously upset the sheriff.

One of the deputies had told Roy that Ches and a friend of his had made a dope pickup for victim Bob Tate about a year before the murders. Mindy Hatton and Anthony Roth were scheduled to come to Texas to interview them and any of the jurors in the Bower trial who would talk with them.

When Mindy and Anthony arrived, Roy took them to Taylor's Tomato Patch in Sherman for an interview with Marjorie Carr. Mrs. Carr was very nice, speaking openly about the case and her testimony. After all the questions they had planned were asked, Anthony showed Mrs. Carr the picture of Bear that Roy had taken a month before in Ardmore, Oklahoma. She stood and stared at the picture for well over sixty seconds. Anthony asked if she recognized the person in the picture. Marjorie Carr said she was not sure.

Carr came forward with her story after Les's picture in a full beard had appeared in the local paper. As she stared at the picture of Bear, she wasn't sure whom she had seen that day at the Tomato Patch: Bear or Les.

Mindy, Anthony, and Roy proceeded to the office of the county attorney to make a courtesy call, prior to checking in to their motel and interviewing the jurors and some witnesses who had come forward. This county attorney was not the one who conducted the trial in 1984, so he was of little help and directed their questions to the sheriff's office.

Jack Driscoll was not happy about meeting with them, and he certainly wasn't happy about their mission. He went into a mini rage about the allegations in the appeal, turning on Roy and berating him about questioning some of his deputies. Driscoll would not answer any of their questions, stating, "I will not provide you with any information of any kind unless I am ordered to do so by a court!" This conversation was held in his office, and he had opened his desk drawer to make sure they could see his pistol.

When they arrived at their motel, there was a Channel 12 News van and a reporter with a camcorder waiting. The first juror they were scheduled to interview was employed by Channel 12, so obviously he had tipped off the news producer so they could get video and perhaps a story for the news.

The second interview scheduled was with the woman who had turned around in the drive at the ranch on the day of the murders. She had seen several men standing near the hangar and had reported it to the FBI in 1984, but no one had spoken to her, nor was the information she called in given to the defense before or during the trial.

The witness called Anthony to say that she was afraid to come to the motel, because of the news report she heard on the midday newscast. They agreed to meet her somewhere else.

She arrived at the meeting with her sister, telling them what she saw the night of October 8, 1983, in great detail. The picture of Bear was shown to her. She immediately identified him as the person she saw at the B&B Ranch. She was shown the original report she gave the FBI when she contacted them and was visibly upset. The FBI had not written down exactly what she told them. They failed to put in several key things about the scene she had witnessed at the ranch that day. Things such as how many men were outside the hangar, what their descriptions were, the descriptions of their cars, and most importantly, the time of day, which was after five.

The witness had brought her sister to this meeting, as she had seen the men outside the hangar that night as well. She confirmed the description of the men.

The sister had been a very close friend of the daughter of Marjorie Carr (the Tomato Patch witness) in 1983 and spent a lot of time in the Carr home. She said that Carr told her several times she wasn't sure the man she saw in her fruit stand was Bower. The DA's office kept on her, though, telling her it had to be Les, until she finally believed that it was. Later, in the post-conviction investigation, Mrs. Carr was shown a picture of Bear and a picture of Les. She seemed quite confused, even upset, and refused to identify which one of them she had seen that day.

The next day, Roy drove Mindy and Anthony to the McLeod Unit, a prison south of Atoka, Oklahoma, to interview Ches. When Ches was introduced to them, he looked at Anthony and said, "I know you. I've seen you before." Anthony assured him he had not, even though Ches may have seen him on the Channel 12 News broadcast, which included pictures taken at the motel in Denison the day before. Anthony chose the seat farthest from the one Ches sat in so as not to be so conspicuous.

Roy started questioning Ches about the dope trade in southern Oklahoma, and Ches began to open up and tell them about his past exploits. He bragged about how good a "cook" he was and about his bust in Arkansas where he spent time in jail with Bear. Ches said he knew Ricky, Bear, and Larry.

When Ches was asked about guns, he really opened up, talking about how many automatic weapons he once owned. As they were on the subject, Mindy slipped in a quick but crucial question.

"Have you ever used Fiocchi ammunition?"

"Yeah," Ches answered. "I've used it a lot."

Bingo! So much for *rare* ammunition.

Ches told them he or one of the others would find a backer who was willing to pay for the chemicals. In return, the backer would receive a prearranged amount of product. When asked if he had any backers in the Sherman area, he said he did but wouldn't reveal any names.

When asked if the cops were on the take, he told them the sheriffs in Durant, Oklahoma, and in Sherman, Texas, were on the take for drugs, money, and girls from a brothel in Cartwright, Oklahoma. Everyone referred to the brothel as "Mama Feel Good." He and Bear met cops often at the Texoma Gun Club to coordinate the dope deals.

Ches confirmed that he had a light-blue Blazer with a white top and that Lynn drove a dark-blue Blazer in the early part of the '80s. These matched the vehicles that were identified by the lady in Denison who saw the men at the B&B Ranch around 5:30 on October 8, 1983.

The following day, Mindy and Anthony drove to Huntsville, Texas, to interview a man who had been identified as a drug runner for Bob Tate. He confirmed he was in the dope business and was one of Bob Tate's runners. This was one of the tips that was called in before the trial to the sheriff's office and one we found on a call sheet when putting the notebooks together. But we couldn't use it at trial because of the deal that was made between Klein and the prosecution about disparaging the reputation of any of the victims.

On September 20, 1990, Roy drove attorneys Grace Speights and Mindy Hatton to Ardmore, Oklahoma, to meet with Bear at a local restaurant. When he arrived, he was clean-shaven and his shoulder-length hair had been cut.

Bear talked freely, saying Ches was a gun freak and always had several with him. Ches was a specialist or sniper while in the army in Vietnam. He admitted knowing Larry and Ricky. He was very proud he had helped set up Larry and Ricky to take the fall on one of the drug busts, in hopes they'd get caught and arrested. He tried to do the same to Ches, but it didn't work.

After bragging about that, Bear said he didn't want Ches to know where he was. It was obvious he was afraid of him. Two Oklahoma sheriffs had told Roy that Bear was capable of murder "without a doubt." If that guy was afraid of Ches, then Ches must be really bad.

Roy had put the word out that he wanted to talk to Larry. At 10:30 A.M. on September 25, 1990, Larry finally contacted him. Roy asked him about Ches, and he said he did know him. He was reluctant to talk about him, though.

When Roy mentioned Bear, he could almost feel the phone heat up. Larry hated Bear. He drove for him on some jobs, he said, but he knew Bear set him up and did the same with Ricky. Bear wasn't too smart, but he was the one who dreamed up all their deals, according to Ches.

When asked if he knew about any contacts Bear had in Sherman, Ches said he heard about a cop in Sherman that Bear knew, but he didn't know his name. He asked if Bear carried a gun on their runs, and Larry said he did. Roy asked Larry if he carried a gun when he drove for Bear. He did for his own protection, he admitted, but he would not give Roy a description of his weapon.

Roy decided he might as well go for it, as they had been dancing around the obvious. He told Larry he had been named as a participant in a quadruple murder in Sherman, Texas. He described the murders, including the man in the doorway. Larry was silent. Roy told him he needed information to get Bear and Ches. But Larry wouldn't budge.

"Larry, do you understand what I'm telling you?" Roy asked.

He broke his silence. "Yes, but I don't know anything about it."

That was the end of Roy's only contact with Larry.

The only one left to find was Ricky. On October 13, 1990, a deputy from Kingston, Oklahoma, called and told Roy he had seen Ricky in a car he stopped the night before on a minor traffic offense. He gave him a description of the car and the name of the driver.

Roy traced the owner to Valliant, Oklahoma. The car belonged to Ricky's mother, the mother who didn't want anything to do with him. In a telephone interview with someone in Valliant, Roy was able to find out that Ricky was living with a girl in Idabel, Oklahoma. He discovered where the girl lived and got directions to the house.

Rather than take off to Idabel on a wild goose chase, Roy called the county attorney's office in Idabel and spoke with the secretary. He explained who Ricky was and why he needed to talk to him. He gave her the directions he had to see if they made sense and might lead to a real place. After reading the description, she said, "I live just down the road from that house, and I've seen that man in the front yard."

Finally, Ricky had been located, and the last suspect could be interviewed. Anthony Roth flew in from Washington this time to interview Ricky. They found the house where Ricky supposedly was living. The girl had been identified through a search, and the black Pontiac Fiero parked in the drive was registered in her name.

She answered their knock, and when asked if she was the woman who had been identified as living there, she said no. They asked her if she knew Ricky or if he was staying at the house. She said she didn't know anyone by that name and closed the door.

The trail had dried up.

Roy left Ricky's picture and details with the sheriff's office, and Anthony went back to Washington.

In July 1991, Roy got a call from the assistant chief of police in Idabel saying they had his guy Ricky in their jail. He had been picked up the night before for driving without a license and for possession of marijuana. This time, Grace would fly from DC to hopefully interview Ricky.

One of the detectives with the police department sat in on the interview. Ricky said he and Larry had met Witness #1 and her friend at Texoma in the summer of 1983. They had lived together for a while, he confirmed. He had known Larry since he was about sixteen and heard he was running with a guy named Ches.

Ricky casually talked about the good old days. He knew Bear and got started by selling narcotics for him. It was an easy job, and he made a lot of money until he ended up serving a seven-year sentence for the manufacture of a controlled dangerous substance.

Roy told Ricky that he and Larry had been implicated in a quadruple murder as the triggermen. Upon hearing this, he became less talkative, not as cocky as he had been when talking about some of his jobs. He leaned in more and clasped his hands together, looking down at them.

Grace asked him where he lived in 1983. He told her that he and his wife lived in Denison.

Roy asked him if he had ever heard of Larry driving and being a back-up man for Bear. He said yes, and Larry made big money doing it. He denied being involved with them, even though he already admitted he ran narcotics for Bear.

The detective took him back to his cell and told Anthony and Roy it was obvious that he knew more than he was telling them just by the way he was acting.

Roy Taylor began his investigation on November 6, 1989, to find the actual murderers of four men in Grayson County based on information from the woman we now referred to as Witness #1. He worked tirelessly on much more than what is reflected in this chapter. And the more he uncovered, the more he was convinced of Les's innocence. Les's acquittal became almost an obsession for Roy Taylor, as everything he discovered made it more evident that Les was innocent. And he was determined he could get him out of prison.

The new attorneys were putting together an appeal to the federal district court, and Roy was an essential part of the team. All the information he uncovered made it possible for Roy to discover much more information than we had at the original trial and was used during the evidentiary hearing in 2000 to try to get Les a new trial.

Witness #1 had handed us the clues to uncover what happened on the evening of October 8, 1983, and Roy Taylor had taken those clues and found all the hidden answers, the truths, and all the players. He had become part of our family, our team, searching for justice. He wanted it as much as we did.

Roy was diagnosed with lung cancer in the early months of 1998 and died July 12, 1998, at the age of fifty-six. He left a lovely wife, Jane, and three beautiful young daughters much too soon. I stay in contact with all of them and treasure their friendship, grieving that loss tremendously. Roy shared with his family that he regretted that he was not able to do more to get Les Bower out of prison.

Interlude

Time goes on, yet our love stands still,
Anxiously awaiting the breath of life
To fill us once more, granting us permission
To love again.
Time is gone forever, yet our love will never die,
For it is rooted deep within each other
And deep within the love of God,
Who is the author of all things,
The creator of time
And of love.

October 27, 1984

CHAPTER 21

Appeals

People often ask why those who are given the death penalty remain in prison so long before they are executed. The shortest answer I can think of is the appeal process. Yet the appeal process is necessary to prevent a jury from finding someone guilty, marching him or her out the back door of the courthouse, and hanging them as we once did.

Those who strongly advocate for the death penalty feel the process is too lengthy and costs the taxpayers too much money. One of the most illogical and idiotic terms I have heard within the judicial system is "an automatic appeal." I was told after Les's conviction and death sentence that he would have "an automatic appeal." There was nothing automatic about it. I think his took about five years. As good as our justice system may be, it is flawed.

The purpose of this book is not to condemn the system or anyone associated with it. Before Les was arrested, we took it for granted that innocent people were not put in prison, much less executed. One might call us naive or even ignorant, and perhaps we were. We trusted that justice would always prevail. We were wrong. And if you are wrongfully convicted, it is not easy to get that wrong made right.

Working on college campuses for almost ten years, I was constantly in the middle of discussions and debates with the professors, as well as the students, on subjects like the death penalty. Oddly enough, it was 1982, just one year before the murders in Texas, and several students and faculty members were in the housing and counseling office at Mesa College in Grand Junction when a very cerebral discussion on the subject was held right at my desk. Les happened to be there, as he had come to take me to lunch, and later we commented to one another that we had never really thought much about it before.

I could write a whole book about the injustices that have been wrought on innocent people, but that is not my purpose here, and there are plenty out there already. I'm sharing the story of what happened to us, how we took our rights for granted, and how we trusted in "truth, justice, and the American way."

When you see someone's picture in a newspaper or flashed on a television screen because they've been accused or maybe arrested, your mind almost immediately decides they are guilty. That's not a tested theory, but I bet it would be an interesting survey to take at your next dinner party.

In a country where we are presumed innocent until found (notice the slogan says "found," not proven) guilty, I fear that concept is often upside down. We've seen it go either way. The innocent are found guilty, or the guilty are found innocent. Every now and then, we get it right.

Our system—as good as it might be and better than some—needs some changes. There's a reason there are hundreds of movies, TV shows, and books out there portraying the fallacy of the judicial system. Most look at them through the eyes of someone who has never been in such a situation, and also as someone who thinks, *Surely that can't happen often, if ever.*

I think one of our brilliant appellate attorneys, Anthony Roth, said it best in 2008 as we waited for a stay of execution for Les:

"Whatever you think about the benefits of having capital punishment, no one could possibly argue that executing an innocent man is in the interests of the state or our society. Our interests as lawyers and as people should be that our government, when in doubt, should not go forward with an execution. There is ample evidence to give people reasonable doubt about whether Les committed these murders. In my view, the evidence is compelling that he didn't."

When Les was arrested on January 20, 1984, we knew nothing about judiciary procedure, politics, and especially about "the good old boy club." One might say I have a tainted opinion on this subject. I would argue that I've had life lessons on it. I'm certainly not an expert, but I am much more enlightened than I was before.

With the exception of the Fifth Circuit in New Orleans, Sherman was always the location of hearings. I dreaded going to Sherman because of the reporters and all of the attention we seemed to draw. As more information became available to the public, I began to see a nod of a head in my direction or a smile on someone's face when they passed me.

One day, I was coming out of the courthouse after a hearing as a woman drove straight toward the sidewalk I was standing on, pulled her car up to the curb right in front, jumped out, and ran through the throng of reporters to get to me. She grabbed my hand, looking panicked and flushed.

"Is the hearing over?" she asked, gasping for breath. "I meant to get here earlier, but I couldn't. Is it over? What happened?"

"Yes," I answered, somewhat confused and not sure whether to be afraid. She was a woman about sixty or so, and I didn't recall ever seeing her before.

"They denied his appeal," I said, assuming she would be pleased. But I was wrong. Her face fell, she began to cry, and she reached over and hugged me.

"I'm so sorry," she cried. "I have lived in Sherman all my life and was here for the trial. I pray for him, for you and your children. He didn't do this! I know he didn't do this. I'm so sorry."

We both stood there for a moment, my family looking over to make sure I was all right, reporters watching this unfold, while she and I stood, hugging one another and crying. Her racing to get there in time, desperate to know what the outcome was, gave me hope that I couldn't judge a town by my experience. That's what some had done of me, of us. We weren't the monsters they thought we were, and neither was Sherman. I still had a lot to learn.

During those thirty-one years between 1984 and 2015, there were multiple filings, appeals, hearings, and investigations. There were also long stretches of time that would seem to never end as we waited for decisions from various courts and judges.

Les had eight execution dates set, each one causing a flurry of briefs and appeals to stop them. There were seven stays of execution, most coming within a week or two of the execution date. Thankfully, those seven stays of execution came in enough time that they did not have to transport Les from the Polunsky Unit in Livingston where death row was to the Walls Unit in Huntsville where executions were done. He was only taken to the Walls Unit one time. That was at noon on June 3, 2015, to face his 6:00 P.M. execution order.

Les had been granted an evidentiary hearing in 2000 by Judge Richard Schell of the United States District Court for the Eastern District of Texas. That was a huge win for us. I was not aware that a motion for appeal like this had to be based on a constitutional amendment. In his case, we used the Sixth Amendment, stating that Les had been denied his right to an effective defense attorney against the charges he had been accused of.

To give an example of some of the reasons our system needs to be reassessed, one death row inmate filed an ineffective assistance of counsel appeal, stating his attorney slept during most of his original trial. Investigations showed that this allegation was true; however, the appellate court ruled against the inmate, as it was felt the attorney sufficiently performed his duties as a court-appointed attorney for the inmate.

The information Witness #1 gave us allowed the appellate attorneys and investigator to find corroborating testimony by other witnesses, revealing what happened on the night of October 8, 1983, showing Les was not the killer. But that information would need to be put to the judge in a way that showed Les's trial attorney did not do an effective job in handling the case, researching the facts of the case, and finding others who were out there to corroborate the facts, thus granting a new trial.

During the evidentiary hearing in Judge Schell's court in 2000, our appellate attorneys brought several witnesses to corroborate Witness #1's story. One of the witnesses was someone she had met at a Narcotics Anonymous meeting shortly after the murders. She shared during the meeting about her boyfriend telling her that he and some other guys had killed four people in Denison and that she was afraid of them because they had threatened to kill her.

At a break in the meeting, a young man came up to her and said that one of the men who had been killed was a very good friend of his. They talked for some time about his loss and her fear of the killers.

When our attorney approached him to corroborate Witness #1's testimony, he was reluctant to come and testify mainly because of the "anonymity" pledge of Narcotics Anonymous. It was imperative that the judge hear this testimony, because she had told him about her boyfriend before she knew Les was arrested. We gave him the title of Witness #2 to protect his anonymity so his testimony could be sealed. He came to Sherman and corroborated Witness #1's testimony.

Prosecutors were not considering Witness #1's testimony as being reliable because of her history with drugs. Bringing in another witness who had been told the story so soon after the murders and prior to an arrest gave more credence to the information being correct and not something she just made up after seeing the papers.

Through some of the investigation that was done after Witness #1 came forward, the team found a former drug user in Sherman to testify at Les's hearing in Schell's court. The man had a dealer he bought drugs from who lived in the Sherman/Denison area. He went to buy drugs one day, and his dealer said they weren't there yet but would be in about thirty minutes. He advised the buyer to go run some errands and come back later.

Instead of leaving the neighborhood, the buyer had a friend who lived down the street a few houses on the other side. He went to see his friend, and they sat out on the front porch drinking beer and waiting for the drugs to arrive.

It wasn't too long before they saw a law enforcement officer's car drive down the street and pull up in front of the dealer's house. An officer got out of the car with a zippered bank bag in his hand. He walked up to the front door and walked right in. In less than five minutes, the officer walked out of the house—without the bank bag—and returned to his car and drove off.

The two guys on the porch had watched this scenario. As soon as the officer left, they got up, walked across the street, and went into the drug dealer's house. On the coffee table in the living room was the bank bag. It was lying open on the table, and the drugs were inside. His dealer now had product to sell. It had always been known by some, suspected by others, that local law enforcement often sold confiscated drugs back to the street dealers, rotating the product in the front door and out the back.

Two other witnesses came forward after the trial to testify in Schell's court that they had been in or around the scene of the crime around 5:00 P.M. on the evening of the murders and saw several cars and men around the house and hangar. They were able to describe some of the men, many who fit the description of the real killers, as having been on the property. The time of day they saw them would also corroborate Les's account of his leaving the hangar prior to that time, as well as the time that he arrived at home.

Witness #1 testified once more about what she knew and what she saw and heard from the killers at one of Les's last hearings in district court in 2012. She never gave up on trying to help him get a new trial. Once more, she was considered unreliable, even though she had been clean for years. We were always hopeful they would believe her, but again, we were devastated. So many other witnesses backed her up on her story; it was hard to believe we could not get some relief.

The hearings again were before a single judge. We were still in a small town where the murders took place, and despite the fact that there was a different judge than the one at the trial and a different county attorney, the camaraderie of the judicial seat and the prosecution was one that could not be overlooked, especially when winks were exchanged between bench and table. This particular day, I had been sequestered. Probably the only time in all these years I found myself literally ten feet outside the doors of the courtroom. Sitting on a backless bench in a courthouse hall for eight hours wondering what was going on inside is very exhausting, both mentally and physically. If you've become accustomed to being "on the inside" at every hearing, seeing the mannerisms and the nuances of each witness, of each attorney, and most importantly, of your husband, being left on the outs can drive you crazy.

But that is exactly what the county attorney asked for and what she got. I had never missed a day of trial or a hearing since this had begun.

The first witness was called to testify, and I found myself sitting on that bench with a petite woman with short, curly hair, glasses, and very nervous hands shaking ever so slightly. I had never met her before, but I knew who she was. It was Amy, the widow of one of the four men our investigators had uncovered as being the actual murderers.

She would be called to testify for the first time. I was busy being annoyed at not being inside, where I felt I should be, trying to figure out what I was going to do out there in the hall for who knows how long, when I suddenly felt like introducing myself to her.

"Hi," I said as I turned toward her. "I'm Shari Bower. You must be Amy."

A surprised look came over her face as it registered for the first time who I was. The confusion turned into a smile, and she suddenly threw her arms around me, hugged me, and then pulled back to say, "Oh, it's you. I'm so glad to meet you finally."

And so began a three-and-a-half-hour journey I never dreamed I would take.

I immediately thanked Amy for coming and for what she was doing for us by testifying. She admitted to me that she was very nervous. I assured her she would be fine and not to worry about it. She then told me that she had not seen the witness who was now testifying, Witness #1, in over twenty-five years.

Amy and I began to talk about anything and everything, yet nothing about the case, which was exactly what we had been instructed to do. We covered children and where we lived, what we did for a living; we discussed parents and aging, death of loved ones, and how it impacted us. I asked her how she and her husband had met and when they married. She began to dig in her purse and pulled out some pictures to show me of her and her husband, taken sometime in the early '80s. She handed them to me, and I stared at a black-and-white picture of this huge man, as tall as the Christmas tree in the background. He had his arm around this petite woman whose head was snuggled beneath his arm. She had long, curly hair, and they were both smiling big for whomever was on the other side of the camera.

He had a huge head of dark, unruly hair that stuck out from all sides, and his bushy beard hung down to at least where the second button on a shirt would be. I stared at him for some time. It was the man who was there the day those four men were murdered, the man they called Bear—supposedly the biggest meth cooker in southern Oklahoma at that time, the man some thought resembled Les. I didn't see the resemblance. Maybe because I knew his personality. From a distance and with a hat on, they could have been mistaken for the other, but I knew better.

I was sitting next to his wife, and we were sharing pictures from our wallets. I looked at the picture once more and said, "You are so tiny next to him and look so happy." That's all I could think of. The picture was taken in December. It was Christmastime. *Was it December of 1983? Had he just killed those men two months earlier?*

She went on to tell me that she met him right after he had gotten out of prison. He had been in for eight years, and she never knew what he was in for. She said Bear had met Ches in prison. Amy and Bear got married and began a life of methamphetamine. Somewhere along the way, they started an insulation company, and in 1987, their son was born.

I asked her if she was doing meth and alcohol when she was pregnant. As the question came out of my mouth, I couldn't believe I was being so personal, but she didn't seem to mind. We had already established a very strange but connected relationship.

She told me that she quit using while she was pregnant and even gave up caffeine. I commended her for her decision and told her that was one of the greatest gifts she could have given her son.

Amy went on to tell me her story of them living in Lone Grove, Oklahoma, and running their insulation company there. I didn't mention to her that was where Les's sister had lived for years. I also didn't tell her that my sister-in-law had kept up with them since we had found out he was one of the murderers. She didn't need to know that.

I asked Amy how long she had been clean, and she shared her journey to sobriety with me. She had quit meth about twelve years ago but had started heavily drinking instead. Eventually, she and her husband divorced. Amy made him leave; once he did so, she and her son were all alone. She was drinking a lot, but Amy and Bear were still working the business together. She decided if she continued down the path she was heading, she was going to die. She planned to detox herself but knew it would probably kill her. So she went to a nearby rehab facility and begged them to take her.

I asked if she still went to meetings, and she said no. She took each day of sobriety with the idea of doing this for herself and her son. She told me her son uses, though.

"When I returned from rehab right before Christmas in 2002, I told him I didn't have a present for him. He said that my getting sober was the best present I could give him."

I smiled and said to her, "Then maybe you should tell him you want that present back but from him."

She looked at me thoughtfully and said, "That's a good idea. I like that."

Amy went on to tell me that her then ex-husband Bear was diagnosed with cancer. He lived alone, and there was no one to take care of him. She felt that he did not need to be alone in his last days and that he certainly needed to be with his son before he died. So they remarried, and he returned home where she cared for him until he died.

I was taken by surprise when she asked me why our attorneys had not come to them in 2000 like we had Witness #1. I told her she came to us—we didn't go to her. But still, she asked, "Why did no one ever come to see her husband before he died?"

I just looked at her for a minute and said, "Do you really think he would have talked to us?"

With a deep sigh, she answered, "Probably not. Probably not."

She then asked me the one thing that almost everyone asks: "I don't know how you have been so strong all these years. How do you do that?"

I told her that only through God's love and grace did any of us manage to get through all of this for this long.

"Do you believe in God?" I asked her.

"I'm not religious, but I believe in God."

"I don't consider myself religious either. Religion is a church, a denomination, but I believe in God and know, without a doubt, that had I been the only person on this earth, Jesus would have *still* gone to the cross and died for my sins. Being religious doesn't have anything to do with it. Accepting Christ as our Savior is what it's about."

She was listening carefully, clearly interested in my passion behind such an important topic.

"Do you know, Amy, that He did that for you too?"

She just stared at me and said, "I really hadn't thought about it that way."

"Amy, would you like for us to pray together, and you can ask Christ to be Lord of your life?"

"I'm pretty nervous," she said. "But let's go for it."

So there in that hallway, on that padded but backless bench, she took my hand and we put our heads together and I prayed. I prayed that God would engulf her in His loving arms and calm her mind, her thoughts, and her words. She prayed with me and asked Jesus to be her Savior. I prayed for her continued sobriety and thanked Him for getting her this far. I asked that she remain a steadfast example for her son and that he, too, would feel the love and comfort of God all around him and he would choose to give up using drugs. I prayed that God would go forward in their lives and show them His mercy and love. And then I thanked Him for bringing the two of us together on this day, in this hallway, on this bench to become sisters in Christ in a very unlikely situation. As I said amen, she looked up, tears glistening in her eyes, and hugged me once again.

Who would have thought?

Amy went on to testify and tell her story about her husband's involvement with the group of guys that Witness #1 had testified about. She and Bear's now-adult son testified as well that his father had bragged about the killings in Denison. Still, no one in the county attorney's office or the judge took them seriously because they were or had been drug users and dealers and were surely lying. *But why would they lie?* We weren't paying them. Our family could not even find help for Witness #1 and her family when they needed it, when her grandchildren were ill, when her washer broke. Our attorneys told us we couldn't help. It was cruel, and we felt awful, but it would appear as a bribe if anyone found out.

After the first day of this particular hearing, a couple in Durant, Oklahoma, not far from Sherman, was watching the news and saw what was going on with Lester Bower's appeal. Both of them knew and had worked with some of the men who had been accused of being the real killers—Bear in particular.

They decided they had to drive to Sherman and talk to the police. They knew Les was innocent. The next morning, they pawned some things to get enough money for gas and drove to Sherman. They first went to the police station to give them a report of what they knew, but the police referred them to our attorneys at the hotel where we were staying, as they would be testifying on Les's behalf.

They, too, testified that Bear had told them about murdering the four people in the hangar in Sherman on October 8, 1983. When asked, they said he definitely was capable of such a crime. As the couple left the courthouse after hearing their testimony had done nothing to help Les, they cried bitter tears. After years of getting clean and trying to turn their lives around, they wanted to do something right and help an innocent man. But no one would believe them.

Odd that all these former drug users who all lived and worked around or with these alleged killers told the same story and had nothing to gain by coming forward to do the right thing and no one would believe them. No one, that is, behind the bench.

At the end of the hearing in 2012, when Judge James Fallon had denied Les a new hearing, Fallon made a strange statement that said much about the judicial process: "While Bower's evidence that someone else committed the crime *could conceivably have produced a different result at trial, it does not prove by clear and convincing evidence that [Bower] is actually innocent*" (emphasis added).

Many lawyers and scholars of the judicial system across the country not only read that statement by the judge but also condemned the double standard of justice when appealing a conviction.

My Heart Is So Full

My heart is so full and yet so broken. As I look into your eyes,
The pain of the memories behind the gaze is almost more than I can bear.
Yet the joy in the love that passes between us causes my heart to leap.
You guard your heart so carefully, for fear that it might break.
So instead, I weep for us both, giving way to the overwhelming
Grief of separation, loneliness, and fear.
And though you smile as if to say, "Don't cry,"
Your own tears filling your eyes betray your valiant façade.
There are no words to tell you how very much I love you.
Instead, look into my eyes, past the tears, and see my heart.
Because though it appears to be breaking, it overflows with love.

February 15, 2000

CHAPTER 22

The Girl in the Pigtail Braids

We made some of the best friends while living in College Station. We hadn't been there long when we met our neighbors, Joe and Bobbie. They lived one row over with their six-month-old daughter, Laurel. We became good friends with them and several other young couples in the area, sharing many meals as we all struggled to pay tuition, study, hold down jobs, and raise new families. It was a fun time, and we made some long-lasting friendships.

We babysat Laurel now and then, giving her parents a night out or when they were in class. Les and I were newlyweds and had no plans to start a family any time soon, but we enjoyed spending time with that little one.

Our bed was covered with a handmade quilt given to us by one of our grandmothers as a wedding gift. Les and I would play with the baby on the quilt after she woke up from a nap, teaching her to identify the various colors in the different fabrics.

She was a quick learner, always pointing to one of the squares on the quilt and waiting for Les to call a color. He would say blue, red, or yellow—whichever the color might be. Once she pointed to a multicolored plaid square. He paused for a moment, then quickly said, "Muckle-dee-duck." She obediently answered, repeating back in her little toddler voice, butchering many of the words she was trying to say. We looked at each other, surprised that she had managed the word as well as she had, but also concerned about how it might sound if she were to use it again, perhaps mispronouncing it a bit.

When her parents came to get her, she proudly showed off her new skills by repeating all the colors she had learned, including Les's new word for plaid. She stumbled a bit over the word, and her mom gave us a look that said, "What have you done to my child?" Joe laughed under his breath, shaking his head in dismay. That story, however, became one of our favorite "bringing up Laurel" stories from our early days in College Station.

Laurel got a new brother about a year later, and we helped welcome him into the world just before leaving A&M. We kept in touch with a lot of the friends we made there. Laurel's family was one we not only kept up with but also visited and vacationed with for many years.

They moved back to west Texas, and we ended up in Colorado. They were excited about being able to come visit us in Colorado, as they all shared a love for hunting. Our firstborn came along about the same time their third child did, and our families shared many memories together thereafter.

When Les was arrested, their family was one of many friends that were in shock and disbelief. Soon after Les's arrest, I had to move from the house we were living in to another house, as the owners were selling. Joe traveled to Arlington to help me sell household and sporting goods in order to have money to live on. He inventoried and took all the guns back home with him where he was going to sell them for me. I had no idea how to do that or what they were worth. They were always a constant source of encouragement during that time, calling, sending me letters, and writing Les often.

They were living in Houston when the trial began. They packed up the kids, taking them out of school, and headed for Sherman. They sat through all the proceedings. Laurel was fifteen, and her brother and sister were thirteen and eleven. It really didn't occur to me then that their kids were sitting through the trial and the testimony, hearing all the things I was trying to keep our own kids away from.

I would find out years later that our twelve-year-old daughter was quite upset that her friends, who were her own age, were allowed to be in the courtroom when she wasn't. I never thought about it from her perspective. She had a point. But I'm not sure Les and I would have done it differently even knowing how she felt.

From the time Les was arrested to the end of the trial, he and I decided to keep our children out of Grayson County. The jail was so dismal, the community so hostile. We chose instead to let them talk to their daddy on the phone now and then but not to take them to visit. He wrote them letters, and they wrote him back. It was a horrible place, and Les did not want them to see him there. He was trying as hard as he could to keep his emotions intact, and he was afraid he would fall apart if he saw them—or if they saw him—in jail.

We believed he would only be there a little while. Hoping to get this all worked out and protect our children from the hell we were going through, we didn't realize how hard it was on them not seeing their daddy. We just thought the more we kept them from the crisis, the better off they would be. Would I do it differently if I had it to do over? Probably. But I'm not sure how. Of course, if it were even possible to have a do-over, there would be so many things on my list.

It would be many years before I would learn only a little of how my children felt during that time. I'm sure I still don't know all that they suffered, felt, and grieved during those months before he was convicted. Or even the years that followed.

I thought we were being open with our children, encouraging them when they wanted to talk about it, but telling them as much as one can tell a twelve-year-old and an eight-year-old about why their father was not at home and why he was in jail. But I don't remember exactly what I said to them or what was said by the myriad of others who helped care for them during that time.

I remember putting Hollie to bed one night when she asked me a question.

"Mom, do you have any money?" she asked as I tucked her in.

"I might have a little," I answered. "What do you need money for?"

"I thought if we had some money, we might be able to get Daddy out of jail," she replied with a pained look on her face and a catch in her throat, holding back tears.

"Honey, I'm afraid we don't have that much money right now." That's all I could say as I took her in my arms and tried to comfort her. "But don't you worry about it. We'll figure something out."

I realized that we had been talking about raising bail money and money to pay the attorney, and she thought if we could get enough money, he could come home.

Years later, our oldest daughter told me that she dug newspapers out of the garbage and watched news stories on TV without our knowledge in a desperate attempt to be informed. She was very upset that we didn't tell her everything that was going on. And she had every right to be. But she was our little girl. And as parents, we were trying to protect her.

And so, on Friday evening, April 27, 1984, after hearing the four guilty verdicts handed down by the jury, we found our family and friends who had been at the trial all week gathered together with Les's attorney to decide how to proceed the next day with the punishment hearing.

Klein, with his usual drink in hand, sat with us around the pool and told us that he needed only five or six people to testify the next day as character witnesses for Les. He said he felt like it would be best if only women spoke on his behalf. Then he started pointing to various women sitting around the pool and said, "One, two, three, four, five, six."

There was no discussion as to why he chose the ones he did nor any direction for them as to what they were to say. He only told them not to insult the jury or to make them mad in any way, as the guilty decision had already been decided.

The six women Richard Klein called to the stand the next day were Cheryl Smiley (Les's younger sister), Denise Bower (Les's youngest sister), Jo Wreyford (my mother), Wilma Bower (Les's mother), Kelli Hamilton (my sister), and fifteen-year-old Laurel.

I thought Laurel was an odd choice given her age, but I knew she was bright and articulate and had a deep love and respect for Les.

I especially thought it odd when she appeared in court the next day in overalls with her hair braided in pigtails—a look I had not seen on her before.

April 28, 1984
Punishment Hearing and Sentencing of Defendant, Lester Leroy Bower Jr., 15th Judicial District Court, Grayson County Justice Center, Sherman, Texas

Klein asked Laurel to state her name and tell the jury what her relationship with Les was. She replied that she had known him all her life, as we were friends with her parents in college.

He also asked if she knew anything about Les that would make her think he might do something violent in the future. She replied no, he wouldn't.

He then asked her to turn and tell the jury what she knew about Les. She told the jurors the history of our families' relationship and how he had helped raise her. He had taught her how to walk and talk. He would tell her stories and read books to her. He often took her with him to run errands or go to the library when her parents were in class.

She told them he would take her and her brother and sister and his own two daughters on camping trips. He taught them a lot about nature and about animals. "He gave us a love of the outdoors that we never would have had."

It was strange to watch her sitting on that witness stand, an adolescent who was dressed as a child recalling childhood days. Everyone sat and listened carefully to her testimony, as it was obvious she was smart and intuitive. I just couldn't imagine why Klein had requested the costume.

"Les would play with us for hours. We would play on the hay bales. He taught us how to shoot a bow and arrow. On holidays, he would take time out of his life to do special things with us."

The jurors were all turned toward her, listening intently. Klein walked back and forth in front of her as he asked his questions.

She went on to say how Les was always fair and just. "He never raised his voice to any of us. If anything ever needed to be said, he would say it quietly and firmly, and we knew what was expected of us. He was always a good father and a good friend. He has always had a good sense of humor. And no matter what, he always found a way to smile about things."

As she grew older, Laurel explained, Les took time out just to talk to her. He would spend time not only to talk to a little girl but also to listen. And he had been a better friend than most people she ever met.

Laurel was the last character witness of the punishment phase of the trial.

She went on to finish high school and then graduate from Abilene Christian University with a Bachelor of Arts degree in mass communications with a specialization in radio and television. She began her career in radio and television in Abilene and went on to larger markets, expanding her career along the way. Laurel kept in touch with Les and with our family, as he continued to appeal his sentence.

Laurel had not shared with anyone, including her parents, about Klein's behavior toward her, a fifteen-year-old girl, during the time she was in Sherman for the trial. She became aware of the appeal that was being prepared, accusing Klein of ineffectiveness of counsel, and called the Morgan Lewis law firm in Washington, DC, to speak to one of Les's attorneys. She gave them information regarding Klein's behavior toward her during the trial. She felt they should know this piece of information prior to the hearing.

She didn't have to do that. Sharing her story could be harmful to her career. But Laurel was and is a person who does the right thing.

June 12, 2000
Evidentiary Hearing of Lester Leroy Bower Jr.
United States District Court, Eastern District of Texas, Beaumont Division, Sherman, Texas

After the swearing in of all parties who would be testifying in the evidentiary hearing to determine if Les was denied effective counsel in his original trial for murder in 1984, Richard Klein was the first witness the state called on June 12, 2000.

He testified for some time, answering questions from the state's attorney and then subsequent cross-examination by Les's attorney, Peter Buscemi. He ended his testimony, claiming he had done an exceptional job defending his client during the trial, and neither Les nor Shari had voiced any concerns or unhappiness on how he conducted the defense. He also testified that we were all in agreement that Les should not testify.

Once the questioning was finished, the court asked Mr. Buscemi if he had any further questions for Mr. Klein. He did not. The judge asked the other attorneys if it was all right to excuse the witness. Mr. Buscemi and Mr. Marshall both said it was. The judge informed Mr. Klein that even though he was excused, he was welcome to stay for the rest of testimony during the hearing.

But Klein said, "Thank you, Your Honor. I believe I'll be on my way back."

And with that, Richard Klein left the federal courthouse in Sherman, where the rest of the testimony during this hearing would be about whether he was effective or ineffective in representing his client, Lester Bower, in a quadruple capital murder case.

That seemed a little odd to most of us, as this hearing was all about him. There would be witnesses testifying about things he had not handled professionally. I was shocked he was going to leave.

Instead of going to his car, however, he stepped outside and gave an interview to the local TV and newspaper reporters as to what a good job he had done and what an excellent attorney he was.

Sometime during the course of the hearing, our appellate team called Laurel to testify on Les's behalf. She was tall and as beautiful as she had always been—only now, a beautiful woman and not a child. Her hair was blond and fashionably styled, and her smile was as illuminating as ever. She rose gracefully from her chair when she was called and took the stand.

She started by telling the court that she was currently employed as a television news anchor and reporter for an NBC affiliate. She anchored the 5:00 P.M. and 10:00 P.M. weekday news. She had been in television news for eight years and had worked in radio previous to that.

She recalled her story of how she knew Les and me from the time she was an infant until now. She described Les as a father figure to some degree and that she attended his trial in 1984 when she was fifteen years old.

Peter Buscemi, our brilliant lead attorney, was handling her interrogation. Peter had tried many cases in his career, some in front of the Supreme Court. He was a man of average height with dark, curly hair and a northeastern accent that was probably very odd to the many Texans who sat in the courtroom. Peter could fill a room just with his presence. He was articulate and spoke in a loud voice that commanded one's attention. He was always precise in his questioning and in control of his emotions. Now and then, I could see he was angry, but he would control it so as to be more effective than offensive. He stood before Laurel and continued his questions.

Buscemi: Ms. Middleton, what, if any, impressions did you form during the trial?

Middleton: My general impression was that the conduct and attitudes didn't seem to suit the gravity of the situation facing Les Bower or the charges that he faced.

Buscemi: And in what sense do you mean that?

Middleton: His attorney, Richard Klein, did not appear to me to be addressing questions and issues that were raised by the prosecution throughout the case.

Buscemi: Did you have occasion to meet Mr. Klein at Les Bower's trial?

Middleton: Yes.

Buscemi: And could you tell the court, please, the circumstances in which you first met Mr. Klein?

Middleton: We first saw Mr. Klein when we arrived and sat in on the last afternoon of jury selection.

Buscemi: And did you have occasion to speak to him at that time?

Middleton: Yes, we spoke. We were introduced, and we spoke in the elevator as we went downstairs in the courthouse.

Buscemi: Did Mr. Klein say anything to you on that occasion?

Middleton: When I met him, he complimented me on my appearance.

Buscemi: Was that your only conversation with Mr. Klein during the trial?

Middleton: No, I had other conversations with him throughout the week.

Buscemi: Tell the court, please, what you recall about other conversations that you and the people with you had with Mr. Klein.

Middleton: We would ask him questions about things that had happened during court that day.

Buscemi: What kind of questions, and how would he respond?

Middleton: We had concerns about issues that were raised by the prosecution that we did not feel were particularly addressed. He was very self-assured and reassured us by saying that all the evidence was circumstantial, that the jury would not convict Les on circumstantial evidence, and that he himself had never lost a circumstantial evidence case.

Buscemi: Now, in addition to these mealtime conversations with Mr. Klein when you were in the presence of the Bower family and other friends of Mr. Bower, did you ever have any conversations with Mr. Klein when others were not present?

Middleton: Yes, two conversations.

Buscemi: Would you tell the court, please, the circumstances and the content of the first of those?

Middleton: About the second day of the trial, during a recess in the courtroom, Mr. Klein walked up to me. It was only the two of us. No one else was immediately surrounding to hear the conversation. He told me that he had been having dreams of the two of us having sex at night and asked if I had the same dreams. I was too shocked to answer him.

I discreetly looked around the room to see the reaction of the spectators. Everyone seemed surprised by her statement, and there was a low hum in the room as some were talking to one another.

Laurel sat in the witness box, cool and collected, her hands folded in her lap. She looked at Peter when he was talking and the judge when she was responding. She showed no signs of being nervous or emotional.

Buscemi: And how did you respond?

Middleton: I walked away.

Buscemi: Would you tell the court, please, the circumstances and the content of your discussion on the second occasion in which you spoke to Mr. Klein outside the presence of others?

Middleton: I was walking down the sidewalk that's in front of the hotel doors, and he was standing in the doorway of his room with a drink in his hand. His wife had arrived in town at that point, and I assumed she was around. I asked him how he thought things were going in the case. He asked me to step inside for a moment; he offered me a drink. I declined, and, again, asked how he thought things were going—if we had a chance. He said once again that all the evidence was circumstantial and that he didn't think the jury would convict on that basis.

Buscemi: And did he say anything else to you at that time?

Middleton: Then again, he turned the conversation toward a sexual nature and said that he was still having sexual dreams about me and wanted to know if I was having the same dreams, and I said no. He asked if I would like having sex with him, and I didn't answer the question. And then about that time, his wife came back.

I was totally disgusted and wished that his wife was there right now to hear all this.

Buscemi: Came back from where? Do you know?

Middleton: She pulled up in her car and had ice cream. I assumed she had gone to get it.

Buscemi: Now do you recall when in the course of the trial this second conversation with Mr. Klein occurred?

Middleton: Toward the very end of the trial, but before Les was convicted, before the last day.

Buscemi: Before the day of closing argument and deliberation of the jury?

Middleton: I believe it was Thursday night, correct.

Buscemi: Did Mr. Klein choose you as one of the character witnesses for the penalty phase of the trial?

Middleton: Yes, he did. After a guilty verdict was returned, we were all basically in a panic. We met with him that evening, and he started to choose—pointing out people he wanted to testify, saying, "You, you, you, you," and I was one of the people he pointed to.

Buscemi: Did you have any meetings with Mr. Klein in which he prepared you for your testimony?

Middleton: I didn't meet with him at that time. He said, "I want you to talk about the ABC story." Earlier during the week during a dinner conversation, I had told him of how Les would babysit me as a young child and how he taught me to read, taught me letters, taught me numbers. And he said, "I want you to tell that story."

Buscemi: Did he give you any other advice about how you should appear or testify at the penalty phase the next day?

Middleton: He told me to appear as childlike as possible, to dress as much like a child as possible.

Buscemi: Did he give you any instructions or information about the kinds of questions that he would ask you?

Middleton: No.

Buscemi: Did he ask you, in addition to the ABC story and the story of Les teaching you how to read and your alphabet, whether you had any other information to offer to the jury about Les?

Middleton: No.

Buscemi: Thank you.

Court: Mr. Marshall, do you have any questions?

Marshall: We do not, Your Honor.

Court: You may stand down.

She rose from the witness stand and walked gracefully back to her seat, all eyes watching her. That is, all eyes but those of the state's attorneys. They busied themselves at their table pretending her testimony was irrelevant.

June 16, 2000
Evidentiary Hearing of Lester Leroy Bower Jr.
United States District Court, Eastern District of Texas, Beaumont Division, Sherman, Texas

The assistant attorney general called Klein back on the last day of the hearing to ask questions regarding some of the testimony that had come up during the week. The following is the questioning of Klein in regard to Laurel's testimony.

Marshall: The next question is a little interesting. Did you sexually proposition any members of Bower's family or his friends during the course of trial?

Klein: I think not. First of all, I don't remember there being any unattached females floating around. Second of all, I was busy with the trial. If I'm hired on a case, I figure to give it my best, and that's not the time to hustle girls. And like I said, I don't remember that there were any stray females around there, and whenever we met, we were in a group. But my answer is no.

Laurel, a successful, accomplished woman, risked having her name flaunted in newspapers and dug up to be used by Klein's opponents in future political battles when Klein ran for judge; she flew halfway across the country at her own expense to testify about something that was obviously a very uncomfortable event in her life. There was no reason for her to do so if it were not true.

More Like You

God, speak to my heart
So that I may know
What it is
You would have me to do.
Erase from my mind
All the pain and the fear
So that I might be
More every day like you.

August 24, 1985

CHAPTER 23

Encounters

August 2002

It was too hot to be running errands on that August afternoon. I chastised myself for once again buying something without making sure it was the correct replacement part and then having to return it. I found a parking spot near the entrance to the drugstore just as a black sports utility vehicle pulled in beside me. A tall, slender man got out of the vehicle and disappeared inside as I followed.

I explained to the young woman behind the register that I needed to make a return. She took my receipt and items, looked them over, and called for a manager. I stepped aside to wait, and the man who had come in ahead of me walked from the back of the store and got in line next to me. Looking up as he approached, I saw something familiar about his face. Immediately, I knew who he was.

We had never met, he and I, but I knew him. He was casually dressed in perfectly pressed jeans and a crisp white T-shirt. As we waited, I began thinking of ways I could start a conversation with him. This was the opportunity I had wanted for years and might never have again. There was so much I wanted to say to him. I had survived one of the worst nights of my life because God used this man to help me cope. I had waited so long to thank him.

"Is your daughter still at UTA?" I asked.

Surprised, he looked down at me and answered, "Yes, she's still in school." He was so much taller than I had expected. And still so very handsome, despite the years that had passed since his hit recording became so popular.

"She's a lovely girl. I met her at the coffee shop some months back when I was there with one of my friends who knows her."

"Yes, she works there now and then."

"My, but they grow up fast, don't they?" I responded, not knowing what I was going to say next. I never said his name, but he knew that I had recognized him. *This must happen to him a lot,* I thought. I knew he lived in Arlington, but I had never seen him around before today.

"I have another daughter getting married this year," he offered.

"I know how you feel," I replied. "Both of my daughters married a couple of years ago. And in the same year. That was a lot of fun," I said sarcastically.

"Wow! That must have been a lot of work." We shared a laugh over the thought of two daughters getting married just six months apart.

There was a brief silence as we stood there, strangers talking about important events in our lives. I felt the butterflies in my stomach and knew I needed to get to the point, or I might lose his attention.

"May I tell you a story?" I asked.

He tilted his head a bit, scrunching his eyebrows together, and said, "Sure."

I began to tell him the story I had wanted to tell him for so long.

"Sixteen years ago, my husband was arrested for something he didn't do." I rubbed my hands on my pant legs. "To our horror, he was tried, found guilty, and sentenced to death for four murders he did not commit."

"I'm sorry." His smile turned into a frown. I could see he was wondering why this stranger was telling him this.

"The night he was arrested," I continued, "twenty-three law enforcement officers came to our home and searched it. They pretty much tore it up from one end to the other."

"I can only imagine." His eyes never left mine.

"When they took my husband away, I couldn't believe what was happening," I said slowly, willing myself not to cry. "I was left alone with most of the officers still in my house, continuing their search." I paused for a moment, and he continued to keep eye contact. "It was almost midnight, and I could feel their eyes staring at me, waiting to see how I was going to react. Some of them were lying across our bed; some were smoking in our house." At this, he shook his head, frowning again, and I felt camaraderie with him, as if he were feeling my pain.

"They were going through all our drawers, cabinets, and closets. They had even searched our children's rooms. I had no idea what they were looking for or why they were there. I thought I might lose my mind."

He stood there, shifting his weight from one foot to another. "I'm sorry."

"God helped me keep my sanity for the rest of the night while I was alone and afraid," I said, "and it was *you* who He chose to help me get through that terrible nightmare."

His head rose slightly as a look of surprise registered on his face. But he said nothing.

"I asked the sheriff if they were finished in our children's bedrooms, and he told me they were. So I went to the kitchen, got dust rags and furniture polish, and went to my kids' rooms and began cleaning up the mess the officers had made. I couldn't just sit there and do nothing. I had to keep busy. I needed something to distract me from what was going on around me."

By now, we had stepped out of the line and stood in the middle of the store as people passed by.

"We had given our oldest daughter a stereo with a cassette player, and it was in her room. I reached down in her collection of cassettes and pulled one out to play. I began cleaning, trying somehow to put our lives back together . . . at least visibly, all the while singing along with you, 'The Faith of a Little Child.'"

There was a brief pause as he took this in, and then a soft smile appeared. We both stood there quietly in the middle of the busy drugstore, people coming and going around us.

"I have always wanted to thank you for that," I said softly.

B. J. Thomas, the legendary country and gospel singer, made famous by singing "Raindrops Keep Falling on My Head" from the movie *Butch Cassidy and the Sundance Kid*, looked at me and said, "You're welcome."

"I almost didn't recognize you," I said. "But when I looked into your face, I knew it was you."

"I've cut my hair and gained some weight," he replied with a slight chuckle.

"Well, you look great! And I firmly believe you and I were supposed to be here at the same time. Are you still performing?" I asked.

"Not gospel, but I do country and western. In fact, I'll be performing next week at Billy Bob's. What's your husband's name?" he asked.

"Les Bower, and my name is Shari."

He reached out, and we shook hands.

"I'm glad I had this opportunity to tell you how much you helped me."

A sweet smile formed on his lips. "I'm glad you stopped me to tell me your story."

"I often thought about writing you a letter, but this is much better in person. Good luck with the wedding."

"Good luck to you and your husband," he replied.

We finished our transactions and walked out of the store together. He got in his truck, I got in my car, and we drove away. I wondered if he told anyone of that strange encounter that day in the drugstore.

I also wondered if God placed B. J. there for me because he needed to hear my story. Or was I placed there because I needed to tell *him* my story?

Did I need to tell him after sixteen years how much his music had helped me make it through one of the worst nights of my life?

Or did he need to hear how much his music had helped someone he had never met make it through one of the worst nights of her life?

We'll never know. God knew who needed it the most. I'm guessing it was both of us.

I'm so glad I never got around to writing that letter. It was so much better telling him myself. And it was even better that God gave me the opportunity to do so.

To My Friend

If I could paint a rainbow,
I'd color it with love
And give it to you gladly
To hang in the sky above.
If I could make a flower,
With petals soft and sweet,
I'd fill it full of fragrance
And lay it at your feet.
If I could write a bird's song,
Its melody sweet and clear,
I'd write it filled with joy
And sing for you to hear.
But only God can paint a rainbow,
Make a flower to bloom in spring.
And only God can write the songs
He gives the birds to sing.
And God gives to me that special love
I feel for you, my friend.
Like God's perfect rainbow,
My friendship has no end.

March 22, 1987

CHAPTER 24

That's What Sisters Do

November 20, 2013

I often look back on those first years after Les was arrested and convicted and wonder what I was thinking. Knowing what I do now, there are a lot of things I might have done differently. I think about what I could have done to spare our children some of the pain and confusion they were feeling. I had my own pain I was dealing with, and I spent a lot of my time trying to take care of Les while keeping a roof over our heads and food on the table.

I'm extremely grateful I had my family who came in to help care for the girls when things got really hectic so I could be available for Les. Despite the fact that those around me told me what was going on with my children, I don't know that I always knew. It's more likely that I don't remember. Between my parents, Les's parents and siblings, my sister, and a myriad of other friends and sisters-in-law and aunts and uncles, I didn't have to worry about the girls, but I did. I still worried. But I have never felt so surrounded by love and care as I did then.

My sister Kelli had just turned twenty a few months before all this happened. She'd been married less than a year, and within a few weeks of her marriage, her husband Tracy lost his leg in an oil field accident. He was twenty as well.

Less than a month before my husband's arrest, Kelli and Tracy's beautiful baby boy, Justin, was born on Christmas Eve in 1983. His arrival seemed to make all the pain and suffering they had experienced a little better. It had been quite an eventful year for her, and I had no idea what a tremendous emotional impact my husband's arrest and conviction would have on Kelli until many years later.

When Les and I met, I was just a month shy of my sixteenth birthday. My parents had surprised my brothers and me less than two years before with a new sister. I think it was a surprise for them as well. My brothers were only ten and twelve when our baby sister came along.

I don't remember ever feeling resentful or embarrassed by the fact that my parents were having a baby while I was in junior high. In fact, I only remember us being happy. My parents allowed me to be a part of choosing a name for her. Mother would go through a list of names, and I would give my opinion of whether I liked them or not, usually based on girls at school, and whether I liked *them* or not.

"If it's a girl, she can't be named Lisa," I told her.

Lisa was a less-than-virtuous girl at my school, and I would never be able to have a sister with that name. (This is where I say sorry to all my friends named Lisa.) Mother liked Wendy and then came up with Kelli. We all agreed on that one.

I had a thing for creativity and loved fancy words. Maybe it was because of my own name and how it was spelled. So Mother let me pick a middle name. Diahann Carroll was a beautiful, popular singer at the time. I thought her name was so unique and pretty, but we couldn't spell it just the way she did, as it was much too long for our last name, which was Wreyford. So after many different variations, I came up with Diahn, and that was it. Kelli Diahn.

Kelli's middle name later became the middle name of her daughter, Shelby Diahn, my daughter, Hollie Diahn, and her daughter, my first granddaughter, Bailey Diahn. I'm pretty sure we haven't seen the last of that name. And so another tradition began.

My relationship with my sister was not like those of most siblings. I was very mature for my age and took her places with me, even on dates. As I grew older, I realized our relationship at times felt more as if she were my firstborn.

When Les and I met, she was less than two years old. My sister was a precocious child from day one. She remembers everything and is wise beyond her years. She was very particular in how she wanted things done. One of those things happened to be dealing with the humiliation of wearing diapers. She informed our mother that she wanted to wear those panties that a little girl at church wore. Mother said she was much too young for training pants, but Kelli prevailed. She was indignant to think Mother thought she might wet her pants.

On my second date with Les, we took Kelli to the park on a Sunday afternoon. I remember him carrying her around, sometimes on his shoulders, and I worried constantly that she would have an accident. She knew I was nervous about that situation and also perturbed with me for not trusting her at twenty-two months old; she knew she had a two-day "dry record" and was not going to pee all over my boyfriend. She was quite annoyed that I continually asked her if she needed to go to the bathroom. Les finally told me she was okay, and if she needed to go, she would tell him. Well, he became her hero right then and there! She had a bird's-eye view of the world on his shoulders, and if she had anything to do about it, that's where she was going to stay. She also remembers us walking that day, each of us holding one of her hands and swinging her up in the air. She was fairly certain, to this day, that she coined the word *again*.

Kelli told me about another time she and I were "getting ready for one of our dates with Les." Yes, she said *our*. I was helping her get dressed and brushing her hair. She claimed I kept jerking her head back as I pulled the brush through her fine hair. She complained that I was too rough and was hurting her. She finally begged me to let Les do it when he got there. And he did. Kelli sat on the closed toilet seat and, I quote from her in later years, said, "This big football hero was in our bathroom, taking the rest of the space up, gently brushing my hair into two perfect pigtails over my ears."

One night in January 1968, I knocked on Mother and Daddy's bedroom door when I came home from a date. I opened the door to go in, and Kelli was nestled in bed, sleeping with Mother and Daddy. She was about four. I came in their room and announced that Les had proposed and I had said yes. Everyone seemed excited except for Kelli. When I left the room, she asked Mother what *married* meant. Mother told her that Les and I were going to be a family. We would go to church, and the preacher would make us husband and wife, like she and Daddy were. Les would be part of our family now. Kelli wasn't sure what all the excitement was about. Les was already part of our family. The part she wasn't happy about was when she found out that we would live in our own house.

When we married eight months later in August, Kelli was our flower girl. In addition to making my beautiful wedding dress, Mother made Kelli the most adorable lace dress with lace pantaloons. After we married and I moved out, she would look at my room and my neatly made bed and wish I were there to do the airplane game. I would lie on my back and put my feet on her stomach and chest and lift her up as she stretched out her arms and pretended to fly. Later, we would all move to Colorado, and Kelli became an even bigger part of our life.

When Les and I came home for a visit from College Station, my parents went out to eat, so I made dinner, which included a chocolate layer cake. Kelli was about five or six. On the menu was corn, and Kelli hated corn. I told her she couldn't get down from her booster chair until she finished her corn, and she certainly couldn't have any chocolate cake.

She called my bluff and sat at the table, arms crossed, while Les and I cleaned up the kitchen. I don't remember how long I made her sit there, but Les was urging me to give it up and let her get down. Finally, I did, but I sent her to her room, and she let me know how she felt as she stomped all the way upstairs. Just this one story gives you a pretty accurate picture of the personality of all three of us: me, militant; Les, compassionate; and Kelli, headstrong. I don't know—militant may be a bit strong.

We watched television while she remained in her room. Les would go up now and then to check on her. She finally went to sleep, and I felt like I had won the battle.

It would be years later that Kelli told me, "You know I got chocolate cake after all, don't you?"

I had no idea what she was talking about. She was an adult, had children of her own. Years had passed, but she remembered everything.

After reminding me of that night, she grinned at me and said, "Les brought me a piece of cake because he felt sorry for me. But he told me not to tell."

Guess I didn't win *that* battle. Those two were thick as thieves from day one. He had two sisters of his own, but he always considered Kelli as his third sister. And she had a special place in his heart, as she did his.

I don't even remember talking to my sister during those days, weeks, and months after his arrest. I know I did. I had to have known what was going on with our girls. *Didn't I?*

But I did not realize that there were times she was caring for my children when Mother and Daddy were with me.

My oldest daughter, Leslea, mentioned to me not long ago that my twenty-year-old sister—who had been married less than a year, whose husband had lost his leg only six months earlier, and who had a newborn to care for—was taking care of her and Hollie in their tiny garage apartment in Weatherford, driving my kids the fifty miles to school each day and back while we were in trial.

These were the selfless acts that allowed me to be with my husband, that allowed me to throw myself completely into taking care of him as best as I could. And yet I was not aware that these moments of compassion were taking place. I think I was in survival mode. Or the pain of the memories of that time was so great I just blocked them out.

I know Les would ask me about the girls, where they were, what they were doing, if they were all right, and I always had an answer for him. Years later, as I reflected on that time, I like to think that my relationship with my family and especially my sister was one where we just automatically took over where the other was needed. We would discover this was a characteristic my sister and I shared.

Not long ago, Kelli and I were having a late-night conversation on the phone. It was one of those deep, reflective talks that would eventually turn into an hour or more. Often our conversations turned to Les. She had told me on other occasions that she felt like Les was another one of her brothers. Her big brother, her knight in shining armor. She did not remember a time in her life when he wasn't there.

When I thought about that, I realized it made perfect sense because she was so young when he and I began seeing each other.

"Do you have any idea how traumatic Les's arrest and conviction was for me?" she said.

I hesitated for a moment because I knew in all those years, I had not really considered the impact it had had on her. How selfish of me not to have thought about what all this had meant to her and possibly other members of our family as well.

"Les was more like a father to me at times than a brother," she said. "He was much more than your boyfriend or your husband." She took a moment to compose herself, but I could tell it was difficult for her. "He was the one who taught me to ride a bike."

"I had forgotten that," I replied, almost in a whisper.

"He was the one I went to when I wanted something fixed. And not just mechanics."

Memories of him fixing things for everyone came flooding back to me. He was *that* guy. The one you could call on. The one who would come over in the middle of the night if you needed something done. He was the one who would drive twelve hours to be at family events. And many times, the things he fixed were not tangible. He knew how to listen to friends and family. Be an advocate for someone who needed one. Talk someone out of being angry or even sad. I was probably his hardest adversary. He thought carefully about everything before making a move. I jumped. He was slow to anger. I was quick. He was confident. I needed assurance.

"I knew I could always count on him to take care of me and keep me from being hurt. I adored him," she said. "When he was gone, it was devastating to me."

Neither of us spoke for a while as we wept silent tears, our heads on pillows in our own beds, in different towns. We lingered, phones to our ears, thinking about him.

"Later, when things got bad in my marriage and with all the things I was going through with Tracy, I knew that if Les had been here, he would have rescued me from my pain. He would have taken me away and protected me from all the bad things that were happening to me."

I knew she was right. He would not have allowed that to happen. He would have rescued her, just like the knight in shining armor she had always believed him to be. How many other things would have been different if he were still around?

"With each one of my children, I grieved over the things that he could have taught them, the wonderful adventures they would have had with him. Sometimes it was more than I could bear."

At this point, she was crying harder and so was I.

I had no idea. And yet it made perfect sense. How could I have been so blind not to see? Not to realize the relationship she had with him and the feelings she was going through. But just as she often did, she kept all this to herself, putting on a good front so no one would see her pain, trying to protect our feelings.

"I'm so sorry." For a moment, it was all I could say. "I never thought about it like that. I only thought about my pain and my children's loss, not yours. But you're right. There's a whole other generation that has missed out on the joy and the knowledge that he could have brought to their lives."

So it was no surprise that her name was one of the ten on his visitation list, and she would often travel alone or sometimes with me to visit with him. She and I shared a hotel room during those last three days when we visited him before the state at last got their way and took him from us. She was also with his biological sisters and with me when we stood together and watched him take his final breath.

That's what sisters do. Even if you never grew up together, shared a room together, wore each other's clothes, or fought for the bathroom. Even if one of you is almost old enough to be the other's mother and treats her children as if they were her own grandchildren. That's what sisters do.

We still have long phone calls late at night—if we can stay awake. We still try to solve each other's problems and sometimes cross boundaries to do so if needed. I don't think I could have made it through life without her. I have a feeling she might say the same about me.

We still get in a car and go anywhere, at the last minute, for any length of time. We take detours and end up at places we might never have seen. And they're always crazy, memorable trips of a lifetime. Complete with awesome traveling snacks. (She's a caterer, you know.)

Needless Pain

Oh, what needless pain I bear
When my back to God I turn.
Why can't I give it all to Him?
When will this lesson I learn?
He patiently waits and watches
As on my own I fall.
His arms outstretched and waiting
For me His name to call.

June 1988

CHAPTER 25

Forgiveness

April 19, 1988

No one knows what the future holds. As Christians, the only thing Les and I knew for certain was that we would one day spend eternity in heaven. When you haven't seen your fortieth birthday yet, eternity seems a very long way off. Millions of decisions are made between birth and eternity, and they are not always good ones.

I found myself making one of those decisions just four years after Les was sent to prison. I had immersed myself so completely into his trial that, once he was gone and reality had set in, I found myself facing a future of not knowing what lay ahead.

I tried to keep Les abreast of what was going on at home and with the girls. His letters did not come nearly as often as I would have liked. Letters to the girls came even less frequently, and this did not go unnoticed by them. When he did write, his letters were usually short, and I was often disappointed that he had not responded to some of my questions regarding how he was doing and about household matters and decisions that needed to be made.

I tried to keep him as the head of our household as much as I could, but the distance, physically and emotionally, was just too much. I felt him withdrawing. He had never been as open with his feelings as I wanted him to be or as I was. I especially needed him to be open and communicative with me now that I felt so alone. In reality, I wasn't alone—he was. I was frustrated with him for keeping us at arm's length, so I'd confront him for doing so and then feel guilty because of where he was and the conditions in which he lived.

I was just the opposite. I never held my feelings back in our relationship. I put it all out there. I had a strong personality and was very independent even though we were a team. It was nothing for me to travel home alone to visit our parents when Les had to work, especially after the girls were born. It was normal at spring break to drive fifteen hours from Colorado over snowy mountain passes, spending the night at a hotel somewhere near Amarillo, and then getting up, packing the girls back into the car, and heading on to visit our families in Texas and Oklahoma while Les remained at work.

We had made decisions together, but now we weren't able to do that over dinner or in the quiet of our bedroom as we prepared for bed. We didn't have opportunities to talk about things while driving in the car as the children colored pictures in the back seat. Those moments were now relinquished to two hours every other week. Or once a month or every two months as time went by.

Weeks turned into months and months into years. We knew we had to choose what we were going to talk about during that short time. If something big was happening, if there were legal matters that needed to be attended to, the time would be gone before we knew it.

I became more and more depressed, feeling overwhelmed by the responsibility of raising our children alone, even though I had tremendous support and help from our families. I began to resent the fact that he seemed to have distanced himself from us, despite knowing he was coping with his own loss, in his own way.

I had no idea as I tried to draw him in to be part of our lives in the free world that he was protecting himself from the pain of not being there for us—from the isolation and loneliness he was experiencing on the inside. We began to talk only about things on the surface, things we could talk about without going too deep.

I wanted him to know and be a part of everything that went on with us 275 miles away. And yet when the car broke down, when we weren't sure how we would pay our bills, I hated telling him those things because he couldn't do a thing to help. Likewise, he didn't want us to know anything about what was going on with him in prison as he sat on death row.

Sometimes I would write to him or talk to him when I visited about opening up to me, expressing his feelings, or even writing to me more often. His letters that came on a regular basis when he was in county jail and facing trial now began to dwindle. My pleas met a giant wall that seemed to grow more and more over the years. I'm not sure what his walls looked like from his vantage point, but from my side, they looked a lot like the ones I had to pass through to see him. Tall, covered with barbwire, locked doors that he wasn't ready, if he ever would be, to let me in. It did not occur to me then that the wall he was building was for his own self-preservation.

It took me awhile to figure out he didn't want us to know how bad it was. There would be no postcards saying, "Having a wonderful time! Wish you were here!" I would ask him to "just write me something—anything!" He would remind me at visitation that there wasn't anything to tell. Yet he would always be upbeat, smiling, and even laughing at our visitations. Except for those times when we fell silent for a moment and just looked into each other's eyes. We had been together for too long for us not to see truth deep within. But he never stayed there for long, nor did I. It was too painful.

I began to deal with my own pain and feelings of abandonment. These issues were not new with us. Despite the love we shared for one another, I needed and asked a lot of him emotionally, mentally, and physically. And he was not always able or willing to provide that for me. Those issues had been there way before he left our home; we had just bandaged them along the way, as so many other couples often do while they are busy raising a family. His absence only made those hurts more glaring. I felt as if he had abandoned us, knowing he had not willingly walked away. But the emotional abandonment was as painful as the physical.

He was always eager to see us and hear from us. And I never doubted how much he loved us. But conversation was always about what was going on at home, how everyone else was, my struggles to find work, and occasionally something on the legal front with him.

It wasn't long until I began construction on my own walls. Mine had windows that I might occasionally open and doors that others could move in and out of if I unlocked them. Sometimes, I would hide inside; other times, I would come out. I painted my walls to give them a festive look, giving me hope for a brighter future, full of experiences and people I felt could embrace me as well as my pain. My walls were designed to protect myself from the pain of separation, abandonment, and loneliness when I needed a place to run and hide.

We had only been back in Texas for six months when he was arrested, so we had very few friends, most of them from church. I began to make new friends as I took various jobs and continued to go to church regularly. It was difficult to know exactly where I fit in. I was married, yet I was alone. I was a mother raising two children alone, yet they had a father.

I struggled those first years to make a living, working one job, sometimes two, occasionally none. Decisions had to be made daily, and I could not wait to ask Les what I should do. I had to make them immediately. I became more and more independent out of necessity.

One of the most painful things for me at the time and even today was to sit alone at church, watching other couples worship together. We had met at church; we dated at church; we married at church.

I gravitated to the people at church who were my age. I was thirty-five and raising my children alone. Most of my friends were learning how to live all over again. That was the common denominator we shared. The only difference was, most of them were coming out of bad marriages. I didn't know one person who shared my special circumstances.

I started to believe that I, too, deserved a second chance. After all, I was alone, just like they were. I didn't have anyone to come home to, just like them. I had half my life or more before me and absolutely no hope of anything ever being any different. They were able to make choices for their future. My future was as imprisoned as my husband was.

As I began to mingle among the newly liberated singles, I experienced friendship and social interactions that I had missed as a teenager. Les and I began to date when I was almost sixteen. Although we had friends, most of our time was spent together. Not only were our friendships limited, but we didn't date anyone else after we started dating. I had a couple of guy friends in high school I sometimes went to dances with, but they were never romantic friends or dates.

Suddenly I was approaching forty, had been alone for several years, and found myself in the middle of a social world I had never experienced, filled with people who liked to be with me and found me interesting, fun, and attractive. It was intoxicating to say the least and seemed to temporarily fill a void that grew greater each day.

As I began to search for answers to what lie ahead for me, I sought the advice from many of my new friends as well as some old ones. I even sought advice from some of my spiritual leaders, people I held in high esteem, as to what I should do.

Most of the advice I heard, or perhaps wanted to hear, was that I needed to go on with my life. I began to take inventory of my life and my marriage and found them both damaged. Even aside from the present circumstances, I rationalized that I could repair my life, but my marriage was irreparable because of past hurts. It was only logical, if I were to have to live in this world alone, I might as well be able to have some control over what I did with it.

It was a very difficult thing I did that day. It was not a surprise. Our discussions and correspondence had led to this for some time. I sat before my husband and told him I wanted to go on with my life and the best way to do that was for us to get a divorce. Even now as I write these words, it overwhelms me to think of the pain I brought to him. My heart breaks as I think of how he must have felt. I would give anything to be able to take that day back and do it over again. He was so stoic when I told him.

If that is what I needed to do for me, he said, then he would agree to it. He didn't want this, but he wanted whatever would make me happy. I told him that I would always love him and support him, that I would always be there for him—that would never change. How hollow that must have sounded.

And so I wrote my check for $135 and filed the divorce papers at the courthouse on April 19, 1988. I went before the judge, ironically alone, and he granted me what I thought I wanted in just a few minutes.

Les had signed the papers and waived his right to be there. How easy it was. I walked out of the courthouse with what I thought would make me happy. Yet I cried as I walked down the steps of that courthouse, knowing I had just made the biggest mistake of my life. I drove home, again alone, and sat in my living room, waiting for my new life to begin.

You know the saying, "You can run, but you can't hide"? I found that to be so true. I ran as fast as I could and tried to find a new life, to start over and put all my problems behind me. It didn't happen.

No matter how fast I ran or how much I searched, I could not escape from the truth. I was deeply, madly, hopelessly in love with the man who was now my ex-husband.

I cringed at the word. I could not bring myself to say it. I never used it. I continued to refer to him as "my husband." And I continued to write to him and he to me. My visitations didn't stop, and I felt I had the mark of a scarlet letter on me, BETRAYER, as I carried the paper inside with each visit marked RELATIONSHIP: EX-WIFE.

What had I done? If I was feeling this way, what must *he* be feeling? Alone. Abandoned. How could I have done this to him?

He said he forgave me. I should have believed what he said. I finally did one day. Yet I was never sure I had forgiven myself and didn't know if there was penance great enough to absolve the guilt I felt for that betrayal.

You remember those walls I referred to earlier, the ones I built yet decorated? I redecorated, taking all the windows and doors out, stripping the walls of paint and wallpaper, removing the pictures and putting a giant No TRESPASSING sign outside.

I made sure no one would come near my walls, much less want to come inside and visit. That was my penance for my sin. Not only did I make sure no one got inside my emotional walls, but I made sure to take care of the physical side too, gaining one hundred pounds, ensuring I would not be attracted to the single world nor the single world to me. After all, I was not trustworthy.

It never ceases to amaze me how God brings us full circle, allowing us to stumble along the path when we have chosen our own way instead of His. It became crystal clear to me that Les was the love of my life, my husband forever, and that God had joined us together, till death do us part. No man can put that asunder, not even for $135.

It didn't matter that he was there and I was here. It didn't matter that there had been hurt before; there are always hurts in a marriage—you just work through them. It didn't matter that I had no control over my future, or that I didn't know what lay ahead, because no one really does. God had chosen my mate, and I had chosen disobedience. I had taken my eyes off Him and looked to the world to find my comfort and joy. Instead, I found only emptiness and pain.

When you were a child, you sometimes asked for and got a do-over. On the edit key of the computer, there is UNDO. How simple that is! Life is not like that. Sometimes we have to live with the choices we make.

My divorce (emphasis on *my*) was one of those choices I had to live with. I asked Les to forgive me. I begged that we remarry and put an end to the accursed title I had been given and had given him. He graciously forgave me yet refused to remarry, citing that when we did, it would not be under the current circumstances. He was not there, he said, when a judge declared our marriage null and void, but he planned to be there when we renewed that vow.

We both agreed that a $135 piece of paper did not mean a thing to either one of us. We knew how we felt about each other and the devotion we shared for one another. In our hearts, and in God's eyes, we would always be husband and wife.

But knowing that did not stop me from bringing up the subject of our remarrying over and over again. And Les calmly fought me all those years, citing that as far as he was concerned, we were still married. And being his usual self, it would often take him a long time to respond to me, putting a lot of thought into what he wanted to say, as he always did. This was part of his character that normally would be considered a positive quality in a person but drove me crazy when we argued over things and he would want "a few days to think about it and then get back to me."

He finally responded to one of many letters I had written him, begging him to say yes. I knew it had taken him a long time to write this. It said:

February 26, 1991

Dear Shari:

I'm sure this isn't exactly what you meant by a quick response, but it took me awhile to figure out what I thought I wanted to say in response to your letter. As I have stated to you several times previously, I have been torn between the two extremes of what to do about our relationship.

On the one hand, I can support and nurture a relationship between the two of us. To me, this sounds a bit one-sided and selfish, but they say love is sometimes blind. If we knew there would be a positive end to this situation at sometime in the future, then there would be a reason for optimism. We're now seven years into this situation, and although the past fourteen months have given us some reason for hope, all of this is far from being resolved, if indeed it can be resolved. I don't seem to have been a very good husband for the first sixteen and a half years of our marriage, and I don't think I improved much over the next three years. I can understand you need to get along with your life given the probability of any future relief, and I didn't hold that against you then, and I don't now.

My situation has improved somewhat since acquiring these new lawyers. I am cautiously optimistic about what might happen in the future, but I've been around this situation too long to hope for any immediate relief. Time and the courts are not on our sides. I'm not giving up hope, but I know that the road ahead of me is long and rocky, and even if at sometime I'm lucky enough to get out, I have no idea what I'll do then. I'm not sure, given my track record up to this point, what I could offer you in the future. For me to hold on to you would be extremely selfish and not at all fair to you. I don't feel it fair to try to make up for past shortcomings by offering you only possible hell in the future.

The reverse side of the coin is that neither of us is the same person we were seven years ago. By setting aside what has happened in the past and striving to build on something for the future, there might still be hope for us. Many relationships start and blossom at the age of forty, but probably few have had so much working against them as we do. No matter what, I will always love you. You were my wife and are the mother of my children; that will never change. By the time we resolve this problem, if we can, the girls will be gone, so when we speak of family, we're really talking about just the two of us. Neither of us seems to have anything hot going on at this time, or I haven't heard of anything, so a loving relationship between us, setting aside these unusual circumstances, could be possible. The family isn't too hot about you right now, but like I've said in the past, if they can't join in, they'll be left in the past. I have no real wants to start over looking for someone to spend the rest of my life with; after all, I've got too much invested in you to let you go that easy—just kidding.

I'm not sure just what to do in this kind of situation, and I don't think they write books about it. I don't know what to say to you, so I just haven't. You take that as a rejection, and it really isn't that. I don't feel much in a loving mood and haven't in some time. I'm not sure I could write a love letter now, and when I've tried in the past, it's all been made up with no feelings—I don't want to do that. Given that the basis of a loving relationship is trust and honesty, I'm not sure I can deliver right now. Of course, I can try to love and try to be honest, but even if I were successful, if some time in the future we're unable to resolve this impossible situation, you'll be left alone again. I won't risk that. If you keep thinking about when all this will be over and when you can come and pick me up, you'll lull yourself into a false sense of security that I may not be able to deliver on.

I know the world out there is drastically different from even seven years ago. I know you go out to social events, and I know you see people, but I don't know if you're the least bit serious about anyone. When you think about your life today and tomorrow, does my being here and possibly still in your life play a factor in how you look at a companion? I think you're correct when you say that I don't talk about love because I'm afraid of the hurt. I don't think it's my hurt that I worry about—it's yours. It's all too easy to say that I don't know what to say about you and me, but in actuality, deep down I do. I don't know what I have to offer a relationship. I'm lousy at expressing love anytime, but especially in a letter, and that's about our only means right now. The car breaks down, the this-or-that breaks, money is tight, and this-or-that daughter has done such or so. I can't do a damn thing about it, and that's hard to put aside. I'm not sure what contribution I could give you now or in the future, even if I do get out. I don't want to push you away from me, but then I don't want you to depend on me and be left holding the bag in the end. Until I break this tenuous bond between us, you won't honestly pursue a life of your own. This in no way means that I don't want to be a good friend, and I hope we can still maintain that relationship.

The response wasn't quick, and this might not be what you wanted to hear, but I thought you needed to know how I feel. No one likes to write a letter like this, and I'm no exception. Maybe all this negativeness is due to the fact that they killed a friend last night, and with that killing, it showed me that, even when things seem to be going your way, there is always the possibility of failure. I've caused you a lot of problems over the years, and I deeply regret that. I don't want to hurt you anymore now or in the future, and this possibility prompts these words. I hope you can find a way to forgive me; I never set out to hurt you. My battle continues, and you're part of the team until the end.

I love you,

—Les

I have no idea how long it took him to write that letter. It was one of the most heartfelt, most thought-out letters he had written to me. And even though he did not consider it a love letter, it certainly was. It was more important than any letter he had ever written, as he was telling me what was really in his heart. He never said no to me. I was always part of his team, and he continued to love me.

He wrote this to me three years after our divorce. I had been asking him for the most part of those three years for us to remarry. But that letter wasn't the end of the story, and it would take me twelve more years to finally get him to come around. (I think you can really see the difference in our personalities about now. Maybe militant was a good description of me.) It wasn't our only topic of conversation over those years, but it was on the top ten list of things we talked about.

After fifteen years of being divorced, Les finally agreed to marry again. We had been married fifteen and a half years when he was arrested; he had been in prison for nineteen years.

Les had put my uncle, Reverend Gayle Baucum, on his visitation list, and we drove to Livingston together. I had obtained a marriage license by proxy, something I didn't know you could do. Gayle and I walked into the visitation room on Valentine's Day in 2003, as if it were any other day to visit. We did not ask for permission from the Texas Department of Corrections, as they probably wouldn't have allowed it. We were assigned seats—Preacher Gayle with his Bible in his hand, me with my heart in my throat.

Gayle and I sat on one side of the visitation window with phones to our ears as Les sat on the other, and Gayle began the "ceremony" of reuniting us in marriage.

I don't remember what was said or what I had worn that day. It didn't matter. There are no pictures to celebrate that wedding day. But on February 14, 2003, Les and I married again and celebrated our union as I donned a new wedding ring with three diamonds on it, symbolizing today, tomorrow, and always.

After our two hours were up, Gayle and I drove back to my home in Arlington, and we let it be known that Les and I were married that day, and the preacher, my uncle, who had been through so much of our life with us, spent the night at my house before heading back to west Texas the next day. Talk about your crazy weddings!

Forgiveness, like love, is something that we profess to do but do not always allow for ourselves. How often do we forgive ourselves for things we feel we have done wrong, for mistakes we have made, for choices we regret? Do we really love ourselves? I think forgiving ourselves and loving ourselves are two of the hardest things for us to do. I know they are for me.

I have done many interviews with reporters over the years and have been asked all sorts of questions. But there was one time I was asked to comment about my commitment to my husband after all these years. We were sitting in my living room, the reporter, his cameraman, and myself, just talking. The reporter, someone I had known for several years, was asking me a few casual questions to get us started.

"One thing that stands out the most with you is your strength, your courage, and your commitment to stand by him all these years," said the cameraman. "Talk about that." He balanced his camera on his shoulder, waiting for me to speak.

I sat there, silently looking into the blinding light of the camera, not able to speak. A silence fell across the room while they waited for me to answer.

"I don't know that I want to talk about that." It was all I could say.

The camera continued to record the awkward moment. They looked at each other, confused by my reply.

"I'm not sure I want to talk about that," I said once more as tears began to well up in my eyes. This was the one subject that would always touch my heart, my soul, my very being and rip me inside with feelings of guilt and shame that could not be described.

"I don't feel like I am strong or was as committed as I could have been," I whispered. "I divorced him." Tears came harder now. "And it was the worst mistake I ever made in my life."

I know Les forgave me. Maybe when you have a hard time forgiving yourself for something, it's hard to believe that anyone else can. The thing about Les was that he was one of those people who stood by what he said. When he said he was going to do something, that was that. And I was always one of those people who seemed to need reassurance again and again.

I know from everything I have been taught and from Scripture, God has forgiven me, but sometimes I have a hard time believing it. I can sit and talk and counsel with someone else, assuring them of God's grace and forgiveness, but I cannot seem to accept it for myself. I often felt as if I were the exception to the rule, the one person in the world who was not worthy of grace.

Many times, I have told someone who felt worthless that "if you were the only person on the earth, God still would have sent His Son, Jesus, to die on the cross so that you might be saved. That is how much God loves you. That is how worthy you are. That is the depth of God's grace."

I continually remind myself that kind of grace applies to me as well. And I'm pretty sure I'm not alone. I'm thankful I can forgive myself, and He alone grants me the confidence to know that I am worthy.

Eleven months have passed since Les's death. I am at odds with what terminology to use when I speak of it. His death? The day he died? His execution? Or the day the state of Texas finally won their battle to kill an innocent man? Perhaps that last one is a bit too harsh for some to hear spoken out loud. Some believe it is not true. I use the latter description now and then, perhaps depending on my mood at the time, or who I happen to be with, merely for its shock factor and to generate some thought as to what really happened on June 3, 2015. It catches people off guard and forces them to think about the possibility that the state so many brag about, love, and claim to hold in high esteem would allow something like that to happen.

I wrote the chapter entitled "Forgiveness" many years ago, and now I sit here to pen this part of an extremely painful chapter of our lives. Painful for many people—not just for Les or for me. The decisions we make in our lives affect a lot more people than we realize, altering our universe, our future, our relationships with others, and how we are judged or perceived by the world in ways we might never have imagined. Should we care about that? I think we should. And even if we don't think about the effect our decisions have on others, do we consider how God feels about those decisions?

God has a plan for all of us. Whether or not we get on board with His plan is our choice. Too often, we don't know what the answers are, and we may not be listening to hear what God's will is, so we strike out on our own, making decisions that we feel are best for us, listening to the counsel of others instead of God. Too often, we ask God to give us the desires of our heart without first asking what *His* desires for us are.

I know now, despite my belief that I was doing the right thing for me and was praying about the decision I was making, I was not asking the right questions. I was not considering what God's heart wanted for me, for my husband, for our family, and for our extended families. Yet even though those decisions may have been wrong, God loved me through them. He never abandoned me and continued His work in me to bring me closer to the woman He intended for me to be.

But it wasn't until now, eleven months after Les's death, that I truly understood how much more God did for me during that crisis of belief. As I sat in the living room of a friend's house, surrounded by several ladies studying God's Word during our weekly Bible study, a seemingly innocent question was presented to the group for discussion. At that moment, God reached out and revealed something amazing to me that I had missed all these years.

The question was quite simple: "Who has extended great grace to you in the past?" I paused as I read how the question was worded; it was obvious this question meant what *other* person, someone other than Christ. Suddenly the words from the old hymn began playing in my head: "Grace, grace, God's grace . . ." and I realized I had never associated grace as a gift from anyone else but Christ.

We had just defined grace in our study that morning as God's unmerited gift of His favor and kindness. How did other people extend grace to us? The answer was so obvious to me at that moment as I sat silently staring at the question on the page, reading and rereading it.

The voices of the others in the room who were discussing the question became like white noise around me as God unfolded right there, in that moment, that Les had extended an act of grace, a gift of unmerited favor and kindness to me by loving me and forgiving me despite the most hurtful decision I had ever made throughout all our years of marriage.

As this revelation continued to unfold in my mind, I was convinced this truly was God speaking to me, showing me another form of grace I had not considered, had never recognized; this suddenly opened up avenues of forgiveness (me forgiving myself) and opportunities to recognize other acts of grace and to offer acts of grace to others.

My husband—who by my choice I made my ex-husband—continued to love, accept, and cherish me despite the decision I made to sever the covenant he and I had made before God. Would he have continued to love me had I chosen to abandon him? I don't know. It doesn't matter, because I didn't. And Les extended grace to me through his human capacity but was driven by his walk with God.

Having read this chapter, you know after many years of asking—no, begging—for his forgiveness, something I continued to do on a regular basis, despite his assurances of his love he made to me, he finally gave in to my pleas for us to remarry.

His protestations were not because he didn't want to. He didn't want to do it the way we did, separated through a wall of glass and citing our vows over a telephone. He assured me that we would marry again, but he wanted it to be when we could be in the same room, together, as it should be.

He never gave up that we weren't married, because he believed the covenant we made the first time, in a house of God, blessed by God, was a lasting covenant. And as he said so many times, "A piece of paper from a judge saying we weren't married didn't make any more difference than a piece of paper saying we were married again."

We had always been married as far as he was concerned, from the day we made that first covenant to God. The only difference it made, he said, was he now had to send me two anniversary cards each year. He called our August 24, 1968, date our Alpha, and February 14, 2003, when we remarried, the Omega. And we celebrated both dates for the remaining fifteen years we had.

He sent me an anniversary card on both dates, as well as a Valentine's Day card. And in keeping with his personality, he was still a man of few words, but one who never forgot.

Bittersweet

You loved me today as only you know how.
Reaching out to me, beyond the barriers,
Past the walls. You looked into my soul,
Touched my heart, and met my needs.
You looked at me today as only you can.
And in that look, I saw how much you loved me.
I remember so much and felt so special.
What bittersweet pain!

September 1986

CHAPTER 26

All My Love Forever

I've always loved Christmas. As newlyweds, Les and I would buy a huge Scotch pine tree, spray it with fake snow, drape multicolored lights around the boughs, and then throw silver icicles all over it.

The tree took up almost a quarter of the living room in our apartment at Texas A&M our first Christmas. We purchased two boxes of multicolored ornaments, mixing them with the vintage ones given to us by Les's parents. I made felt stockings by gluing felt letters of our names along with cute Santas, reindeer, and wreaths. I was doing my best to be "Suzy Homemaker" on a college student's budget.

A tradition was born that first Christmas. After our girls came along three and a half years later, decorating the tree was a significant part of our family's Christmas tradition. We added a new felt stocking with each new addition to our family. Living in Colorado, we often traveled to the mountains to choose a tree and cut it ourselves. The girls loved spraying the fake snow all over the tree. Les would lift them up high in the air so they could reach the tallest branches, making sure it was covered from top to bottom. What was a Colorado Christmas tree without snow on it? Even if it was from an aerosol can.

We purchased a crèche, or nativity scene, from a variety store in College Station our first year. It still spends Christmas holidays on our coffee table, reminding me of holidays past. The Spanish moss on the roof of the manger has seen better days, but the figures are still intact. The crèche, one of my most prized possessions, is one of the few original decorations I have from those first years.

There are many Christmas memories I will always cherish. We usually made our gifts for our family. And wherever we lived, we always traveled for Christmas celebrations in Texas, Oklahoma, and Missouri. Both our families had Christmas traditions, and as we started our own family, we blended the various traditions, making them our own. Those first years when we still had all four of our grandmothers, we would make appearances at six Christmas dinners and gift exchanges.

Les's dad, Lester Sr., was a very meticulous man. I always remember him tinkering with something, whether it was a broken toaster, the 1958 Oldsmobile, or the most perfect fudge recipe at Christmas, each piece wrapped in precisely cut pieces of aluminum foil. It was quite a process.

I didn't recognize it early in our relationship, but later I came to realize how very much like his dad Les was. He, too, was meticulous about the things he did. He was precise in all the things he built or created. He researched tirelessly when making purchases, ensuring he bought the best product. And that was before we had the luxury of surfing the internet to compare and read reviews.

It was no surprise to me, when many years after Les was incarcerated, he figured out a way to carry on the tradition of making fudge that was handed down to him by his father. It wasn't exactly the fudge recipe that Les Sr. used, but as usual, Les Jr. figured out a way, given what he had. Here is Les's recipe for the perfect fudge, if you find yourself in prison during the holidays.

When Are You Going to Make Fudge?

I don't know what it is about making fudge, but it seems to run in the family. My dad always made fudge around Christmastime, so I guess it was only natural that I should continue the tradition. My recipe is not original. A friend who has long ago made the drive to the Walls Unit gave it to me. But it is one of the better ones floating around down here. You may look at the list of ingredients and say, "You can't make fudge from that," but looks can be deceiving. The hardest part in the process is getting all the ingredients together, and then, of course, there is the expense: not everyone can afford to do it. This recipe makes a lot of fudge, so you will find you have a lot of friends when they figure out you're "cooking."

There are only a few things that are truly important to you down here. Your Bible is one thing they can't take from you, but there are a few other things you hope they don't take. The typewriter is understandable. I've already written about the radio. Your fan is less important here at the Polunsky Unit than it was at Ellis, but nice to have, nonetheless. And then there is your hot pot.

Wet Ingredients:
Peanut butter (10 oz.)
Snickers (4 bars)
Chocolate syrup (6–8 oz.)
Instant milk (6 heaping spoons)
Cashews (4 bags)

Dry Ingredients:
Cookies (two 14-oz. bags)
Vanilla wafers (1-pound bag)
Hot chocolate (half of a 2-pound bag)

You want to do all this on a day when you have several hours of uninterrupted time. I like to do it on a Sunday, and if there is a football game on the radio, all the better. Those who have looked at these ingredients soon realize there is a lot of stuff here, and indeed you have to split this project up into two batches, because we only have two-quart bowls to work with, and even then, it takes two of them. The hot pot comes with an insert that operates as a sort of double boiler. Into the insert you place your peanut butter, Snickers (crushed, of course), chocolate syrup, instant milk, and the cashews. You then take your cookies, twist them apart, scrape out the filling into the insert, and set aside the bottom and top halves for later. Once you get all this into your insert, it's pretty well full, but you can add a little water now if you want. You have to be real careful with the water, because if you use too much, you will make the final product too soft to mold into fudge bars. Put your insert into the hot pot and start heating your wet ingredients.

This next part would be easy with a wooden rolling pin or a blender, but down here a spoon and your thumb will have to do. It's nice if there is a game on to listen to, because this will take some time. With your thumb pressing down on the spoon, crush up the vanilla wafers and then the cookie halves as fine as possible. A couple of coffee breaks later, you are ready to begin the mixing process. In one of your bowls, put in the crushed-up cookies, vanilla wafers, and the hot chocolate. Wash your hands real good (culinary standards). Take the insert out of your hot pot and slowly pour it into your dry ingredients as you mix everything up with your free hand. With all the wet ingredients in the bowl, it becomes a two-hand process and is somewhat like mixing bread. At some point, you will need to transfer this mixture over to your second bowl to get to the remaining dry ingredients left in the first bowl. Mix, mix, mix until everything is well blended. Take another coffee break.

The cookies come in a clear plastic tray with four slots, which we will now use as molds to form the fudge blocks. These blocks will be about 4" long, 2" wide, and about 5/8 to 3/4" in thickness. Half a batch will make about 8–9. Take the molded block out of the mold, wrap it up in a piece of 24-pound typing paper, then wrap all this up in a sheet of newspaper. Set aside under your bunk and start all over again mixing up the second half of your ingredients. In the end, you'll have 16–18 fudge blocks all wrapped up in typing paper and newsprint. The next day, pull out your wrapped fudge, unwrap each one, throw away the oil-laden paper, rewrap each with a new typing paper and newsprint, and put back under your bunk for another day. What's happening during this process is you're pulling off as much peanut oil as possible, and the block is hardening up. On day three, you pass out the fudge and ingratiate yourself to your friends until they start bugging you again about making another batch. Your first response will be that your thumb is still recuperating.

I'm sure my dad never thought about the time and effort it took to make his fudge. It was something he was good at, and his family and friends appreciated the effort as they unwrapped the individual squares of fudge from their precisely cut aluminum foil wrapper and enjoyed the moment.

With much love and respect,

—Les (aka The Wiley Ole Veteran)

Christmas 1983 held its own particular memories. We had recently moved back to Texas after living in Colorado for ten years. Les's office in Grand Junction had closed due to the oil recession, and he was offered a job in Dallas. We hated to leave Colorado.

That year, we hosted both our families at our new home in Arlington. My parents lived only forty-five minutes away, but Les's family came from Oklahoma and Alabama, and we had people sleeping in every corner of our house. That was the way we both grew up. Wherever we were, whomever we visited, there were people sleeping on the floor, on couches. It was the way we did holidays.

I never changed the sheets on my bed without thinking about Christmas Eve that year. My sister went into labor with her firstborn. There were complications, so Mother and Daddy went to the hospital in Fort Worth with Kelli and her husband, Tracy, while Les and I were at home, preparing for the arrival of more family members. Kelli had wanted a natural birth, but complications indicated the doctors might have to do a cesarean. Mother would call me periodically with updates.

I was in our bedroom changing the sheets and lifted the clean top sheet to wrist-pop it out, as I always do, letting it float down to cover the bottom sheet I had just put on the mattress. But this time, I let it fly too high, and one corner of the sheet caught a light bulb in the ceiling fan above the bed. Though the sheet was thin, it connected with the thin glass, shattering the bulb and making a loud pop when it broke.

Les was standing nearby as I crumpled into tears. My tears were not about the light bulb or the glass that would have to be cleaned up. They weren't about the sheets that would have to be redone. The tears were about my worry over my sister and her baby—things I had no control over. He quickly came to my side, took me in his arms, and told me everything was going to be all right. We could clean it up and start over. I continued to sob as he held me close to him, confused as to why I was so upset. He tilted my head up to look at him, searching for any cuts or signs of glass that might have injured me.

"I'm worried about Kelli," I said to him through my tears.

"She'll be okay," he soothingly assured me as he tightened his arms around me. "She's in good hands. Soon, she'll be holding her baby, and this will all be behind us."

It wasn't long after we got the call that Justin had arrived and everyone was fine.

Our guests arrived, minus the new parents and baby, and we celebrated our traditional Christmas Eve Mexican dinner and opened gifts. As

Christmas morning dawned, Les and I found a large basket and gathered up all the presents that had been placed under the tree for Kelli, Tracy, and Justin. Once the kids were up and crawling all over their gifts from Santa, Les and I bundled ourselves up, as it was a very cold day. I remember watching Les carry the basket of gifts out to the car. He looked so handsome and so like him, in his cowboy hat and boots and his sheared-lined suede vest. The two of us sneaked off before anyone else woke and went to the hospital to get a look at this new nephew of ours who had caused me to cry on Christmas Eve. We walked into Kelli's room and met Justin, who had been brought to Kelli in a Christmas stocking. We visited with the new family as they opened their Christmas presents while I held the baby.

I had no idea that would be the last Christmas Les and I would share together. I didn't know we only had twenty-seven more days together until he would be arrested and taken from our home forever.

Thirty years later, in 2013, our daughters, Leslea and Hollie, and their husbands and children gathered once more in my living room to celebrate Christmas. It was a family gathering once again without Les.

It was a different living room, a different house. A home Les had never seen. My Christmas trees had changed over the years. I now had artificial ones, with clear lights already strung on them. And rather than the hodge-podge of multicolored lights and ornaments, my Suzy Homemaker had turned into Martha Stewart, as all the decorations were color-coordinated throughout the house. What a long way I had come.

We had just finished our now traditional Christmas morning brunch as our grandchildren dove into their gifts, squealing with delight over their new clothes and toys. I was struck at how very much Les had missed. And how very much we missed him. Not just Christmas Day, but so many other days, so many other moments. I wondered what he was doing as we sat in front of a crackling fire in the comfortable home I enjoyed, a table laden with food in the other room.

Leslea asked me to open a small box sitting on the stack of gifts ad-dressed to me. She readied her camera as I reached to pick it up. I always knew something big was about to happen when she made that move.

Opening the box, I found a single silver bangle bracelet with a silver disk attached. I looked closely at the disk and was surprised to see Les's handwriting engraved on one side. I would recognize that writing anywhere. It was engraved with an acronym, AMLF, and his signature, Les, beneath. I began to cry.

The laughter stopped in the room, and everyone began to look at me. The little girls were concerned that Mimi was crying. Why would a Christmas present make her sad? All their presents made them happy. I assured them that Mimi was okay; she was happy with her present yet sad as well. I looked up and saw that Hollie and Leslea had tears in their eyes too.

As long as I could remember, Les had always signed his letters to me with "All my love forever, Les." That signature began when he had gone away to college and wrote me almost every day, until we were married two years later. Every card and letter thereafter were the same. When he was arrested and went to prison, he still used the same sentiment to end his letters to me, oftentimes signing just AMLF.

During the few court hearings we had while appealing his conviction, we were never allowed to pass notes, talk, or even acknowledge each other's presence. But he would slip a piece of paper to Anthony to give to me. I would unfold the note and see in his very distinct handwriting, "AMLF, Les."

Broken Pieces

I'll cry myself to sleep tonight from the hurt of missing you.
I'll fill my life with busywork and try to keep up such a front.
When my cup fills to the brim with grief,
And I can no longer bear the burden of pain,
Only then will I allow my heart to wrench itself in two,
And my life's blood drains from my body,
Forming streams of tears, dissolving silently on my pillow.
My soul cries out, "Please, God, no more!"
Yet I know there will be more, and my heart will break again.
So please, dear God, instead of letting my heart crumble
Into tiny pieces, only to be lost in the wind,
Let me instead share myself by giving each
Broken piece of my heart away to those I meet.

August 1986

CHAPTER 27

Don't Mess with Texas

June 3, 2015

W e had Monday, June 1 and Tuesday, June 2 to visit from 8:00 A.M. until 5:00 P.M., and Wednesday, June 3, the day Les was scheduled for execution, from 8:00 A.M. until noon—two of us at a time, two-hour increments. It was like marathon visits.

Six of us were there, making up three groups of two, to visit. Kelli and I were one group; our daughters, Leslea and Hollie, were another group; and Les's sisters, Cheryl and Denise, were the third.

We were running shuttles to and from our hotels to the prison. I calculated the time it would take for the two who were visiting to come out of the visitation room, go through the double-locked double doors that were mechanically opened and closed, walk down a thirty-foot corridor to the outside door, then travel another fifty-foot sidewalk to the last checkout. The pair had to clear that before the next pair could even step out of their car.

A Texas Department of Corrections van would be coming at noon Wednesday to pick up Les and take him from Livingston to the Walls Unit in Huntsville where the execution would take place.

I mapped out our three-day visitation schedule with exact times for the six of us, making sure I was the last one. My sister and I had the last spot on

Wednesday, and we agreed she would have time alone with him during that block. Les and I would have the last hour alone. No one was going to argue with me about that. I made the schedule.

Kelli told me later that, during their time alone, she asked Les if we were really messing up his routine with this three-day marathon of visits. He laughed and said, "Yes, you're messing up my busy schedule."

He sat in a small box of a room, just a little bigger than the regular visitation cubicles. He sat all day on a twelve-inch-round stool that had no back. He was literally a prisoner in that room for nine hours on Monday, nine hours on Tuesday, and four hours on Wednesday. I know his back must have been hurting badly. *Do you think about that when you know you're about to die? What do you think about?*

He and I didn't cry. There were moments when our eyes would brim with tears. There had been so many of them spilled over the past thirty-one years. We had previously discussed the possibility of him getting a stay of execution on this one, like the last seven execution dates Les had, but we didn't expect it. We even talked about whether he wanted it. He and I had many philosophical discussions regarding this subject in the recent years. We seemed to have exhausted every move that was available. But that didn't mean we would have to stop fighting. But was that what he wanted? Les and the team had even looked at ways to try to get him life in prison, which would move him off death row and into general population.

He was thirty-six when he went in and was now sixty-seven years old. If the execution went forward, he would be the oldest man Texas had executed since reinstating the death penalty in 1976.

There were a few silent moments during that last hour. I wondered how in the world we could have silent moments when they were our last. Everything there was to say had been said already. Yet so much seemed to have gone unsaid as well. We just sat for a while, looking into each other's eyes, which somehow was more painful than I imagined.

I sat in a glass box with a door that only a guard could open. The glass in front of me was so I could see him, and the glass behind was so the guards could see us. I could see the door behind him that opened to a long hallway and then another door, which opened to the outside.

He looked so very weary. And I knew he was. His hair was now sparkled with streaks of gray, and his face was much older than the man they had brought in here thirty-one years ago. I thought to myself how nice it would be if they would just let us hold hands. I wanted to feel his hands once more.

"You know that I love you all very much," he said softly into the phone while looking directly at me, both of our eyes gleaming with tears that would not fall.

"Yes, I know. We all know. And we love you too."

"I've already written and thanked Peter and Grace and the other attorneys on the team for everything they have done on my behalf, but thank them again for me, will you?"

"I will. They know." He was such a gentleman. Even now, his manners in writing last letters to each attorney, the secretaries, his children, his pen pal he had written to in Scotland for years, friends, and other family. It had to be hard for a man who hated to write letters. But he did it to say goodbye. I probably don't know who all he did share last letters with.

We knew that our attorneys, Peter and Grace, were in DC, still making calls and trying to figure out a way to stop this. We trusted that they had done everything humanly possible to keep this from happening. They, along with Anthony, had given Les the last twenty-six years. There was a whole building of people on Pennsylvania Avenue grieving the event that was about to take place.

How do you say goodbye? After so many times, I always knew how to say goodbye because I would be back in another few weeks or so. I knew how to say goodbye, knowing that there was still hope it wouldn't be the last time. But how do you say goodbye to someone, knowing the exact hour he will draw his last breath?

I could see three women appear out of the corner of my eye to my left. They just stood there, outside the door, waiting. Two of them wore gray TDC guard uniforms. One was the visitation guard I had checked in with upon arrival. The other one was a major or some other high rank. She was carrying a gun, holstered on her hip. The third woman was more casual with a white polo shirt, dark pants, and a jacket. She, too, had a gun. My sister stood behind them with a concerned look on her face. I don't think I had ever seen that particular look on her before.

Les had seen them as well.

He smiled softly and said, "It looks like my ride's here."

I turned to look at him. "You mean them?" I asked, tilting my head in the direction of the three women.

"No, *they're* here for you," he said.

I stared at him and looked over his shoulder to the back door where I saw a van parked. I turned to look at the clock on the wall, seeing it was 11:48. We had till noon.

When I told the guards it wasn't time yet, one of them informed me, quite firmly, "Your time is up. His transport is waiting. You need to leave."

Again, I turned to look at my husband. He couldn't hear what they were saying since he was on the other side of the glass. But it was obvious to him why they were there and what they were saying. After all, this was his territory, and he knew all the drills.

I looked at him pleadingly, irritation in my voice and body language, as I said, "But they are interrupting our visit."

"You're not going to win this argument, honey," he said to me through the phone, smiling slightly, as he knew that I was about to make this an issue. He was the peacemaker, and I was about to start a fight.

There were twelve more minutes that belonged to us, and they were stealing them. Whether we chose to sit in silence looking at one another or pour out our undying love to one another, it was our time, and the transport could just wait as far as I was concerned.

I had witnessed scenes and heard stories about last visitations before an execution where family members threw themselves at the glass, hysterically crying and having to be dragged away.

I leaned in toward him sitting on that tiny stool, our eyes locking one last time. My ear was nestled in the center of the phone that was tethered to the wall, the wires running from my receiver to his through the barrier between us, connecting me to him on the other side.

"I love you."

His eyes were moist, as were mine, and he smiled and said, "I love you too."

One of the officers moved toward me and took a stance with her right hand on her hip as I stood and placed the phone in its holder on the wall. His eyes never left mine as he remained seated on the stool he had been sitting on for hours that day in the tiny room.

"Ma'am, it's time to go," she said in a firm voice.

Kelli and I walked out of the small room toward the hallway. We turned, looking through the windows into the room we had just left, and saw Les still sitting there, watching us, his hands folded neatly on the desktop in front of him as we walked away for the last time. We raised our hands as if to wave goodbye. He responded with a wave of his own, along with the stoic smile he reserved for our exits. My heart was wrenching in two, and I knew his was as well, but he kept smiling at us, watching us walk away.

Every inmate who was in the regular visitation room turned to look at us as we walked through the door. They all knew it was the last visit for Lester Bower, or as they called him, Mr. Bower, a man they admired and respected.

Kelli and I walked toward the electronic door that led out of the visitation area and waited for it to be opened by the guard sitting behind a control panel overlooking the small hallway. The huge door in front of us suddenly lurched, creaking and crawling from one side to the other. The four of us—two of the three guards, my sister, and myself—stood in silence while the first door closed and we waited for the second one to open. I assumed the guards were leaving at the same time we were. The second door finally opened, and we passed through before it lumbered its way closed once again.

We traveled in silence on the bright linoleum tile that had just been polished by one of the prison orderlies, our shoes clicking on the floor as we walked. The two women continued to follow behind us.

Kelli looked over her shoulder and then leaned toward me and said in a low voice, "I think I'm going to walk backward just to see what happens."

I wasn't sure what she meant at first, so I quietly asked, "Are they following us?"

"Looks like it. I think we're being escorted out."

I looked over my shoulder, and they were only a few paces behind us.

Reaching the outside doors, we opened them and walked into the blazing June air and onto the long sidewalk leading to a small building where visitors and employees checked in through metal detectors and pat-downs to get inside. Beautiful roses bloomed in the perfectly groomed beds along the almost forty-foot-long sidewalk. A stark contrast to the walls covered with razor wire.

The women were still in perfect step with us.

We entered the building, collected our driver's licenses, and continued toward the door on the other side that led to the parking lot. I could see that Leslea had brought my Rogue around and was parked right in front, waiting to pick us up. The women continued to follow us out the door. Leslea had the engine running and was standing on the curb next to the driver's door, watching us as we walked out. Hollie was in the back seat.

I began to move toward the back of the car when I heard Leslea say loudly, "Just get in the car, Mom!"

"But I need to get my purse out of the back."

"Get in the car, Shari!" Kelli chimed in. "We'll get your purse later."

"It won't take but a minute," I said as I walked toward the back of the car, my hand reaching out to push the button to open the hatch while looking back at Kelli to respond.

"*Get in the damn car, Shari!*" yelled my daughter, louder than before, with urgency in her voice.

I immediately stopped, as Leslea had never spoken to me like that. I turned to look at the two women who had been following us out of the prison, just as one of them placed her hand on her weapon. Suddenly it dawned on me. Yes, they definitely were escorting us out and didn't want any trouble.

And as far as they knew, trouble might be in the back of that red Rogue.

"All right, all right," I said as I walked over to the passenger side, opened the door, and got in the front seat. I barely had time to buckle my seat belt before Leslea pulled away from the curb and toward the gate to exit.

I turned around to look back, and the two women were standing at the curb, watching as we drove away, their hands still on their guns.

"What were you thinking?" Leslea asked incredulously. "They had no idea what was in the back of your car." The tension inside the vehicle was palpable for everyone else. I found it a bit amusing and laughed as we drove off, which I believe convinced Leslea and Kelli I really had lost my mind.

We drove out of the Polunsky Unit and took a left onto Highway 350 toward Livingston. Leslea and Hollie had packed the car with our suitcases while Kelli and I were visiting with Les those last two hours. We were going to the Hospitality House in Huntsville, which was about an hour away.

In 1986, just two years after Les entered the Texas penal system, the Texas Baptist Prisoner Family Ministry Foundation began a ministry in Huntsville, Texas, where they could meet the needs of families visiting their loved ones in prison, as well as families that lost loved ones either through natural death or execution.

In May of that year, 270 men and women volunteers, led by Texas Baptist men, built a house in only twenty-four hours. By August, the house, located just three blocks from the red brick prison known as "The Walls," was open, welcoming and ministering to family members of inmates.

Les's parents had spent the night there a few times when they would make the long trip from Tulsa, Oklahoma, to Huntsville or Livingston. The services of the Hospitality House were free of charge.

One of the many things they do is provide a place for the family members of death row inmates to gather, stay overnight if they like, and eat during the hours prior to and just after the executions. They provide a safe place for them to be free from the press and other people they might not want to encounter during that time. Chaplains are available and explain to the family exactly what happens and minister in whatever way might be needed, including staying with any family members who remain at the house during the execution; they're also there to console family members who attend the execution. They literally act as a liaison between TDC and the families.

About 4:00 P.M., Grace called me from Washington to say that there had been no word from the governor and the Supreme Court had refused to hear an appeal. I could tell she was very upset, and she apologized several times. I assured her they had done all they could to try to stop this execution and told her Les had asked me to thank her for all her work. Peter called within a few minutes, and he, too, was very upset that nothing more could be done. My thoughts went to Anthony, who had died only nine months before of cancer. He had said his biggest regret in life was not getting Les Bower out of prison.

Leslea and Hollie remained at Hospitality House with my aunt, Pat Baucum, and her daughter Ronda. Gayle Baucum, my uncle and Les's spiritual advisor, my sister Kelli, Les's sisters, Cheryl and Denise, and I were driven by two chaplains to the Walls to witness the execution. There were one or two chaplains who remained at Hospitality House with the girls and other family members. At least three other chaplains accompanied us.

After the execution, two chaplains quietly led us from the execution chamber sometime after 6:40 that evening. They led us between the buildings and out a side door, away from the family members of the victims who had chosen to be there. We were able to avoid the press, the protesters, and the other family.

The sun was still shining brightly outside as we approached the glass doors on the front side of the building that faced the main street of Huntsville. I saw a lone man standing on the sidewalk outside the building. It appeared as if he were there waiting for us.

There were no cameras, no reporters, no spectators—just this one person, backlit by the sun as it was going down on the horizon. Still standing inside the prison, the others with me saw him as well and asked if I knew who he was. The TDC chaplains and escorts were looking somewhat concerned, wondering who he was, why he was there, and how he had managed to find where we would be coming out.

"Yes, I know him," I said to my entourage. I recognized his profile even from a distance and backlit by the sun. It was David Dusek. Of course it was David. Our faithful friend, our next-door neighbor from our days in College Station. David and his wife, Sandra, had lived next door to us for several years, sharing the top floor of the two-story, married-student housing fourplex we lived in while Les and David attended Texas A&M. We were both newlyweds, and those were some of the best memories of our lives. We shared paper-thin walls, meals and movies, road trips and life during the first few years of our marriages.

They had been faithful supporters of Les during the past thirty-one years, as had so many other friends. David would randomly show up at hearings and fight behind-the-scenes to get justice for Les. He was terribly frustrated that there wasn't more that could be done.

I wasn't surprised at all to see him that day. David would always arrive unannounced, at the right time, at the right place, in solidarity for Les. And today he had found the out-of-the-way door we would exit, away from the spotlight of the news, away from the protestors. That was so David.

As our group walked toward the cars, I stepped away and went to David, who was standing off to the side. We embraced and we cried. I thanked him for coming so far to be here, if even for just a few minutes. And then he left.

We returned to the Hospitality House where the others were waiting. We gathered once more, thanking everyone for being so kind and compassionate to us. Our hosts offered us dinner and to spend the night. We took them up on dinner, but we would not be spending the night. We all just wanted to go home and sleep in our own beds. It was about a four-hour drive to Arlington and another hour or so for Les's sisters to go to Irving. The chaplains had Les's remaining property, and Leslea accompanied them to my car where they loaded the bags. He had given his fan, hot pot, typewriter, and other personal necessities to others who could use them on the row. His property was mostly books, his Bible, and personal items.

It was nearing dusk as we said our goodbyes to all the kind people and got on I-45 and headed north, with Leslea behind the wheel. It was a solemn ride home. At one point, I realized we were in Corsicana and glanced at the time. There was no way we could have driven from Huntsville to Corsicana in that short amount of time. I looked over at the speedometer and asked Leslea how fast she was driving.

"Welcome to Red Rogue Airlines" was all she said as we passed through Corsicana and continued north toward DFW. Around 10:00 P.M., we were dropping Hollie off at her house and headed to Leslea's to drop her off as well. I pulled into my driveway and looked at Kelli in the back seat. She, too, wanted to sleep in her own bed, with her own thoughts. So she gathered her bags, got in her car, and headed to Weatherford.

I was home. It was over. For now.

True love
Is like a fire.
First there's a flicker,
Then a flame
That becomes a roaring
Blaze burning madly
Until it turns
Into a fiery coal
That doesn't warm
With the passion
Of the blaze
But is steady,
And it warms
And it lasts
Forever.

June 22, 1984

CHAPTER 28

The Day After

June 4, 2015

I knew I really didn't need to set an alarm for the next morning, but I did anyway. It was June 4, 2015, and at 8:45 A.M., our nine-year-old grand-daughter Katie would have her awards ceremony and graduate from third grade. I planned to be there.

I sat there the next day, watching all the excited kids, parents, and grand-parents taking pictures to commemorate the big event. I looked around and thought to myself, *No one has any idea where we were last night or what we were doing.*

Life goes on.

I saw the enthusiasm on Katie's face as she marched in with her class-mates, interacting with them, tossing her head back to laugh at something someone said. I delighted in the moment and snapped pictures as her name was called and she walked over to receive her graduation document. She went to stand on the risers in formation, looked down at her diploma, and burst out in raucous laughter.

I looked closer at the document she held in front of her chest and saw there was someone else's name on the diploma. It wasn't hers. Instead of getting upset and pointing out the mistake to the teachers, she found it hilarious, and her personality shone as she took it all in stride, laughing at such a silly thing. It brightened my morning, and I smiled with tears welling in my eyes, for I knew, if Les had been here, he would have found it funny as well and laughed along with her. Les and Katie, named after her great-grand-mother Bower, would have been great buddies! Her finding joy in something that was wrong gave me hope that life could go on.

These were the moments he had missed. Moments stolen from him. These were the times I would cling to. She was part of the legacy he had left. And once again, my heart broke, realizing that these grandchildren would never know exactly what they had lost.

While I was watching Katie graduate, Leslea had decided to relax at her next-door neighbor's pool that morning while everyone was off to work. She and her dad had been very close, and he took her with him on many hunting, fishing, and cross-country skiing trips and taught her a lot about the outdoors, nature, and wildlife. Canadian geese flew over our ranch in Fort Collins, and we would stand in the yard and watch them in formation either going south or north, depending on the season. Every now and then, there would be only a pair, and Les had told Leslea that geese never fly alone—they were always in a group of at least two.

As she lay on the lounger next to the pool the day after she said good-bye to her daddy, she was reminiscing about all the times they had shared. Somewhere in the far-off distance, she heard a sound she had heard many times before. A childhood sound, a calming sound, a sound that would always be connected to her daddy.

It sounded like geese. But it was June. She raised up, looking for the source, and saw one lone goose flying low, directly over the pool, honking as he passed by. She began to cry.

Geese don't fly alone.

I Can Be Me

Because you gave me room to be myself,
And yet to catch me if I fall,
I can be me.
Because you hold me close to show me I am loved
But let me go so I might find my own identity,
I can be me.
Because you love me for myself
And not for something that I am not,
I can be me.
Because you expect only what I have to give
And ask for no more than the love I have to offer,
I can be me.
Because you have done this, now that I am half,
Not whole as I once was when you and I were one,
I can be me.

June 8, 1984

CHAPTER 29

The Memorial

June 20, 2015

Les didn't give me many instructions as to what to do after he was executed. However, there were three things he made perfectly clear:

1.   He wanted to be cremated.
2.   He wanted his ashes spread somewhere in Colorado.
3.   Not one tiny piece of ash was to be left anywhere in Texas.

Leslea and Kelli warned me over and over not to open the box when his ashes were delivered to the house. Do not attempt to look in the box and risk spilling anything, they had said. If I did and we had to vacuum any ashes up off the floor, we'd have to take the vacuum cleaner on the plane to Colorado as luggage and throw it over the side of a mountain.

Coincidentally, his ashes were delivered about 1:00 P.M. on the day of his memorial on June 20, 2015. I carefully placed the box in one of my closets.

Les had also requested that if we were to have a memorial, he would like for it to be soon. He wanted us to move on with our lives and try to find some normalcy.

I'm not sure why he thought there wouldn't be a service. I don't think he ever really had a grasp of how many people cared about him, prayed for him, and loved him. Most of them were people who had never known him.

It was a beautiful, simple service with so many people there, most of whom had never met Les. I gave the eulogy. Peter and Grace were there from DC, and Peter spoke, his voice breaking a few times. Reverend Gayle Baucum made us all laugh as he usually does, even at funerals, by recalling silly things he and Les did as friends when they were together. But he also talked about what a wonderful man he was and the best friend Gayle had ever had.

We showed some great pictures on the screen of Les, and someone commented that he was smiling in every picture.

I had found a great song by Kirk Franklin called "I Smile." It was a very upbeat tune he wrote about smiling even when you're down. We played that song at the end of the service, and my pastor, Russ Barksdale, escorted me out of the worship center while we all sang along.

Anticipation

I lay here in the chill
Of the morning,
Remembering the times I awoke, nestled
In the warmth of your arms.
I close my eyes
And listen quietly
As you call my name
In the wind,
Outside my window.
I smile softly,
Remembering the touch
Of your lips
Gently on my neck,
Waking me to a new day.
Oh, what memories I have of you
In the quiet stillness
Of the morning.
Memories that are merely
Expectations of things to come.

October 27, 1984

CHAPTER 30

The Many Sides to Grieving

July 2015

T hings didn't seem right. Everything had calmed down, and there was nothing left to do to take care of Les. For so many years, I made that long trip to visit him, came home, did what needed to be done, and then went back to visit him again in a few weeks.

There were no visible reminders of him living here. He had never lived in this house. There were no clothes in a closet, no toothbrush in a drawer, no razor by the sink. The sights and smells of one's partner in life linger in each room of a home even when they've gone off to work, on a trip, or just outside to mow the yard. Those memories, those telltale signs, had long faded from our home years before. The few reminders left were pictures that were more than thirty years old and a Bible with his name engraved on it that was given to him when he was just a boy of nine. His high school letterman jacket hung in the hall closet; his wedding ring, which he had long ago given to me for safekeeping, was tucked away in my jewelry box. What could possibly be different?

I didn't sit and weep. I didn't crawl in bed, pull the covers up over my face, and sleep for hours on end. I didn't drown myself in hours of watching mindless TV, trying to soothe the pain that did not seem to be there. Instead,

I went back to my schedule of activities that I had accustomed myself to for the past three months since becoming "unexpectedly retired." I went back to my water aerobics classes, to my yoga group. I continued to go to church when it would have been just as easy to stay away. I went to my grandchildren's graduations and end-of-school events and made lunch plans with my friends.

Something had to be wrong with me. I was not grieving as I felt I *should*. I had my moments, I cried sometimes when I least expected; I had the occasions of a deep-seated knot in the pit of my stomach and the need to take deep breaths or to even make sure I was breathing. But where were the breakdowns I had expected?

I shared with my pastor that I didn't think I was grieving correctly. After a slight smile, he asked what exactly was the correct way to grieve? Obviously, I had no idea, but I felt I was not doing it properly. He went on to say that grief was like a bucket of cold ice water. When you lose someone unexpectedly, it feels as if that bucket has been thrown on you. It's shocking and overwhelming, and your reaction is immediate; oftentimes, like the overflow of water from the bucket, the grief comes pouring out.

On the other hand, if you lose someone who has been very ill for a long time or, in our case, if you have been grieving circumstances and absences for three decades, the loss is no less devastating, but it's as if the bucket of ice water is covered with holes, allowing the grief to trickle out now and then, perhaps sloshing over the edge so it comes in smaller intervals rather than a knee-buckling, overwhelming event. I thought that was a very good analogy and seemed to fit exactly what I was experiencing: trickles of grief that just spilled out now and then.

I found myself not being able to look at those pictures on the mantle, as it pained me to see that person who had been my husband. Our day-to-day experiences together as a couple raising a young family had abruptly ended thirty-one years before. All our memories together had stopped, and now new memories replaced them. But they were ones of separation, loneliness, heartache, and unending grief. Our relationship was forever changed, and there were no happy pictures of memories made in the past thirty years.

Fifty-nine days later, I found myself crying—finally. Not just crying for the first time, but *really* crying. Deep sobs of grief and tightness in my chest so intense I could hardly breathe.

I cried before. A little here, a little there. Corner-of-the-tissue cries. Just enough to really mess up my mascara, and then I shut off the valve and stopped the flow. Why now? What set this off? It was a friendly embrace from an old friend, a comforting hello that tugged some memory of another time. A memory not even of them, but it planted a seed, and that seed grew and eventually blossomed into a full-blown kaleidoscope of pictures—no, worse—sensations, thoughts, and feelings filled with tactile memories of what was so much farther back than fifty-nine days.

And then it happened. The kaleidoscope collided with the heart, and all the pent-up grief had no place to go, the dam broke, and the swell was more than could be contained.

Rather than obey the rules of my past, which echoed in my mind and yelled for me to "not let them see me cry," I ignored the voice and yielded to the pain and the tears and the grief. It really didn't matter, anyway, because there was no one there to see me give in to the grief that I had held in for so long. So no one did see me cry. No one but God. And He smiled and said, "Good. It's about time."

A Prayer

Thank you for the love you share,
For your mercy and tender care.
Thank you for joy amidst the pain,
For sunshine through the pouring rain.
Thank you for patience to wait upon Thee,
For faith to see what I cannot see.
Thank you for granting me restful peace,
For untold blessings that shall not cease.
Thank you for life so full of love,
For your eternal guidance from above.

June 25, 1984

CHAPTER 31

A Final, Hilarious, Fun-Filled Farewell

(Les, You Would've Been So Proud!)

August 2016

We all thought Les wanting his ashes spread in Colorado was a wonderful idea, but we had to figure out a way to pay for it. Silly girls, when will we learn? God will find a way.

There was such an outpouring of love and condolences from our friends, family, and people we didn't even know after Les's death. A woman from an organization that ministered to inmates decided to gift us with some money and sent it through her home church to have them send it to me. The church was so moved by the gesture that they matched it. I was flabbergasted. And oh-so grateful. I tucked it away for Colorado.

I was asked to speak at a church in another town about God's love even in our darkest hours and give a bit of my testimony. I thought it would be a twenty-minute talk but found out from Uncle Gayle, who was interim pastor at the time, they wanted me to do the whole service. The deacons gave me a love offering before I left to return home, and it was much more than I ever imagined. So that, too, was tucked away for Colorado. God had found a way for the four of us to go and finally lay Les to rest.

Leslea, Hollie, Kelli, and I made plans to go to Colorado in August 2016. It was a wonderful trip. I arranged an Airbnb in Evergreen after deciding that was a pretty good middle spot for a lot of the places we wanted to go. The trip was not sad at all; in fact, it was a trip Les would've very much enjoyed and approved of. Well, *approved*, anyway—I'm not sure he would have enjoyed some of our shopping excursions.

We had so many great stories to tell from that trip, some we could hardly believe. Every time we came around a corner or looked over a lake, we found something that reminded us of Les. Like the evening we were going back to our Airbnb in Evergreen. As we drove up the winding road, we saw a huge elk about twenty feet away, standing in someone's yard near our house. Kelli took a picture of him as he stood staring at us. He seemed to be posing just for us. When we got to the house, we looked at the picture, and the elk was standing next to a Texas A&M yard sign!

We each had our own baggie of ashes and got to choose where we thought Les would like to be. Leslea chose Mount Evans, which has the highest paved road in the country with the eastern slope of Colorado on one side and the western slope on the other. The summit is over fourteen thousand feet and is home to many mountain goats. Leslea found beautiful views from each side of the summit and dispersed her dad's ashes—some on the east and some on the west, making sure he would be on both the eastern slope and the western slope. If ashes from the east side were caught in a runoff from rainstorms, he would end up being dumped into the Atlantic Ocean. Any ashes from the west side would end up in the Pacific. Yes, that is *his* daughter, calculating exactly where she would leave him.

Kelli took her baggie on a whitewater rafting trip down Clear Creek River in Idaho Springs, which eventually makes it through to several tributaries of the Platte River, emptying into the gulf and into the ocean. Her rafting buddies were Leslea and Stevie, my niece who lives in Denver, along with a couple of other rafters and Juan José, the guide.

Kelli had been rather discreet when tossing ashes out along the way at various spots she thought Les would like, trying not to arouse suspicion with the guide, as she wasn't sure he would like her throwing something over the side. They were on one of the smaller rafts than what we had always used in western Colorado. All the passengers had to row in this small craft. She was almost done. Unfortunately, or maybe not, a big gust of wind came up just as Kelli tossed the last of the ashes out of the raft, surprising the Costa Rican guide with a face full of ashes. After many apologies, and her assuring him it wasn't garbage but ashes, he said it was okay, no problem. He had told them earlier that he was going home the next day to his native country. I'm pretty sure Les made it to Costa Rica somehow with that gracious guide.

Hollie and I chose a beautiful copse of Aspen, just up a mountain outside of Evergreen. The sun was about to go down, the light shining on the leaves, turning them to a beautiful silver. Hollie and I stood back a ways from the still aspens, reached into our bags, and tossed a huge handful of ashes up into the air toward the trees. Just as we did, the wind began blowing, lifting the ashes we had tossed high into the air and scattering them through the leaves and across the rest of the forest of trees. It was beautiful watching the ashes drift through the air and traveling far off as if they were flying.

The leaves were clapping together, as they do when the wind blows, and it sounded like applause as Les's ashes flew past the trees and across a great meadow on the other side. Nature once again was showing off its beauty and awe. Les would have loved it there as well.

We were silent for a moment, as the sun was slipping behind the mountains. We all got back in the car and headed down the mountain to Evergreen. It was quiet for a few minutes when Hollie looked up and saw a deer on the side of the highway.

"Oh! A deer!" Hollie declared.

There was silence again, and then Leslea sang out, "A female deer."

I chimed in, "Ray, a drop of golden sun."

Kelli cried out, "Me, a name I call myself."

And then we all sang out together: "Far, a long, long way to run."

And the four of us continued, "Sew, a needle pulling thread," and sang the rest of the song down the steep highway, concluding with raucous laughter. This is how our group does a road trip!

We came around the bend as we passed Evergreen Lake, and the sun was sparkling off the water. We turned another corner and passed the dam and slowed to look at the ducks that were lined up in a perfect row across the narrow top of the dam.

Kelli, still taking pictures, said, "Look at the dam ducks." We almost ran off the two-lane road; we were laughing so hard. Les would have been so proud that we were having so much fun.

Lift Me Up

Lift me up to heaven, Lord.
Take me home with Thee.
Give me peace within your gates.
Take this pain from me.
I don't know how much longer
I can walk this narrow way.
For my heart is very heavy
As I face each lonely day.
Give me hope to face this life,
Full of doubts and the unknown.
Help me, Lord, to know you're there
And never to feel alone.
Help me learn to love you, Lord,
More than life itself.
Help me learn to love you, Lord,
More than anyone else.

May 20, 1984

CHAPTER 32

Just Breathe

October 3, 2016

I was sick for most of that summer and was even worried about going to Colorado. I had gone to my doctor several times over the summer to try to find out why I was coughing and having so much trouble getting well from what was believed to be some kind of bronchial trouble. I was finally sent to a pulmonary specialist, who did some breathing tests. Everything seemed to be normal. But still no answers. He decided to send me for a CT scan and another test.

I thought I knew how a CT scan worked. I had not given any thought about there being a dye inserted in my veins for this test. I remember filling out all the paperwork in the waiting room when I had arrived, and I remember the page that described the contrast dye. But it did not occur to me how the dye would be put into my body. I certainly didn't expect to experience what I did that day.

As the technician prepared me for the scan, she had me lie down on the narrow examination table that slides in and out of the tube and scans your body. I lay there, looking at the ceiling in the dimly lit room as she asked me if I knew which arm had the best veins for her to insert an IV. I told her my right, but she was on my left and decided to test that side to see if she could get a good vein. *Why did she bother asking?*

She strapped a band around the top part of my arm and put a rubber ball in my hand, telling me to hold it tightly while she checked my vein. It was then that it hit me. I suddenly had a flashback of the scene of Les lying on the gurney in the death chamber only sixteen months before, arms out in a V on either side of his body with tubes coming out.

She rubbed my vein with an alcohol pad, over and over, and as she did, one lonely tear rolled down my cheek and onto the pillow where my head lay. I began to feel an overwhelming panic creep into the pit of my stomach, moving slowly into my chest. Another tear, this one on the other side, dropped, as had the one before.

Breathe, I told myself. *Don't panic!* I began to breathe steadily, trying to force myself to be calm, praying I would not panic. Two more tears began to fall as she took the ball out of my hand, untied the rubber strap from my arm, and moved to the right side to see if that vein was better. *I could have told you that wouldn't work,* I thought.

She began the procedure again, this time on the right side, and quietly told me what she was about to do. *Did anyone tell Les what they were doing when they were inserting an IV into his arm?* I thought. *Probably not.*

Was it quiet in that room when he was being prepared for liquid death to go into his veins? Did the technician even speak to him or acknowledge him as he went about his job? The technician would be the last person to physically touch him before he died. *Did Les have to talk to himself and pray silently to God to keep the panic from overcoming him? Did tears roll down his cheeks as he lay there, looking at the ceiling?* These were things I would never know.

I was about to have a five-minute scan and would walk out of there when we were done. My husband never had that opportunity. What I was experiencing paled in comparison to what he felt, but suddenly I remembered that scene I saw when the curtains were opened, and I felt as if I were reliving it. Only this time, I was inside.

She told me that she would insert a needle in my arm, I would feel a slight prick, and then she would start a saline solution to check and make sure the needle was in properly. My bottom lip quivered, and more silent tears fell. I'm sure she must have thought I was scared, if she even noticed at all. She had no idea what was going through my mind at that moment.

The saline solution went in, and she announced it was a good vein and that she would begin the dye injection. I would feel a warm feeling; don't be alarmed, she said.

Don't be alarmed? This whole scene is alarming.

The solution flowing into my veins was not lethal. His was. *Did he feel the solution go into his body as I was now?* I had no idea. It was all I could do to keep my panic at bay. Not a panic of fear for my life, but the panic of extraordinary grief for a few minutes, reliving a scene that would forever be burned into my memory.

It was soon over, and she helped me up from the table and escorted me to another room to await the next test. I sat there alone, thinking about what had just happened and the overwhelming grief that had enveloped me in a way I had not seen coming. Grief hits when you least expect it. I certainly did not expect this.

My Heart Is Broken

My heart is broken!
See the life drain from me
As my heart crumbles
Into tiny pieces.
My heart is broken!
See the anguish
As I lift my face
To God and ask, "Why?"
My heart is broken!
And only God
In His wisdom and mercy
Can mend a broken heart.

April 29, 1984

CHAPTER 33

Do I Miss You?

January 27, 2016 — 238 days after execution

Dear Les,

Someone asked me not too long ago if I missed you. I'm not sure anyone had asked me that. To tell you the truth, I was surprised by the question and had to think about it. We were standing in my kitchen. The kitchen I had been in for the past twenty years. It's odd how only a few seconds can go by, but a million thoughts can race through your mind during those few seconds.

Did I miss you? Of course I did. But I had been missing you for thirty-two years. And that was pretty much how I answered.

Your death had only been seven months before the question. Yet your absence in our home had been 384 months. Over 11,680 days. You kept up with the exact number of days you had been gone, and somehow I forgot to ask you how many days it had been on that last day we visited, just before they made me leave. I wish I had asked. That is how long I had missed you. However many days that was—11,680 days, 32.444444 years.

I do miss you. But at the same time, I'm glad you no longer suffer the isolation, pain, humiliation, and grief of being in a place few people know the horrors of. I regret your not being exonerated of the false accusations you had to live with for the majority of your life. I regret your not being a part of your family's day-to-day life for all those years. I regret not being able to physically be together, to touch you, to embrace you, to even be in the same room with you. I regret not being able to grow old together. I regret all the things that might have been. I regret all the people who never got to know you and the person you really were versus the person the courts, the press, and some think you were. The list of regrets goes on.

When I told her, "Of course I miss him, but I've been missing him for thirty-two years," she then asked if I missed being able to go and see you and visit with you. Without a beat of hesitation, I answered, "Oh, no, I don't miss that at all." And I don't. I don't miss the vile place you lived in, the comforts you missed, and the loneliness, pain, and suffering you endured.

I don't miss seeing you with welts on your wrist from handcuffs that were too tight.

I don't miss watching you sick or in pain from some illness that could easily be treated in the "free world" but was neglected inside because you were merely a number that the state was in control of and didn't care for. I don't miss that for you.

I find myself, now and then, especially in the first few months following your death, hearing something on the news or receiving a note from a friend, and thinking, *Oh, I need to tell Les.* Then I stop myself in mid-thought, realizing I can't do that. That happened a lot at first.

Oh, I need to write him and tell him . . .

I wonder what Les will have to say about this new candidate . . .

I miss being able to share those thoughts and conversations with you, even if we didn't always agree on everything. At least they made for interesting, if not sometimes heated, and lively conversations.

I miss the look you gave me after instigating such conversations. And you did instigate them, which was part of your fun. It was a look uniquely your own, silently saying to me that you were purposely antagonizing me on a subject you knew would create a lively conversation, just because you could. Those conversations were initially frustrating—and would almost always get my blood boiling—but certainly did not make for a dull visit. And you usually initiated them near the end of our two-hour visit, grinning at me with delight before proclaiming, "Well, that should keep you alert and awake on the drive back home."

I miss your sometimes wicked, but always clever, sense of humor—something I'm afraid I didn't always appreciate or recognize in our time together before your incarceration. Or maybe I just forgot. Maybe it was one of those things that just got lost in life.

I remember when the children were very small and we were living in Fort Collins. We were at a social function with our Sunday school class, and someone said to me, "Les is so funny!" I thought, *He is?* I think it was then that I began to take the time to recognize it.

I miss the things I don't even know to miss. You said it yourself in a letter you wrote to me in mid-1984, only a few months after you had gone to death row. You said you wondered what we would find to talk about during a two-hour visit and soon discovered that there was never enough time. We always found something to talk about.

You then admitted that you weren't sure we ever had really talked, just the two of us, for two hours at a time when you were at home. That seemed to bring you some regret, and rereading your letter recently gave me pause as well, thinking that surely couldn't be true. But perhaps it was.

The fifteen and a half years we were married, before you left, were filled with school, work, children, moves, new jobs, recreation, and the day-to-day living that comes with building a life and a family. And as you conveyed in this letter of reflection, you were not the best at sharing your feelings and talking things out. I'm not sure that changed much during your time in prison, but I believe it improved some. I couldn't help but wonder if your time there helped facilitate that change.

Do I miss you? Yes, I do. Do I wish you were here? Of course I do. But I began missing you at 11:45 P.M. on January 20, 1984, when you took your last step across the threshold of our home, never to return again.

When I began missing you then, I also began the anticipation of seeing you again when I visited you and the hope that this horrendous nightmare would soon end with us once again being united. That gave me something to look forward to.

By the same token, when I think of you now, I remember where you are and look forward in anticipation to when we can be together again, knowing it won't be here on earth.

I remember many years ago, I asked you during one of our visits, "When you get to heaven, isn't the first thing you're going to do is ask God why in the world we had to go through all this pain and suffering?"

You looked me straight in the eye, through that dirty glass that had separated us for so many years. And with a peace about your face, you replied, "When I get to heaven, it won't matter anymore."

Fantasy

A cool, crisp morning, geese high above,
Mist on the lake, the call of a dove.
Wind through the pines, calling softly to me.
The sun peeking over the top of the hill,
Looking down on the morning, peaceful and still.
A small, cozy cabin in the valley below,
Nestled beneath mountains, covered with snow.
A fire on the hearth makes it cozy inside
And beckons the lovers to take refuge and hide.
Lost in a world that's strictly their own,
They come to each other, in love and alone.
They share their love all through the night,
And in each other's arms, they awake at dawn's light.
The picture is clear. In my mind I can see
The scene I've created, but it's pure fantasy.
My mind is a canvas, and I paint what I do
With watercolors of memories, of me and of you.

May 19, 1984

Gallery

Les preparing for his high school graduation
(May 1966 in Tulsa, Oklahoma).

Les's senior class picture
(May 1966, Tulsa, Oklahoma).

Les and Shari at a church Valentine's Party *(1966).*

Les and Shari on their wedding day
(August 24, 1968).

Les and Shari's one-year anniversary picture
(August 24, 1969 in College Station, TX).

Les and Shari on a family-and-friends trip
(June 1967, Royal Gorge, Colorado).

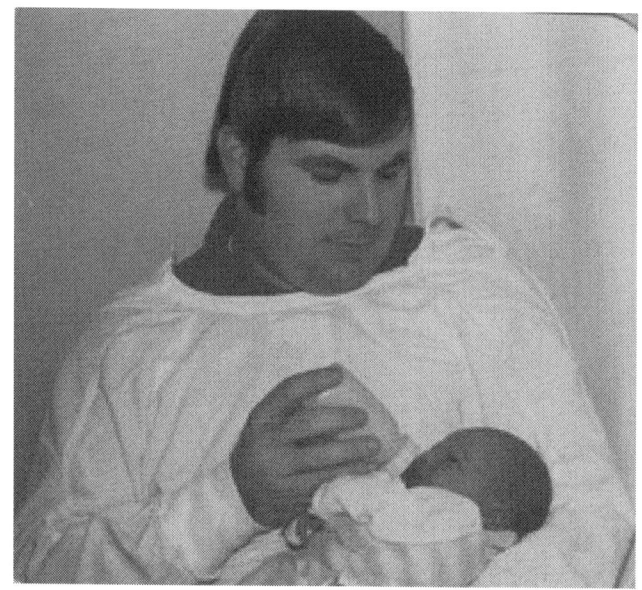

Les and Leslea on the day of her birth
(February 13, 1972, Denver, Colorado).

Les, Leslea, and Hollie as we prepare to leave
Daleville, Indiana, for Colorado *(August 1975).*

The Bower Family *(1977)*.

The Bower Family, three days before the murders
(1983, Arlington, TX).

Colorado River, *(1982)*.

Leslea (11) snapped this photo of her dad *(May 1983)*.

At an award banquet for Les, who had won an award for
top salesman with Thompson-Hayward *(1981)*.

Ellis Unit *(date unknown)*.

Les and Shari waiting on the jury to return
(April 1983).

(1988, location unknown.)

Livingston, TX
(date unknown).

Newspaper clipping *(May 2015)*.

(June 1967.)

Hollie, Shari, and Leslea
on the trip to release Les's ashes *(2016).*

Acknowledgments

This book would not have been written without God inspiring me and encouraging me throughout the many years we lived it. I had no idea when I was scribbling poetry on yellow legal pads in the courtroom in 1984 that God was beginning a work in me and would one day call on me to share with others that God does not bring sorrow, trouble, and heartbreak into our lives. He provides a way *through* those times and calls on us to comfort others through our experiences.

Second Corinthians 1:3–4 (HCSB) says, "Blessed be the God and Father of our Lord Jesus Christ, the Father of mercies and the God of all comfort, who comforts and encourages us in every trouble so that *we will be able to comfort and encourage those who are in any kind of trouble, with the comfort with which we ourselves are comforted by God*" (emphasis mine).

I would like to thank my family and friends for their support and encouragement along the way. There were times it was overwhelming, but so many lifted me up in prayer when my spirits were down, and countless friends all over the world encouraged me and sometimes, literally, cheered me to the finish.

Thank you to Art House Dallas who sponsors writers groups across the Dallas–Fort Worth area. It has been my privilege to be a part of Awakening Creativity, the Arlington group, who not only supported this effort, but critiqued it as well along the way, helping me to become a better writer. Sarah Kay Ndjerareou, Stephanie Suire, Shannon Holt, Maggie Philpot, Sara Hill, Sandra Rhoads, and Krissi Dallas—I couldn't have done this without you.

I am grateful to Writing Workshops Dallas and Blake Kimzey, the executive director, for creating such an amazing environment for writers and would-be writers. I learned of them through my writers group and took many of their classes over the past two years. My work was young and needed nurturing. As I took one class after another, my writing improved exponentially with the help of the amazing writers and instructors I learned from: Blake Atwood, Whitney Davis, Mag Gabbert, Allie Pleiter, Mike Farris, Tex Thompson, and Shayla Raquel.

Thank you to my beta readers, Leslea Miller, Diane Miller, and Linda Miller. You sacrificed your time to read my initial draft, and it was then, with your feedback, I thought I might have something good. I'm sorry, my sweet daughter, Leslea, that I put you through so many readings. I know it wasn't easy for you to read it so many times.

Thank you is not enough for my sister, Kelli Hamilton, and my oldest daughter, Leslea Miller, for helping me remember so many things that had happened over those thirty-four years and telling me if I got it wrong. The addition of many of their personal memories and input of their own made this book even better. Thank you also for being there when I fell apart as I wrote and relived every single minute of those years.

I am extremely grateful to all my "tribes" that I call my friends and do life with, study God's Word with, and laugh and cry with. If you are reading this and you don't have a tribe, go out and find one. Life is much fuller with all of you in it. You know who you are.

Thank you to Kristen McGregor and Brianna Hamilton of Astrea Creative for designing my website so the world can easily beat a path to my door. I look forward to meeting all those people I haven't met yet.

One of the last things to do before going to the printer is having a professional proofreader take one last look at the manuscript to make sure it's a polished product. I want to thank Lisa Thompson (writebylisa.com) for the outstanding job she did proofreading, correcting, and pointing out some things that might have been confusing to the reader. Even though I was working with all of these people who assisted me in this project, by the time we were done, I felt as if I knew them well and had become friends with all of them.

A cover is very important, as it is the first thing that speaks to a potential reader. I was fortunate to find Melinda Martin of Martin Publishing Services to design a distinctive cover to fit this book and this story. She also formatted the interior. Thank you, Melinda, for your patience as we navigated through this crucial part of the journey.

Choosing an editor was one of the biggest tasks. I felt I had to ensure my words, my thoughts, and our life would be taken care of and nurtured and would bloom as I envisioned and as God wanted this story to be told. There were many times when I thought I had decided on an editor, but it didn't always feel just right. Then I met Shayla Raquel when I took one of her classes at Writing Workshops Dallas. I was charmed upon meeting her by her spunk and enthusiasm. After another class, I knew she was the one. When we finally met for lunch one day in Oklahoma City and she read my first chapter and cried, I knew I had a winner. After that, we became great friends, and I have her to thank for the spit and polish of this memoir that I feel very proud of. Shayla is not just a brilliant editor, but she is a cheerleader, a trainer, a promoter, and so much more. And now I can call her my friend. Thank you, Shayla, for loving our family and our story, for being the godly woman who saw what God wanted to do with this book, and for believing in a first-time author you chose to take on.

ABOUT THE AUTHOR

Shari Bower

Shari Bower retired from corporate management in 2015 and now enjoys driving her granddaughters to school each morning, attending Bible studies with her friends, and leading a ladies' Bible group twice a month in her home. She began writing poetry in a courtroom in 1984 after her husband, Les, of almost sixteen years was arrested for a crime he didn't commit. The poems made their way into her memoir when their 32-year battle to try to win Les's exoneration and release ended in his execution. Shari enjoys reading, writing, painting, and binge-watching historical stories and crime series on Netflix. A widow of five years, she has two grown daughters, four grandchildren, and one great-granddaughter. She lives in Arlington, Texas, with her two cats, Bandit and Cali. Shari is the author of *Before They Executed Him: A Wife's Story of Death Row.*

Connect with the Author

ShariBower.com
Facebook.com/sharileabower
Twitter.com/sharileabower
Instagram.com/sharileabower
Linkedin.com/in/shari-bower-34757889

Email

hello@sharibower.com

Printed in Great Britain
by Amazon